Navigating *The Gay Gaze*

Historian Jack Fritscher's newest book, *Inventing the Gay Gaze: Rex, Peter Berlin, Arthur Tress, and Crawford Barton*, is the third volume in his award-winning series *Profiles in Gay Courage* showcasing twentieth-century artists speaking to the twenty-first century in this revealing book of lively annotated oral-history interviews as enjoyable as heart-to-heart conversations in an artist's private atelier.

The artist Rex drawing his pointillist pictures, and the three photographers, Berlin, Tress, and Barton, speak for themselves inventing their own authentic queer eye during the Stonewall 1970s dominated by the politically-correct gaze of censors, and by the influence of their common frenemy Robert Mapplethorpe whose spirit infuses this boundary-breaking book.

Eyewitness Fritscher has known these artists since the 1970s when as editor-in-chief of *Drummer* magazine, he first published their pioneering work. He canonizes his iconic friends by curating their specific avant-garde histories within the context of mainstream gay history that readers will find informative and entertaining.

In four unfiltered conversations, he profiles the reclusive anarchist Rex who designated him to hear his deathbed confession. In his chat with photographer Peter Berlin, celebrating Berlin's 80th birthday, Berlin details how his camera-eye created his strutting alter-ego. In dialogue with ethnographic photographer Arthur Tress, Tress explains using the magical realism of mid-century modernism to develop his unique perspective. In his tête-à-tête visit with the dying Crawford Barton, the key photographer of 1970s Castro Street, Barton recalls escaping the homophobic American South to document diversities of men in San Francisco.

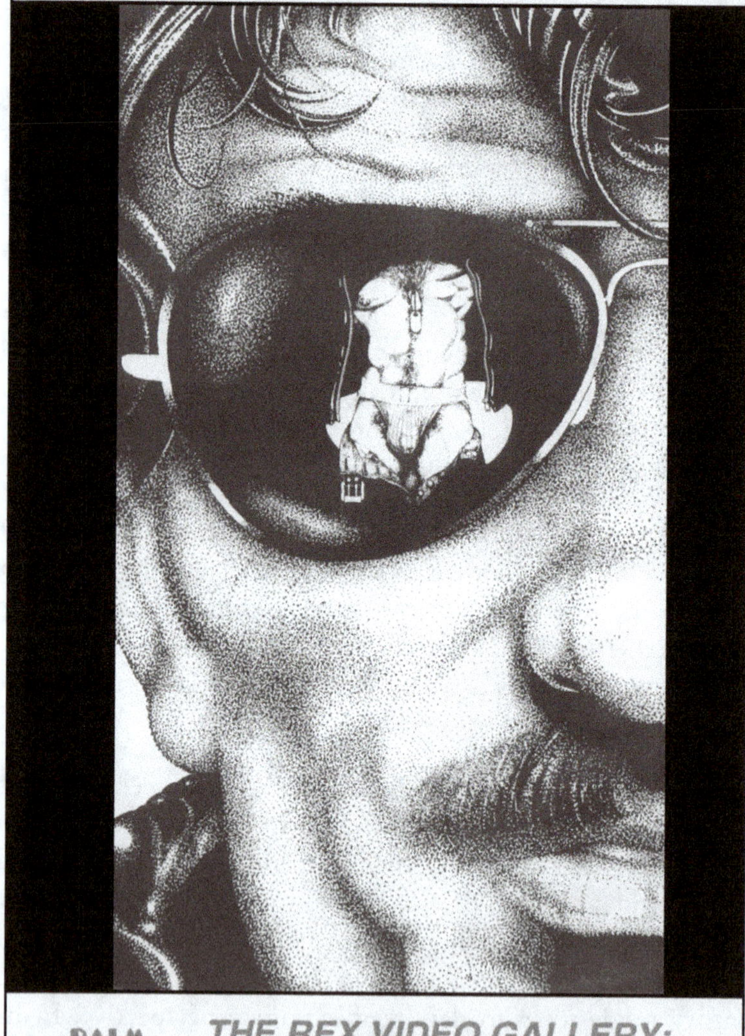

The Rex Video Gallery: Corrupt Beyond Innocence directed/photo-graphed by Jack Fritscher, produced/edited by Mark Hemry, Palm Drive Video, bespoke soundtrack, 65 minutes, 1990

INVENTING THE GAY GAZE

REX
PETER BERLIN
ARTHUR TRESS
and
CRAWFORD BARTON

Jack Fritscher, PhD

PROFILES IN GAY COURAGE
Volume 3

Archival Edition
Jack Fritscher-Mark Hemry Archives

Palm Drive Publishing™

For author history and for historical research https://JackFritscher.com

Cover and book design by Mark Hemry

Published by Palm Drive Publishing, Sebastopol CA
www.PalmDrivePublishing.com
Email: publisher@PalmDrivePublishing.com

Library of Congress Control Number: 2024949895
Fritscher, Jack 1939-
Inventing the Gay Gaze: Rex, Peter Berlin, Arthur Tress, and Crawford Barton
Profiles in Gay Courage: Volume 3 / Jack Fritscher
p.cm

ISBN 978-1-890834-73-9 Print
ISBN 978-1-890834-74-6 eBook

1. Fine Arts. 2. Drawing. 3. Gay Photography. 4. Art History. 5. Gay Art History. 6. Biography. 7. Rex. 8. Peter Berlin. 9. Arthur Tress 10. Crawford Barton. 11. Robert Mapplethorpe. 12. Castro Street History. 13. San Francisco History.

First Printing 2025
10 9 8 7 6 5 4 3 2
PalmDrivePublishing™.com

Special dedication and thanks
to my stoic editor and husband Mark Hemry
without whose remarkable diligence
for nearly fifty years
this material would have been
impossible to collect, analyze, and present

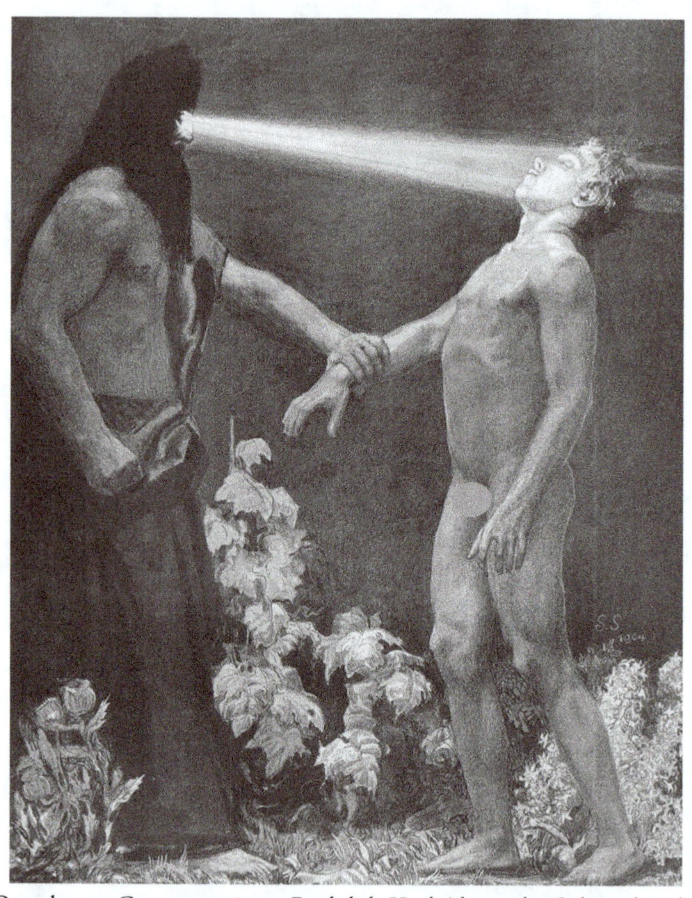

Openly gay German painter Rudolph Karl Alexander Schneider aka
Sascha Schneider (1870-1927), "Hypnosis," 1904

Contents

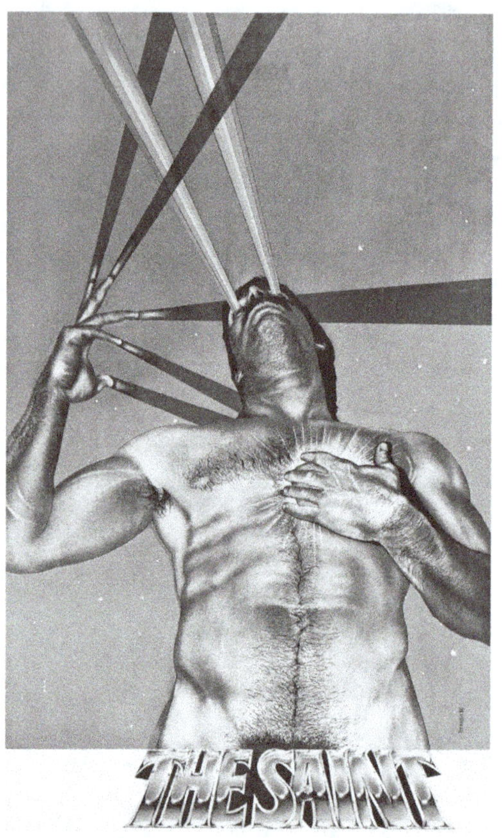

Michael Vernaglia (1956-1991), "The Saint," a "gay-gaze laser poster," 1980, was the invitation to the opening party, September 20, 1980, of The Saint nightclub, "The East Village Vatican of Disco," 105 Second Avenue, New York, 1980-1988.

Robert Mapplethorpe was the official photographer of The Saint's first Black Party for which he shot two horned-god photos for the invitation: "Rites Part I and Rites Part II: A Two-Night Black Party," March 20 and 21, 1981. The next day, he carried his gay gaze from his studio to shoot "selected guests" at The Saint's Sunday Tea Dance, March 22. 1981.

Rex drew the Invitation for "Rites IV, The Black Party," March 19, 1983, and for "Rites XXIV," 2013.

Introduction

Curating the Gay Gaze

by Andy Campbell, PhD

What to say about Jack Fritscher's role in leather culture that hasn't already been said? What about his own gay gaze? In him we still (thankfully) have one of our greatest living leather writers and New Journalists. At 86, he is an embodiment of what decades of observant living and mindful scholarship may offer to new generations. As his fellow writers and artists and photographers who invented the 1970s genre of homomasculine words and images will tell you, such foundational work is done for love not money. The prolific author's psychic income of earned respect comes from the numerous art and alt-communities he fostered during his 65 years of documenting and reporting leather lives in his books, feature articles, and fiction in the leather bible of *Drummer* magazine which was a first draft of leather history.

Luckily and happily, Fritscher, the tenured university professor who taught creative writing and film in the turbulent 1960s, is a writer who is an artist finely attuned to art, and to all the trappings of that wayward, difficult calling to create visions against all the odds of straight and gay censorship. In this book, as editor-in-chief of *Drummer* (1977-1980), and on screen, as co-founder and director of Palm Drive Video, he reveals how evolving visual artists invented the gay gaze. Recalling his unique community eyewitness position as editor, he says it was the centrality of *Drummer* itself that gifted him personal access to recruit and befriend artists seeking publication.

The multi-award-winning author is a Lambda Literary Finalist whose 1994 memoir of his bicoastal lover, *Mapplethorpe:Assault with a Deadly Camera*, is one of his thirty books chronicling the first post-Stonewall generation of artists and photographers including in this book: Rex, Peter Berlin, Arthur Tress, and Crawford Barton. As an intimate of Mapplethorpe, he is uniquely qualified to stir Robert's eye, attitude, and ubiquity into this book of competitive peers. Fritscher, clearly relishing the task of putting language to page, is a pleasure to read. Rollicking, fun, sexy, provocative, and heartfelt, he entertains and informs by opening his deep archives and journals as portals to the past.

He lets the unfiltered artists speak for themselves in their own authentic voices in these interviews of oral history. In this book, the third volume in his series *Profiles in Gay Courage: Leatherfolk, Arts, and Ideas,* these vivid profiles offer readers a basic introduction to the artistic practices of fine artists and photographers who helped create and develop the postwar queer eye in gay media. For this task, Fritscher culls his archive of writing, interviews, missives, and his own journal memories. His point of view canonizes his iconic friends by presenting their specific origin stories within the context of general gay history.

In these profiles of four artists who started up before Stonewall, flourished in the 1970s, and carried on as influencers despite AIDS to the end of the century, Fritscher is in top form. In his annotated interviews, he writes a paean to the reclusive pointillist artist Rex who asked him to write his uncensored eulogy.

In his interview with photographer Peter Berlin on Berlin's 80th birthday, Berlin, speaking under his birth name, Armin Heune, tells how he created his famous alter-ego by refining his gaze both in camera and in post-shoot enhancements.

In his intense chat with ethnographic photographer Arthur Tress, Tress explains using the magical realism of mid-century modernism to develop and frame his unique perspective.

In his conversation with Crawford Barton who was the key photographer of 1970s Castro Street, the dying Barton recalls how he escaped from the homophobic American South to the sanctuary of San Francisco where he developed his multiracial street gaze around the platonic ideal of all kinds of new male beauty.

The coverage of these four essential visionaries will interest readers of gay popular culture, photo historians, and scholars tracking the shifting visual codings of gay life. Taken together these essay-interviews consider the many ways that art moves the mind, body, and the relational feelings we have towards one another.

A new generation of readers may enjoy this book by an eyewitness survivor of the twentieth century.

—Andy Campbell, PhD, author of *Queer X Design: 50 Years of Signs, Symbols, Banners, Logos, and Graphic Art of LGBTQ Pride and Activism*, is Chair and Associate Professor of Critical Studies at USC's Roski School of Art and Design

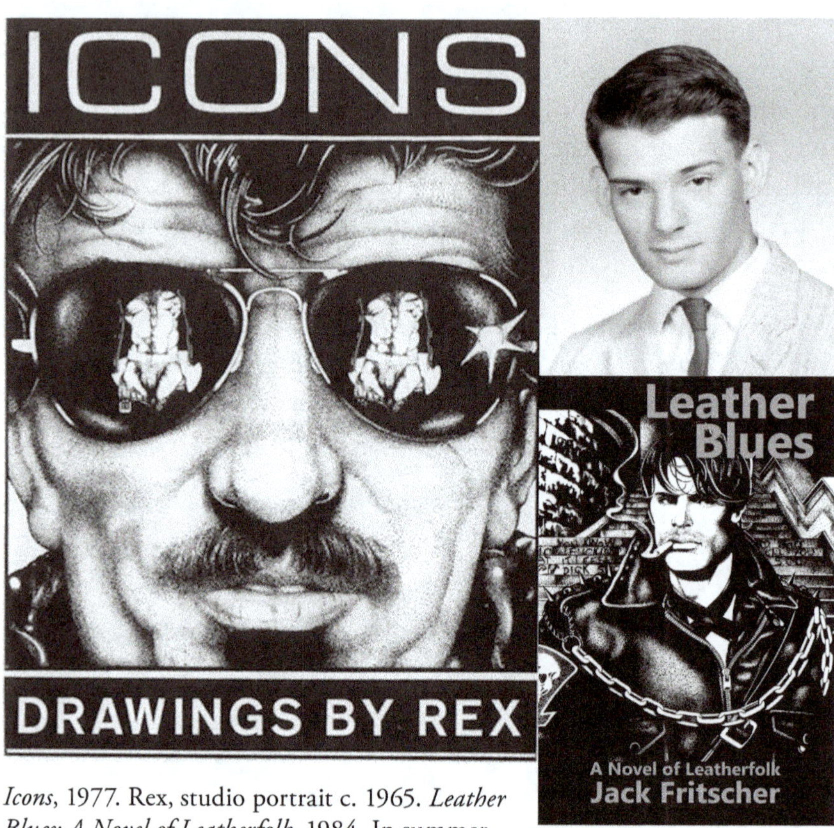

Icons, 1977. Rex, studio portrait c. 1965. *Leather Blues: A Novel of Leatherfolk*, 1984. In summer 1984, the camera-shy Rex permitted frequent collaborator Fritscher to shoot four archival photos during his visit to the Fritscher-Hemry home.

REX
REQUIEM
1944-2024

Corrupt Beyond Innocence
His Life Before His Legend
Became Myth

His Words and Thoughts

"Rex: Persona Non Grata"
—Leslie-Lohman Gay Art Foundation, New York

"The world of Rex excludes you
or draws you in at your own risk."
—*Drummer* magazine

"My drawings define who I became.
There are no other 'truths' out there."
—Rex

1
REX INVENTING REX

Art is a harsh mistress. Art asks everything of the artist. Art keeps the artist alive until all that is left of the artist is the art.

Rexwerk, the summary name of Rex's beautiful book of forbidden sex, smacks of Germanic discipline, of American homomasculinity, and of the authentic homosurreal art that imitates life the way, once upon a time, it was lived after midnight by men hunting other homomasculine men. Beginning in the 1960s, Rex helped create our gay culture that thrives on homoerotica because life enhanced by the renewable energy of Eros is the best panacea for gay men wounded by homophobia. He was a product of his own will. His work was his life. His work is his grandeur.

This isn't a history of Rex (1944-2024). It's a memoir. An archival memoir. A personal eulogy in which renegade Rex speaks for himself revealing a new autobiographical visibility to a mid-century founder of the gay gaze. With the passing of this self-generating genius, the curtain can go up on the dramatic adventure of his highbrow and low-down life.

How strange. How sad to be 86 and waking Rex, 80, the last of the red-hot pioneers. He leaves this editor of *Drummer* magazine the last man standing in the "Tontine of Leather" in what the profound Sam Steward, friend of Gertrude and Alice, dubbed the "*Drummer* Salon." Counting Rex, our vanishing circle disrupted art history, defied gay censorship, and entertained millions.

Our fraternity included a who's who of Stonewall-era inventors of the gay gaze: artist Tom of Finland, emphysema, 71; photographer Robert Mapplethorpe, AIDS, 42; poet Thom Gunn, heart attack from acute polysubstance abuse, 74; author Sam Steward, pulmonary disease and barbiturate addiction, 84; filmmaker Fred Halsted, suicide after death of lover, 47; Oscar Streaker Robert Opel, murder, 39; artist A. Jay Shapiro, AIDS, 56; photographer Lou Thomas, AIDS, 56; artist Bill Ward, AIDS, 69; filmmaker Wakefield Poole, 85; artist Olaf Odegaard, 59; author Larry Townsend, non-AIDS pneumonia, 77; videographer David Hurles, complications from drug-induced stroke, 78; and a few others like artist Dom "Etienne" Orejudos, AIDS, 58.

As editor-in-chief of *Drummer* from 1977 to 1980, I was privileged by the centrality of *Drummer* to review and publish and socialize with these trailblazers. How exciting it was in that first decade after Stonewall when these men arrived at my desk and unzipped their brilliant portfolios that, in fact, helped create *Drummer* and the very leather culture they celebrated. See a "Tom." Dress like Tom. See a "Rex." Fuck like Rex.

In his origin story, Rex legally renamed himself "Rex West" invoking Marlboro cowboys when "Rex King" might have been more apt because "Rex" in Latin means "King" and he, never a queen, ruled the wild kingdom of Rex World. It may as well have been called Rex Neverland because Rex whose self-defining late-in-life portfolio was his *Peter Pan* series was a Lost Boy. He claimed he ran away from home to the streets as soon as he could, first at age eight, and finally at sixteen. He carried the gay gene for *nostalgie de la boue*: the erotic attraction to blue-collar men, low-life culture, skid-row adventures, and ritual degradation—redeemed by the magical thinking of orgasm as male worship. He was a socially distant mystery wrapped in a black leather jacket.

What I write about him is memory struck from our mutual lives after we met in person in 1978. He called himself "Rex West" which is the name on his passport, but his birth name which has yet to be revealed might be "Cameron Fifield," a name I found written on the margin of a 1960s studio photo of him at twenty. Or perhaps the theatrical "Cameron Fifield" was the aspiring model's constructed stage name.

As a child, Rex was a voracious reader. Perhaps the ambitous boy fancied himself to be novelist Horatio Alger's "Ragged Dick," a bootblack who pulls himself to success by his own bootstraps. He claimed he was born hardscrabble in Connecticut. He was desperately, insistently blue collar. He was not one of those gay Beau Brummell dandies who polish their boots with champagne. Rex pissed beer on his kinky boots.

There's a maxim in the closing line in John Ford's cowboy film about outlaws, *The Man Who Shot Liberty Valance*: "When the legend becomes fact, print the legend." Rex worked hard at the mystique of his legend. But history seeks facts.

When word circulated that after Rex finally rejected the United States, he had suffered and died alone in the last of his many self-imposed exiles far away in poverty and obscurity in Amsterdam around April 1, 2024, I suspected, knowing him, always a tempestuous trickster, that news of his death was perhaps an elaborate April Fool's joke, like Tom Sawyer faking his own drowning to see what the world had to say about him. I was several weeks into writing his obituary before we learned his death date was Thursday, March 28, 2024.

At the same time the San Francisco *Bay Area Reporter* published a brief obituary on Rex on April 10, the *New York Review of Books* published its May 9 issue with a cover drawing by Tom of Finland to illustrate its long cover essay, "Tom's Men." What Jarrett Earnest wrote about Tom, who inspired Rex, made the same point I've made for years in *Drummer* about Robert Mapplethorpe's revolutionary contribution to art—which applies equally to Robert, Rex, and Tom.

"Tom of Finland's [Robert's, Rex's] work has transformed from mid-century gay pornography to twenty-first-century art, but its *troubling dimensions* [italics added] as well as the ways it has creatively shaped the desires of a diverse range of queer people, cannot be ignored."

During one of our long conversations when Rex asked me to wait until he died to write about him with permission to quote him, it was as if he wanted the surety of at least one designated mourner who had observed, interviewed, and published him from the start of his long career.

In the Dutch morgue, there were no collectors of *Rexwerk*. And as far as is yet known, there were no personal mourners. But for those dying with no kin in Amsterdam, the Lonely Funeral Project provides a volunteer poet to read a custom poem based on what the departed revealed of his life. What could a poet say about an artist who kept his life secret? About an autistic man who committed social suicide cutting off people, gay culture, and an American nation he felt had betrayed him?

Our lives and careers ran parallel. I am a participatory New Journalist who liked him and never saw a Rex drawing that was not perfection. To promote the struggling artist, I wrote about him in *Drummer* and other magazines from the 1970s through the *fin de siècle* and was a producer of his Berlin exhibit *Rex Verboten* at the Gallerie/The Ballery during Folsom Europe Fair, September 2016.

For years, we collaborated, and talked on and off the record, depending on his mood swings. He always addressed me like I was an audience. I listened. He told me, "My work is very dependent on my moods." He was a genius on paper where as a pointillist artist with both a Rapidograph Pen and a 3.5mm Rotring Ink Pen—inking like a tattoo artist dotting human skin—he controlled the million ink dots that composed each drawing. He was not happy that he could not control, could not dot the i's and cross the t's, of the gay press. He always knew what he wanted to do and how he wanted to position himself for public consumption.

When shooting the *Rex Video Gallery: Corrupt Beyond Innocence* for him in 1989, I suggested we needed a bang-up final shot. He said, "Go for the Dot." He was not being reductive. He was being essential. He showed me how he had used a photocopier to keep enlarging one small dot from one of his million-dot drawings until that one dot grew to fill the entire frame.

In fact, the ultimate Rex drawing is that Dot, alive with breath and pulse, which sums him up.

To honor his art direction, I used my macro close-up lens to enlarge one dot of one picture, drilling down more each take, the dot becoming larger, shedding literal meaning for abstraction, until the entire screen was filled with one last shot of one huge perfect Rex Dot. Now I mourn his life has come to an end. Dot. Dot. Dot. Full stop.

In May 1996, Rex, was anxiously coping with his issues and intense mood changes around abandonment, trust, betrayal, control, and social withdrawal.

> **Rex:** I know I've been terse with you about writing about me in gay magazines. I have no reason to suspect you of anything, but crazy things happen like when my fans don't destroy my letters to them. I destroy all my letters. When I let you publish my interview in your *Mapplethorpe* book [1994], I know it was absolutely quoted perfectly. It sounded like me as I was reading it. All the pauses, the commas, it was exactly the way I talk. It all came back to me. If you're talking to the BBC, then you can talk freely about me. Excellent

stuff. That's a different context than writing something for a gay magazine.

If Alistair Cooke [BBC host of *Masterpiece Theater*] came over today, I'd sit right down and babble my head off.... If my life belongs anywhere, it belongs in an historical book, not in some porn smut gay rag. To sell gay magazines the editors want upbeat sexy articles. How many dogs did I suck and at what parties did I do it? And I don't live that kind of life. I want to be revealed in my best light. I've gotten neurotic about this. That's the way I am.

I don't really mind when JD writes about me in his *Trash* magazine [hundreds of issues 1975-2020)] because no one really reads it. ["JD" was Rex's longtime friend, the vitriolic and aggressively reactionary conservative John Dagion (1935-2020) who retired from New Jersey to cruise young Mexican laborers at reststops in Republican Florida near the same time Rex fled to Amsterdam.] JD's written more about what I've done and where I've been in life than anyone, and nobody actually sees it. He knows everything. I really think the man is a saint in a way. His porn is the best, better than yours, no offense, but I don't think he is appreciated as much as you, and I know he is sensitive to that so I try to support him. When you're 65 like he is, you're shaking anyway by just growing old. That's an age when it's hard to make new friends. Especially if you're in the sex business. He's basically retired. When I see him, I realize he's an old man. When you're growing old, you've got to take chances. We're all isolated. As I was saying to JD, you know, the world is coming to an end.

Someday historians will need to go through his zine. I told [our mutual friends] Trent [Dunphy] and Bob [Mainardi] that it's not that I mind you writing about me, but not while I'm alive. If you're going to write about what I've told you, put it in a book of interviews where it belongs. From my point of view, you've always respected me and you should show respect for me on this. Tell people that's just the way he is. Agreeable till he's not. Tell them, "When he's dead, we can print it. While he's alive, it isn't worth alienating him."

Jack Fritscher: So I've got to outlive Rex? That's a terrible tontine. I've been here before. After I interviewed Sam Steward in 1972, he told me I couldn't publish the interview until he was dead because he had to live off his stories [about Gertrude Stein, Alice B. Toklas, and Doctor Kinsey].

Rex: I don't wish you dead. Of course, I'm going to outlive you. I'll make sure of that.

Jack Fritscher: You're going to outlive me?

Rex: Absolutely.

Jack Fritscher: You'll make sure of it? [Because he worked for the Mafia, I joked.] Have you taken a contract out on me?

Rex: No. No. No. We'll go on forever.

As an eyewitness monitoring his career, I had a constant human regard for him that often went unrequited. He was a voyeur who hated to be observed.

In the world of gay origin stories, Rex would not be the first gay teen escaping the closet of a bourgeois family home and re-wilding himself as an outrageous outlaw with a new street name. Kafka, who liked to lick the legs of blond boys, said, "I am my stories." Rex, who liked to lick the legs of leathermen, said, "I am my drawings."

The self-possessed artist owned himself. He once told me during the many years we chatted for hours on the phone—when I took shorthand or recorded him by agreement—that he, who in his bestiary of men often drew horny canine companions, decided to call himself "Rex" because it was the perfect name for a dog who is man's best friend. When Rex was a bookish teenager suffering the existential pains of an abandoned pup, he dived into Nietzsche and may have read his line, "I have given a name to my pain and call it *dog*."

He repeatedly insisted he had been abandoned at birth—although, in a Greek-Dickensian plot twist, Oedipus Rex later said, in the 1990s, he reconciled with his mother whom he supported in a retirement home where she died and left him a fortune he lost in the stock market. He always concealed the 1944 year of his February 5 birthday which I calculated as closely as possible from his emails. On September 9, 2021, he wrote he was 78. On December 17, 2023, he wrote, "I'll be 80 in less than two months"

A born fabulist hellbent on controlling his narrative, he impeded his own entry into art history. Rumors he himself may have started had it he was the black sheep son of a United States senator. Or some industrial magnate. Or some Mafia boss. In his kitchen-sink drama, he claimed as a young boy he had to work alongside rough itinerant field hands on a tobacco farm in Connecticut. He said he was an orphan who became a double orphan when his adoptive stepparents died. He said he drifted to New York in the 1960s where he told me he was a kept boy in his twenties, had half a dozen lovers, and attended art school on the dime of a sugar daddy. His longtime friend Clyde Wildes has a photo of Rex standing like a fashion model outside the Ritz Hotel, Place Vendome, Paris, December 1965. Whether his tangled origin story was fact or legend, you'd have to ask the man who shot Liberty Valance.

In 1975, he told the *Village Voice*, "I nearly died seven times. I've been chic and elegant. I've had a nervous breakdown. I've been in three institutions. I've ridden with motorcycle gangs…. I'm thirty years old."

After Rex died, a man who said Rex was once his lover told me that Rex, who was tending bar anonymously, told him he had been hired in the late 1960s as a staff artist for a cigar-chewing Mafia publisher who gave him the code name "Rex."

At the time of the 1969 riot at the Stonewall Inn owned and managed by the Mafia, Rex was twenty-five and living in Greenwich Village where gays interacted for mutual benefit with the Mafia who owned most of the gay bars. Two years later, on March 29, 1971, Francis Ford Coppola began romancing pop culture into the sexy allure of the Mafia when he started shooting *The Godfather* on location in the streets of Lower Manhattan.

Rex recalling his first decade in Manhattan said, "I was in New York long before Stonewall. I think I went by, on the night it happened, to the bars on Christopher Street. It was just a little disturbance with people caught between the Mafia and the cops. It was the 60s. There was always a disturbance going on. At the time, no one paid much attention outside the Village. Then, my God, it mushroomed!

"During the next year," he said, "the gay press made a 'thing' out of it. It became like the landing of the *Mayflower*. There were only about a hundred people onboard, but a million people claim they landed on Plymouth Rock like the five million revisionists who rioted at Stonewall.

"I had gone to the Stonewall once when it was a restaurant."

Bonnie's Stonewall Inn, 53 Christopher Street, 1934-1966, advertised itself on its matchbook covers as "New York's Smartest Rendezvous of Celebrities from Everywhere. When in Greenwich Village, Don't Miss Bonnie's Stonewall Inn." The Genovese crime family bought Bonnie's restaurant in 1966 and opened it as a gay bar in 1967.

"Then it became a little dance bar," Rex remembered, "and now a little coffee shop [called "Bagels"] I first read about it in the gay press that turned it into a political symbol."

Suddenly that summer on July 8, 1969, a fast ten days after the riot, Rex witnessed Mattachine activists Lige Clarke and his lover Jack Nichols kickstarting the *idée fixe* of Stonewall as a creation myth, an origin story, a politcal teaching moment, and a battle cry in their column in *Screw* magazine and then in their weekly national newspaper *GAY* (1969-1974). On February 10, 1975, five months before the *Village Voice* attacked Rex, the pretty longhaired blond Clarke was murdered age 32 in Mexico by motorcyclists spraying his car with machine guns. Was he like gay poet Federico Garcia Lorca targeted by macho fascists? Was the *Voice* taking out its frustration and anger over bikers and Clarke's unsolved ambush by ambushing and scapegoating Rex?

"Basically," Rex said, "that night the police arrested some people in a bar raid. It was no pivotal moment in history. Think of all us who were already out for years. We'd already pivoted with our work."

Rex was not quite married to the mob, but he may have fallen for some of the hot *guido* gangsters he met when he worked for Star Distribution where for the first time his gay dirt hit pay dirt and the amateur became a professional. Star, the Mafia's main publisher and distributor of adult material, hired Rex to draw covers and illustrations for its 1970s gay pulp-fiction series *Rough Trade*. During those Manhattan years, 1976-1985, his home bar where he was often hired for specific tasks was the Mafia-owned Mineshaft. Rex who liked association with Mafia tough guys and their attitude might have cooked up his own protective Rexian sense of their Sicilian *omertà*, their code of silence, in his own queer *omertà* refusing to talk about himself even under questioning.

Young Rex was too provocative, disruptive, and subversive for his own good. He had reason to protect himself. Like gayish playwright Alfred Jarry saying "shit" in Paris in 1896, and gay writer Lytton Strachey saying "semen" in Bloomsbury in 1908, Rex said "leather S&M" in New York in 1975. He was a modernist trying to make gay art new. When the Psychedelic 1960s exploded in a glitter bomb at the 1969 Stonewall riot, gay character changed. Rex helped embolden the new decade with his art. He became *persona non grata* for challenging the fixed horizon of short-sighted establishment homosexuals. Rex took them to the edge and pushed them over the edge.

Five years into his career, his shocking pictures debuted suddenly like thunder in the New York press on July 7, 1975, when closeted journalist Richard Goldstein interviewing Rex about his new gay gaze attacked him with an exposé in the *Village Voice* and labeled him a "Naziphile" for drawing explicit scenes of leather-sex and saying, "The greatest S&M trip in history was the Nazis." Hypothetically, was it queer vanilla fundamentalism or musical-comedy satire that a vanity of *Village Voice* writers like Arthur Bell and his erstwhile lover Arthur "The Red Queen" Evans wanted to purify the blood of gay male identity and mortify the flesh of sado-masochistic gay leathermen whose pride and joy is mortification?

To understand Richard Goldstein's hyperventilating investigation of Rex, consider the source about whom I write allegedly. Goldstein, the *Voice* rock critic who in 1967 created a media scandal when he irked Paul McCartney by trashing *Sgt. Pepper* after listening to it on a broken stereo, was a closeted gay man struggling with his identity while married to a woman. He told *The Advocate* in 2015 that his life experience at that time was like, God help us, *The Boys in the Band.* With his myopic gaze on that miserable horizon in 1975, it was four years before he came out in 1979.

Pirandello would have had a picnic with these two characters in search of authenticities in the mix of art and politics. In Rex's first media interview, why did he consent to play defendant to prosecutor Goldstein whose militant scorn was wrong for all his otherwise right reasons of anti-defamation vigilance? Rex told me, "It's what I strive for—to really get their juices going till they lose control." Whether publicity hound Rex called himself an anarchist or was a Naziphile or a Nazi or a right-wing fascist conservative or not, the postmortem answer lies not in Goldstein's confusions, but in readers studying the trajectory of Rex's life and art while using critical ability to consider that my allegations about Goldstein are based on Rex's allegations about Goldstein as well as on research and on internal evidence in the *Voice* article itself.

As an iconoclast making new icons, the truth is, Rex broke the norms of received gay male identity. Like Tom of Finland and Robert Mapplethorpe, Rex glorified the new male selfhood and gender identity of post-Stonewall leather homomasculinity by turning symbols—Nazi, Catholic, Queer, American, and otherwise—on their heads while launching raw and radical S&M content as a bonafide subject in art.

Goldstein, like Susan Sontag who in the same year of 1975 called leather culture "camp," was investigating 1970s "Fascinating Fascism" and "Nazi Chic." If Rex and his kind were camp to Sontag, why not to Goldstein? In an age of Nazi hunters, Goldstein was *en garde* in his article, "S&M: The Dark Side of Gay Liberation: Flirting with Terminal Sex." Calling out Rex as "Exhibit A," he stopped short of calling Rex a "Nazi," but did he overreach Rex—and himself—when he took a broad swipe at leather culture itself for flirting with fantasy fetishes of Nazi drag, insignia, and role play?

There is an irony that Goldstein's article calculating the "horrors" of S&M was so filled with delicious information warning "what not to do" and "where not to go" that perversatile leathermen exiting the closet in 1975 re-purposed his words as a kind of "Gay Guide to S&M Things to Do and Leather Places to Go."

As a 13-year-old in 1952, I hadn't yet noticed that men's dirty postwar pulp magazines existed until a priest clutching the pearls of his rosary warned us altar boys to keep custody of our eyes and avert our gaze away from the sinful girly men's adventure magazines in drugstores where I rushed to feast my queer eye on bare-chested buddies fighting vicious animals and Nazi sex kittens with whips on the cover of *Argosy*. Just one look woke my critical thinking and my dick. Beneath the hetero pictures and text idealizing the sweaty masculinity of rugged guys, I felt the beating heart of a subliminal homomasculine subtext.

Back then before the erotic gay press began to exist, subtext was all we had. Gay boys growing up in a straight world learned to squint the gay squint that turns straight stuff gay. That's the first and basic gay gaze.

Rex and I each cocked an eye to build our own teen spank banks. We both learned to narrow our eyes to blur busty Nazi blondes like "Ilsa: She-Wolf of the SS" on the cover of *Saga*, so we could focus on the well-built American soldiers Ilsa was tying up nearly nude in soft-porn articles like "The Conquering Fräuleins."

In our postwar childhoods, we war babies grew up with American media portraying Nazis as escapist entertainment everywhere in a pop culture created to relieve the stress of a nation of veterans and home-front citizens dealing with the PTSD caused by the war.

In reaction, the 1960s and 1970s became a nostalgic period of swinging sex, transgressive art, and pop-culture cosplay. Rex's contemporaries like the Beatles put Hitler obscured on the cover of

Sgt. Pepper; Kenneth Anger shot gay Nazi bikers orgying across the screen in *Scorpio Rising*; the Residents art-band titled its album *Third Reich Rock 'n' Roll*; glam-rock metal bands and punk rockers like the Sex Pistols wore styles akin to the Nazi-spiked fashions of Vivienne Westwood and Malcolm McClaren; Warhol shot his business manager Fred Hughes and socialite model Maxime de la Falaise wearing Hitler mustaches; Jim French of New York's iconic Colt Studio named his porn studio after a phallic gun and pseudonymed himself as a fine artist after the famous German gun: "Luger"; Mel Brooks went camping with "Springtime for Hitler"; and 1970s films like *Cabaret*, *The Night Porter*, *Seven Beauties*, and Pasolini's *Salo* sold tickets because audiences never tire of Nazi gowns and uniforms.

The activist culture critic, playwright, and university professor Sarah Schulman, a creator of the ACT UP Oral History Project, once asked in general "why some people are micro-critiqued, and others say and do vile, regressive things that get overlooked."

What made Rex different from those diverse artists? What made Rex an easy target? What made Rex a "Naziphile"? Was it his politically incorrect point of view? Was it because he declared the constitutional rights of masculine Eros and the free choice of consensual male-to-male domination and power in a prescriptive feminist age when vanilla gays had no clue that leathermen on Folsom were fisting Foucault, raising his masomachismo consciousness, as he on his sex-tourist weekends climbed into slings at the baths seeking to find power and receive wisdom from the disciplinary games and penal practices of leathermen.

Rex stood out for better or worse because Rex always stood out. His smoldering personality was that provocative. His work was that good. Even before the *Voice* article drove him into seclusion, he was as much a cult artist as Tom of Finland. His fans who never thought of him as a political artist never quit the pointillist seer whose visions of erotic anarchy documented the iconography of the apolitical leather identity they lived.

Rex's cool gay gaze like the *Drummer* gay eye was rooted in that postwar context of those pulp-mag artists who, mining Nazis as sexy gold, created the seductive covers of "straight male adventure magazines." He built his repertoire by queering their aesthetic and redrawing their images for the emerging new genre of "gay male adventure magazines" like *Drummer* and *Honcho* that flourished during the Golden Age of gay magazines from 1975 until their death by internet in 1999.

Although Goldstein actually wrote he was personally "nauseated" by Rex's art, to his credit, he never accused Rex, whose ethnicity remains unknown, of the mortal sin of antisemitism.

As a gay humanist, I have to ask why, as part of the commercial gay-pride establishment in New York, did Goldstein try to sound an alarm on Rex—and insult the community culture of a million leatherfolk? Was Rex in leather drag typecast as a convenient polar opposite of leftist gays in Stonewall drag? Did Goldstein correctly sense that Rex was a nascent conservative leaning right as seems later in Rex's own words in our interviews? Was there gay-on-gay animosity because of leathermen's own brand of gay male masculinity, denounced as politically incorrect, with its erotic rituals and dedicated bars with virile dress codes that, like women's safe spaces excluding men, excluded effeminacy with door signs like "Leathers Not Sweaters."

One short year later, as Goldstein had cautioned, the Leather Apocalypse arrived on a cloud of poppers when the quintessential leather club, the orgiastic Mineshaft, opened its world-famous door, bathtub, slings, and buckets of Crisco to thousands of international leathermen with Rex as its official artist till its closing eight years later.

"It's almost," Goldstein, a constant critic of male power, wrote, "as if gay culture has taken on the Yeatsian task of creating its own rough beast—the leather man." Goldstein throwing a literary punch was pointedly aware that Irish poet W. B. Yeats was an identified conservative nationalist in sympathy with the rough beasts of fascism and Nazism.

After every war, with or without Nazis, there is an afterglow of romantic and erotic nostalgia in popular culture. Did Goldstein really think that garden-variety homosexual hedonists playing at being sexual outlaws sporting hankies, nipple-clamps, designer vests, and Iron Crosses as junk jewelry in leather bars were neo-Nazi Hells Angels? Or that the Eagle name and the spreadeagle logo of almost fifty international gay leather bars is an homage to the Nazi Eagle of World War II?

Dealing with the ambiguity and moral axioms around mid-century imagery, the Jewish Anti-Defamation League calls for critical ability to discern what's Nazi and what's not: "Eagles [in the logo of leather bars, and drawn repeatedly by Rex] are a common symbol among nations worldwide, including the United States, and not every image of an eagle is derivative of the Nazi eagle. It is not uncommon, for example, for some Americans to mistake the Blue Eagle logo of the Roosevelt-era National Recovery Administration for a Nazi-derived symbol."

There is absolutely no apologia for Nazism ever, and there is no better way to counterphobically denature Nazism than in art on page and screen. While everyone today is vigilant if not vigilante about neo-Nazis and Nazi sympathizers infiltrating society, it's not an uncommon prejudice for mainstream vanilla gay people to misinterpret subset leather people, art, and culture the way the audience on screen in artist Mel Brooks' satire *The Producers* at first misunderstands "Springtime for Hitler," or the way composer John Kander and lyricist Fred Ebb use the power of art in *Cabaret* to seduce, teach, and enlighten Broadway audiences who, wondering why Germans fell for Hitler, find themselves suddenly fizzed with patriotic emotion and falling for the gorgeous blond Aryan Hitler Youth, who could have been drawn by Rex, singing their rousing—fictitious—Nazi anthem: "Tomorrow Belongs to Me."

Inquiry, debate. and education about gay men's masturbatory magical thinking about Nazis can create teaching moments around *auteur* Rex as well as around Tom of Finland who said: "In my drawings I have no political statements to make, no ideology. I am thinking only about the picture itself. The whole Nazi philosophy, the racism and all that, is hateful to me, but, of course, I drew them anyway—they had the sexiest uniforms." Certainly there were confusing coincidences. Hitler's politically-correct Nazi party founded at the Furstenfelder Hof pub, his Stonewall Inn, in Munich on

January 5, 1919, was centered around beer halls, homosexuals, camaraderie, uniforms, short leather pants, and slap dancing—just like gay leather culture.

In the 1970s, every American gay-bar customer thirty and older had as a boy lived through the war with the Nazis. Did Goldstein, born in 1944, not understand it was our generation of war babies who alchemized real-life toxic violence and empowered the 1970s culture of liberating resistance with the curative of imaginative orgasm? The violence of World War II was insanely surreal with the kind of terror that can only be survived by making it romantic, comic, or erotic.

In 1972, three years before Goldstein's anti-leather article, the nurturing pioneer leather author Larry Townsend was so aware of the pop-culture confusion of leather and Nazis that he directly addressed the psycho-erotic nexus with many references throughout his *The Leatherman's Handbook* and its sequel *The Leatherman's Handbook II* (1983) in which he wrote: "I can't imagine anyone in his right mind seriously wanting to revert to this [Nazi] period. As with many other historical evils, the fantasy will exclude the reality and the horror. We focus only on the parts we find stimulating, or titillating. The same barrier of time and/or space makes it possible to look on other atrocities in a very different light from the people who had to endure them…. Such sources are often the bases for many of our best and most exciting stories."

If Nazis can be sent up by satire, then why not by eros? What a camp subversity it was when gay uniform clubs hosted events like the "War Games" party at Probe disco in Hollywood, and the Pacific Drill Patrol (founded 1972) hosted uniform parties in Rex's San Francisco home bar, the Brig, later, the Powerhouse, 1347 Folsom Street.

Rex drew the poster "The Liberating Experience" for the Brig which was owned from 1978-1983 by German refugee Hank Diethelm who to Rex's erotic envy was forced at fourteen into the Hitler Youth before his rescue by an American soldier when Rex was a year old. Cringe or binge, laughing at Nazis and reducing them to fetish sex objects in a gay bar is a certain kind of hotsy-totsy-Nazi revenge served cold for ruining our boyhoods. Was it "An Appointment in Samarra" that on April 10, 1983, in the basement of his home at 226 Bemis Street, the jolly Hank Diethelm was found tied in a dental chair, tortured, strangled, and set on fire.

In the February 2025 *Vanity Fair*, the writer and actress Natasha Lyonne joked that her family consists of "my father's side, Flatbush, and my mother's side, Auschwitz." She who began her film career while living in Israel said she believes in the Surreal Freedom of Make-Believe. "I'm pretty honest about that being my kink."

So why not the Homosurrealism of Kink Make-Believe by Rex and Tom? In London on February 26, 2015, *The Guardian* newspaper headlined: "Why are we still so obsessed with the Nazis? How thinking about the Third Reich has changed over the decades."

Goldstein's spring-loaded wisecrack about the "anarchy of manbeasts" and the "end-time chaos" of leather revelations included visual exploitation. At least, the *Village Voice* page design looked very like thirsty self-serving sexploitation. Did the publisher have a double motive? The anti-leather page layout took the opportunity to illustrate itself with two S&M drawings of Rex's "rough beasts" because offering that kind of prurient "Exhibit B" for curious and queer readers squinting to find bits of porn to take in hand before major gay magazines were founded in the mid-1970s, would sell more copies on newsstands.

It's to Rex's credit that the penniless artist won many column inches of free publicity in the *Voice* when he stood up for himself with clever ripostes about the human worth of leather culture, about the evils of corporate culture, and about his theories around American religion, politics, and fascism that eight months after his death came true.

From my interaction with Rex, the *Voice* feature because it found valid reasons to question his art and politics wounded him deeply. Rex never suffered critics gladly. Feeling scapegoated, the autistic artist was all on his lonesome without much fraternal support when the *Voice* hit the streets three weeks after publication of the first issue of *Drummer*. That West Coast leather magazine, then unknown to Goldstein, escaped the *Voice* inquisition even as it became a refuge for Rex, and the international magazine of record for twentieth-century leather culture.

In 2004, Goldstein alleged he was fired by the evolving *Village Voice*. He threatened a lawsuit, and went on writing books excoriating the formal gay right wing of which the independent Rex, who was no Leni Riefenstahl, was never a part.

Whether history finds Rex's avant-garde work Naziana or not, the article deprived the struggling homomasculine gender artist of nuance and cast him as a villain in the cultural narrative of gaystream gatekeepers.

The PTSD he suffered was collateral damage not intended by Goldstein, but the high-profile trauma—which must be addressed—ignited his lifelong distrust of the gay press. He began guarding himself against censorship and cancellation with fierce anxiety.

"The Press!"

That complaint was the first thing that came out of his mouth the first time we met. Was he spinning reverse psychology every time he proclaimed he did not want to be in gay magazines to cover for the fact that the national gay press loudly alerted by the *Village Voice* was afraid of him and his shocking, and sometimes illegal, art in their pages?

To correct that, *Drummer* rode to his rescue and published his first magazine cover drawing on issue 10, November 1976. Years later when Rex was living bicoastally, he told me about his misbegotten return to New York in 1992 to open his own "appointment only" Secret Museum Gallery (1992-2001). It was a little too secret. What a shock when, seeking his canonical due, the legend in his own time began making the rounds of the new young millennial magazine editors who had taken over publishing by default, lacking mentoring from the generation-gap of previous editors dead from AIDS. Anyone can open a gallery. The editors had no idea who he was and they didn't care what embarrassing veterans of the ancient gay liberation wars they left behind. They scratched their heads and touched their man buns because Rex was off their gaydar. The internet did not exist before 1993, and they could not be bothered to look at the extreme portfolio of some vaguely vagrant old guy they did not know was a transgressive beat-punk artist years before Patti Smith sang at Hilly Crystal's CBGB in the East Village.

Jack: As an artist, how do you defend your problematical and often outlaw material? How do you face editors and critics?

Rex: I don't have to face them because I never face anyone.

Jack: But your work does. Your *putti* may be beyond the pale.

Rex: They will talk to the work and the work will talk to them and it will end there. I know a lot of regular people who are appalled by my work, but they never confront me or address me.

In 1976, Rex became the official artist of the legendary after-hours club, the Mineshaft—835 Washington Street, 1976-1985—two years before his friend, the other keen eye, Robert Mapplethorpe, became its official photographer. Rex was two years older than Mapplethorpe who collected his drawings. I remember one day over a late lunch at the Sausage Factory on Castro Street when Robert asked Rex, "How do you do it? How do you make your drawings so erotic?" Rex just smiled and said, "More pasta?" The blistering raw eroticism Robert saw in Rex, and hungered for, he never achieved.

Rex is to drawing what Mapplethorpe is to photography, but Rex is edgier with a *mise-en-scène* more daring than the cool formal world of Mapplethorpe who had to deal with temperamental living models while the unfettered Rex without borders pulled his conceptual models out of his chiaroscuro imagination—or from magazine photographs as did Mapplethorpe in his collages.

If Mapplethorpe flew first-class on private jets with his patrons, Rex rode slouched across the cheap seats at the back of a Greyhound bus jacking off the hard men of his dreams and collecting dots of cum. While Mapplethorpe created his pictures for the eyes of the professional art world of critics and collectors, Rex created his perfect moments for the eyes of ordinary people who relate personally to his images in which they find emotional satisfaction they may not be able to analyze. Mapplethorpe told clients, "If you don't like this picture, maybe you're not as avant-garde as you think." Rex had the very same attitude.

Rex once told me: "I want to draw pictures nobody has seen before."

Mapplethorpe once told me: "I want to see the Devil in us all."

Profiling Rex in *Drummer* 12, January 1977, with three Rex drawings in the article, "Rex: Unusual Erotic Work from a Superb Leather Artist," we rebutted the *Village Voice*. One image we published pictured a muscleman on the telephone, and the other a sailor riding exposed and hard on the subway slouched under a poster that Rex had Rexified of the Marlboro Man whom both Rex and *Drummer* kept in mind as a source image for basic gay American masculinity. The same issue illustrated reporter Gary Collins' exposé of prison sex horrors in his lead feature "Male Rape" with Rex's gang-bang drawing "Male Rape."

As keeper of the DrummerArchives.com, I'm quoting here that Rex article—that has no byline—to give Rex fans, readers, and researchers direct access now and in the future to this hard-to-find classic issue because this is the kind of reportage most likely written by Oscar Streaker Robert Opel who wrote a series about artists in *Drummer* issues 2, 4, 9, and 13, culminating in his interview with Tom of Finland in issue 22.

The evidence of Opel's authorship lies in the symbiotic timeline. Opel would have written this January article for publicity at the same time he was writing press releases for his forthcoming Rex exhibit in April at his Fey-Way Gallery, 1287 Howard Street, where before he was murdered there July 7, 1979, he mounted Rex's first show in San Francisco: *Rex Originals*, April 8-19, 1978.

Rex came to *Drummer*, hat in hand, in the 1970s, almost at the same moment as did Mapplethorpe with his hat because both New Yorkers needed monthly *Drummer* to build their brands with thousands of national and international readers. In 1989, *Drummer* continued its general support of sexy Rexy by specifically promoting him in its "Second Short Story Contest" seeking fiction based on a Rex drawing. Years later, in 2018, the *New York Times* published "A Trio of Short Fictions Inspired by Robert Mapplethorpe Photographs" written by Michael Cunningham, Elif Batuman, and Hilton Als.

Drummer was a first draft of leather art history with its star-making adoration of talents like Rex, its coverage of his drawing process and of his first live-work studio in New York at 178 Christopher Street conveniently next door to the marvelously sleazy Christopher Hotel at 180 Christopher where leathermen rented rooms by the hour, and Rex spent nights, months, and years of sex research on his knees studying *tableaux* of life models in real knock-down-and-drag-out scenes he turned into art. During the Golden Age of Gay Magazines (1975-2000), gay artists from Rex to Mapplethorpe to Bill Ward, who was the artist most published in *Drummer*, to Tom of Finland needed and courted editors to build their careers in the national web of gay magazines that started up after Stonewall, crashed with AIDS, and died at the dawn of the internet.

Drummer reported:

"Uh, there really is a Rex, isn't there?" The voice answering on the telephone is hesitant. It's a fair question. Though the drawings that are signed "Rex" are earthy, highly real and personal, still there is something in that technique that doesn't seem quite human. Something suggests the infinite detail of a photograph. But if you pick up a magnifying glass to check it out, well, it's only lines and dots and black and white after all. A drawing doesn't give itself up to you like a photograph. It eludes you.

There is a Rex, but Rex doesn't give himself up to you either. Not many people meet Rex. An interview? It's out of the question. Reserved, intense, wary of outsiders and newcomers, Rex is an enigma, as disciplined and demanding in himself as the taut technique of his drawings. He's handsome: fine sharp features, dark hair, tight-muscled, the classic grin of a G.I. Definitely handsome, and always soberly dressed in black, always wearing those thick-soled German army boots you sometimes see in Rex drawings.

Rex lives and works in the kind of fortress you get used to in New York. A cool dark space with a precision finish. Photographs are everywhere—men, machines, aircraft hangars, horses, and Tom of Finland drawings. "Everyone," Rex says if you ask him, "owes Tom a lot. He took the rugged American man, made him larger than life, and gave him back to us."

In a room like a bunker, drawings for the next Rex book are tacked to cork walls below a khaki parachute that spills out of an army helmet in the center of the ceiling. Some of the drawings are finished, just the way they'll be published. Others are being worked on, a process that can take months. The outlines are already there, the male flesh still blank, perhaps just a leather sleeve Rex has totally completed, highlights glistening, the teeth of a zipper. Already they are beautiful and hot just like that, unfinished. ("A drawing is complete at several stages," Rex said once. "Something in each stage has to be sacrificed to the final drawing.")

What makes the finished drawings so hot? For one thing, these are not pretty fellows all draped in fetish symbols. The boots and leathers, the uniforms, the clamps and chains express a horny urgency. The men who grapple with each other with such a fierce passion are not always even handsome. Some of the best men in the world of Rex are brutal.

Rex never sets up a narrative series. All the story is there in one flash, telescoped into a single moment and isolated on the page. These are drawings you look at one at a time. In each one, Rex distills the action we have all seen, done, or imagined, but which we get to bring off only rarely and never so well.

The settings are immediate. The action can't wait for a safe place or better time; it explodes on the spot, in the johns, on a subway car, in lockers or a room at the Y. But there's a cryptic quality in the atmosphere, a sense that even the litter on a seedy hotel room floor carries a special message. Though you recognize some familiar images, Rex gives them a private twist. Take the classic leatherman on the cover of *Männespielen: A Portfolio by Rex*. Rex captures the dull shine of his jacket and the topman's traditional leather cap, but you can't read the expression in his eyes; they are strangely remote. And he licks his lip in a disconcerting gesture. Why? In anticipation? A cool appraisal? There is something elusive and seductive in these details, too.

And the titles! Last year, hardly anyone knew the meaning of *Männespielen* (let alone how to say it). Rex explains it as German slang meaning men's games, a kind of rough locker-room horseplay. The games these men are into make heavy horseplay: games of power, games of submission, played out in an intense hush.

His new book is called *Icons*. Images of worship. And new games that express a kind of rugged communion. Rex is finer than ever. He draws his icons from his own world. The world of Rex excludes you or draws you in at your own risk.

Those who never got a friendly flash from a sailor in the subway might see Rex drawings as a pure exercise in fantasy. But the *Drummer* man who moves in this world himself? He knows.

After Opel's January 1977 *Drummer* article, I first wrote about Rex in my feature about the Mineshaft in *Drummer* 19, December 1977.

The Mineshaft Is a Fantasy by Rex. The *essence* of the Mineshaft is found in page after page of Rex's drawings in *Männespielen* and *Icons*. If you get off on Rex, you'll like the Mineshaft and you'll understand why the Mineshaft chose him to design its 1978 poster and T-shirt. Rex epitomizes in his work the concept of the Mineshaft Man.

Within days of publication, Rex sent me five drawings and a letter expressing his gratitude for coverage in *Drummer*. I responded on February 16, 1978.

Dear Rex, Thanks for your letter full of kind words on my writing and for the even more generous gift of your latest work...I'd be delighted to write an article featuring your professional "comeback" [after the *Village Voice* fiasco] with your approval of the copy as well as make a point of your new mail-order availability. I will, as you desire, focus on your work rather than on you personally. The discipline in your work has long impressed me. Yours, Jack Fritscher, Editor-in-Chief

He responded in a letter dated February 21, 1978, airing his smoldering resentment of the New York establishment misunderstanding his art.

Dear Jack: Thank you for your letter of the 16th. I am most grateful for any coverage I might get from your publication, especially at this transitional stage of my career. I'm enclosing the drawings you requested.... I would very much like to see your viewpoint about my work, much as you interpreted the Mineshaft poster. You'll be more objective about the work and I would definitely want some critical points mentioned.... I've a great many critics.... A paragraph exploring my [New York] detractors would prove most interesting.... Many thanks for your help, Rex.

Rex was a visionary artist of gender, of homomasculinity, for men who prefer men masculine. That made him a perfect match for *Drummer* which published his work and his equally hot commercial advertisements for popper companies, leather bars, and telephone sex lines. Durk Dehner, co-founder of the Tom of Finland Foundation in 1984, who labeled both Tom's work and Rex's work *homomasculine*, wrote: "*Drummer*, ground-breaking for its time, set precedence for all male representation to come."

Rex played an important part in creating the virilizing homomasculine standard of positive male gender presentation that became *Drummer* policy. Rex's gay eye helped usher in the New Wave of gay masculinity that came out of the closet in the 1970s in life and on page and screen. To conceptualize this, I coined the word *homomasculinity* and published it first in *Drummer* 24, September 1978. While Rex drew the faces of homomasculinity, critics often mistake his homomasculine work as toxic hyper-masculinity.

But gay homomasculinity is not straight hyper-masculinity which is a negative term embracing mid-century military toughness, misogyny, and male supremacy wrongly applied to the gender-positive work of Rex and Tom of Finland. Critics liking labels might do well to consider that the work of Rex and Tom is not hyper-masculine. Durk Dehner emphatically insisted, "Tom's work is homomasculine."

Hyper-masculinity is an exaggeration of aggressive XYY male behavior and bodies that like Neanderthals don't fit in our majority XY culture. Studies report a large percentage of the American male prison population is locked up for being XYY.

Ringmaster Rex was fascinated by the menagerie of gay desire in the zoo of gay bars where thousands of manimals in leather hides presented themselves magically zipped up, and shape-shifting identity like ritual animals—anthromorphic bulls, bears, pigs, ponies, dawgs, and pups—vested head to foot in the virilizing fetish of blue-collar clothes cut from full-grain cow hide.

He established his zoological art as edgy and bad-ass when he broke the taboo against bestiality which he made literal by adding man's best friend to many of his scofflaw pictures. He assaulted the gay gaze, and panicked the gay press, by turning taboos into totems representing emerging new queer masculine animality. He drew Montague men for hero worship by Capulet men who, like him, were homomasculinists born with a fatal attraction to bad boys and the dangerous straight hyper-masculinity of onward-marching soldiers of religion, nationalism, and capitalism.

Rex drew his men to look "straight" because he liked men that way and because of the gay fetish "in search of" straight men. His men read as masculine-identified men "in search of" one another, like a pair of straight Marines on leave drunk-fucking each other in a cheap motel with not a gay culture thought in their buzz-cut heads. Freud warned in *Three Essays on the Theory of Sexuality* that "concepts of *masculinity*, like those of *femininity*, whose meanings seem so unambiguous to ordinary people, are among the most confused that occur in science." So, why not query *homomasculinity*?

Rex's sophisticated drawing for the cover of the landmark twentieth anniversary issue of *Drummer* 100 (November 1986) is an icon of his platonic ideal of a leatherman. His hard-boiled image of a hairy-chested muscle biker with a cigarette dangling from his insouciant lip evokes a cynical underworld anti-hero in a lobby poster for a Hollywood film *noir* unreeling in a fleapit theater that's seen better days.

Rex was a fine artist with a keen eye who prowled "half-deserted streets" and dared "visions and revisions." He was a skid-row existentialist of "J. Alfred Prufrock" proportions. His rented rooms where men come and go fucking with Michael and Angelo were inspired by the archetypal rooms he cruised in the molly-house of the Christopher Street Hotel. As a virtual "landlord" managing the virtual rooms in his voyeuristic drawings, his proprietary point of view was the gay gaze of a slum lord silently spying on his tenants through keyholes.

In his 12-10-2015 picture "The Nightwatch," he "drew from life" documenting the scene in the sex-cellar Darkroom of Amsterdam's Cuckoo's Nest bar. As an ancient eye revealing his lifelong voyeurism in the 9"x18" drawing, he included a tiny selfie of his own face hiding in a corner of the drawing spying on the leathermen carousing in the actual basement orgy room where he who never smoked cigarettes spent many a night standing next to his own face, smoking dope, and sniffing poppers.

His real-estate locations in his erotic imaginarium read like a road guide to YMCAs, saloons, toilets, flophouses, carnivals, prisons, shipyards, and truck stops cruised by itinerant construction workers, greasy gas jockeys, muscle bikers, tattooed fighters, succulent young bums, pissing ex-cons, armpit suckers, studs seeking head, and the rogue cops who roust them.

Rex's men are unshaved lone wolves in jockstraps, leather, boots, and torn tank tops, who ring their tits and pierce their dicks tied off with leather thongs, who pay-per-hour in sleaze-bag hot-bed hotels where sailors, Semper-Fi Marines, cops, and drifters flop back on cum-stained mattresses—the smoke of their cigarettes drafting out the crack of their door down the hall to the common washroom where other grifters running power games of humiliation and domination stand around the funky urinal dripping beer piss, and the graffiti-covered stalls are drilled with gloryholes glazed like donuts with cum.

Rex told me, "Everybody thinks I can draw everything whereas I am extremely limited. I give that impression because I am so shrewd about limiting my repertoire. What I can't do, I don't do. So when you think I can draw everything, I don't show you the things I can't draw. In my pictures you never go outside because I can't draw nature. That's why I have to stage my sex scenes indoors at night, because I can't draw nature."

Rex's work invokes the human solitude of straight painter Edward Hopper who featured lone men and women waiting in the *noir* spaces and all-nite diners in his suggestive night paintings "Office at Night " and "Night Windows." Hopper's superb "Nighthawks" became such a pop-culture icon it was parodied by Austrian artist Gottlieb Helnwein who, recreating Hopper's exact interior, inserted four movie stars to replace the original figures in Hopper's midnight diner: Elvis is the soda jerk serving James Dean sitting solo at the counter to the left of Marilyn Monroe laughing with Humphrey Bogart. How interesting if Rex had ever tried to Rexify "Nighthawks" with a quartet of Rex men.

His pictures feature men dealing erotically with masculine isolation and existential loneliness, killing time with sex during restless nights in single-room-occupancy hotels, dive bars, and gas stations warming hot dogs on roller grills. He limns a short-order cook out of "Nighthawks" in his chrome-plated diner drawing dated 1-9-82. Created from his study of his life lived on the skids, his art, exquisitely corrupt beyond innocence, is authentic.

He once informed me: "I've had enough sex to know what happens in the world. I don't think I've ever drawn something that I haven't done or known someone who's done it."

On July 2, 1979, when William Friedkin, the Oscar-winning director of *The Boys in the Band, The French Connection,* and *The*

Exorcist, began filming *Cruising* on location in the streets of the Village, Rex was traumatized once again by the *Village Voice* whose war on *Cruising* was yet another of its assaults on leather culture. In the July 16 issue, staff reporter Arthur Bell (1939-1984) attacked the film, leather decorum, and Rex's Mineshaft when he incited violence by calling up mobs to "give Friedkin and his production crew a terrible time if you spot them in your neighborhood." Bell and his henchman, the equally troubled Vito Russo, the author of *The Celluloid Closet*, impugning the shooting script, tried to cancel the creative process of director, cast, and crew whose film, as art-in-progress, they were disrupting with no idea of the holistic final cut. So much for critical thinking in the gay civil war.

Even John Rechy, no lover of leather, spoke out against Bell's "prior censorship." Distressed by Bell's propaganda, Rex, forever the consummate New York artist, realized he had to exile himself from New York. So in 1980, he followed gay migration westward moving like Harvey Milk, who had his own "Appointment in Samarra," from the gated cliques of Manhattan to the open city of San Francisco. Like his peer, fine artist and photographer Jim French aka Rip Colt of Colt Studio, he left behind his dark New York studio to open up his second act to new West Coast vibes.

On March 1, 1981, Rex, the recluse, hosted the opening exhibit of his San Francisco studio and gallery and home South of Market Street in a three-story Victorian, fifty feet off Folsom Street, at the deep dead-end of the Hallam Street *cul de sac*. Like his New York home next door to the Christopher Hotel, it was conveniently located sixty feet across the narrow lane from the entrance to the orgiastic Barracks bathhouse that opened in an abandoned blue-collar flophouse hotel, May 15, 1972, where the action was also what Rex witnessed at the St. Mark's bath at 6 St. Mark's Place in the East Village. The crisp designer interior he created for his studio in the light-industrial slums of SOMA was very New York: black walls, gray carpet, and track-lighting spotting his framed drawings and his work in progress.

Three months later, on July 3, the *New York Times* announced the news: "Rare Cancer Seen in 41 Homosexuals: Outbreak Occurs Among Men in New York and California—8 Died Inside 2 Years."

One week later, on July 10, outside Rex's studio windows, the mythic Barracks, vacated for renovation, exploded in an arson fire that traumatized him on top of the traumas he suffered from the *Village Voice*. The worst fire in San Francisco since the 1906 earthquake burned his new Rexwerk atelier to the ground and made him so famously homeless that the Mineshaft back in New York hosted a fundraiser so he could keep on working in San Francisco. Mineshaft manager Wally Wallace told me in our 1990 video interview, "Rex is our Michelangelo. So is Tom. So is A. Jay."

In the *Mineshaft Newsletter*, Wally Wallace wrote:

CASINO NIGHT TO HELP A BUDDY OUT. (Rex Benefit) TUES. OCT 20 [1981] 9-12 PM. In July the largest fire since its earthquake swept the Folsom Street area in San Francisco leaving 120 totally homeless. One of the victims was Rex, the artist of the Mineshaft logo, who lost all his earthly belongings in one night. The Mineshaft gave a benefit for him in San Francisco and now we are having one in New York from 9 until Midnight on Tuesday, October 20th. It's a Casino Night with lots of prizes for the winners…with some recent Rex work on display…. Please note that another Casino Night will be held in early November for the Gay Men's Chorus and their Bux for Tux Fund.

With the Mineshaft proceeds, Rex rented a squat in a warren of rooms at 199 Valencia above the popular gay leather biker bar, the Rainbow Cattle Company, which was later renamed Zeitgeist. He told his German gallerist friend Bernd Althans that because of his post-traumatic stress about the fire, he did not leave his room and did not draw for a year. When finally he quietly picked up his pen, he drew some of his best work. Overcoming his depression, he rose like a phoenix from the ashes of the fire, and created a poster offering his new drawing "Phoenix" as an original signed Rex picture to support AIDS research in New York: "Win the Rex drawing 'Phoenix.' Support Karposi's Sarcoma Research at the NYU Medical Center. [Raffle] Drawing at the Spike, 120 Eleventh Avenue, September 22, 1982." "Phoenix," signifying his recovery and resurrection, then became the cover of *Rexwerk* published by Les Pirates Associes Editeur, Paris, 1986.

One of the few pre-fire works to survive was his drawing "Leather Bar"—picturing seven leathermen standing side by side— which he had drawn and then leased as a poster-advertisement for French director Jacques Scandaleri's 1978 erotic film, *New York City Inferno*, the first film shot inside the Mineshaft. The movie featured leather poet-artist Camille O'Grady, fresh from CBGB, singing her piss song "Toilet Kiss" with her band Leather Secrets. Scandaleri returned the original drawing to Rex in New York in the 1990s. In 2013, three years before Rex would be inducted into the Tom of Finland Foundation Hall of Fame, he gifted "Leather Bar," his earliest surviving original, to the permanent collection of Tom's Foundation.

Later during Covid, Rex said his life always lurched from disaster to disaster. Nevertheless, it seemed no headlines, plagues, fires, and politically correct critics could ever dent his true grit.

Rex told the Tom of Finland Foundation in 2017:

People say I'm stubborn just for the sake of being difficult—just to have my way. But I'm someone who has had to fight for decades against society, the law, church and state—even the art world itself—in order to get my art before the public uncensored. There is simply no "polite" way to battle against these great odds that I have had to battle against for the past five decades. Saying "please" does not work when taking on these powerful, entrenched institutions. So I fear fighting the status-quo in the long run has made me rather abrasive and abrupt at times when trying to get my art before a society that essentially won't allow it to be seen. Or rather, allow it to be seen on "my terms." But my bark is worse than my bite.

Durk Dehner wrote in the *Tom of Finland Foundation Newsletter*:

Rex is well versed in the knowledge of our base cravings and desires and that same force has driven him to meticulously lay down scenarios that others dare not manifest. He has been adept at creating imagery that pays homage to that nature that gives us *the strongest of erections with the most powerful of orgasms.* [Italics added] Both Rex and Tom of Finland did not want to compromise their freedom of expression in exchange for getting the approval of the greater society in which we live.

From the start of his career, Rex, like Mapplethorpe with his *XYZ Portfolio*, turned to self-publishing keeping in print his run of softbound 36-page portfolio "books" that began in 1975 with *Männespielen* and continued with *Icons* graduating to his first hardcover book *Rexwerk* (1986).

But the politics and ignorance during the long slow-motion fall of the American Empire that—years before 9/11—began with the assassination of JFK in 1963 and picked up speed with Reagan denying AIDS in the 1980s, turned America's greatest living gay erotic artist into the expatriate who in 2011 fled America for Amsterdam where erotic joy and backrooms reminded him of the best of the 1970s in New York and San Francisco.

2
SWINGING SIXTIES: PIONEER GAY POP ARTISTS

The artists who were Rex's contemporaries were an international underground of homomasculine art appreciated for its aesthetics inside the pop art of the Warhol 1960s. When the Tom of Finland Foundation named Rex to its Hall of Fame in 2016, Rex, still loathing the *Village Voice*, wrote in the *TOFF Newsletter*:

Mine was the first generation that came out of the closet to the art world a decade *before* Stonewall. We paid a heavy price in those early days for drawing dirty pictures as they were then called, sacrificing in many cases, our lives, jobs, family ties, and homes for daring to depict "The Love That Dare Not Speak Its Name." Our art was burned and destroyed in raids by police and postal authorities. The work was condemned and spit upon by church and state, and especially by the legitimate art world for whom we were rude intruders storming the gates of their conservative ivory towers. What we dared to depict of the naked male form were criminal acts back then and those of us who portrayed them, criminals.

Tom of Finland, who as a teen in occupied Finland had sex with Nazi soldiers whose politics he hated, but whose uniforms he loved, drew clean-cut blond Aryans while Rex's barbarian Aryans have their own Nazi genes courtesy of Rex's own Nazi fetish. If ritual S&M fantasies became real, they'd be homophobic nightmares—and that's the counterphobic thrill of the magical thinking of masturbation and sex role play as sexual healing that Richard Goldstein never considered.

The New York S&M artist Mike Miksche aka Steve Masters (1925-1965), who in the 1960s excited the young Rex, was the six-foot-five bomber pilot and real-life Marlboro Man model and sadistic suicide who beat up Sam Steward (1909-1993) consensually for the camera of sex-researcher Alfred Kinsey. In his crisp tattoo-inflected Vitruvian-man style, Miksche drew the strength of post-war gay men, posturing tattooed cousins of Rex men, made defiant by their military service, and made proud by winning the war.

Masters and fellow New York artist Jim French (1932-2017) who was the founding photographer of Colt Studio in 1967 with my longtime friend Lou Thomas (1933-1990), founder of Target Studio, who shot a dozen *Drummer* covers, were both Madison Avenue advertising men with formal training who drew and photographed butch guys in the New York S&M leather scene. French aka the fine artist "Luger" aka "Rip Colt" photographed and then sketched the same kind of alpha men Rex drew. Rex, however, flipped French's aesthetic of Colt men who were aloof, unavailable, clean-cut sex gods to be worshiped. His Rex men were alternative sex gods, muscular, aggressive, sweaty brutes to be served.

Chicago artist Domingo Francisco Juan Esteban Orejudos aka Dom aka Etienne aka Stephen (1933-1991) was co-founder with photographer Chuck Renslow (1929-2017) of Kris Studio, the Gold

Coast bar, and the International Mr. Leather contest. Like Rex, Dom also created kinky bar ads, posters, and illustrations of leathermen evoking folk-art circus banners not unlike the mustached "Strong Man" and tattooed "Sword Swallower" in fantasy paintings flapping on canvas panels hanging outside peep shows and freak shows lining carnival midways. His images, like Rex's intense carnival and *Sex-Freak Circus* images, were primal and had romantic appeal because they tripped leathermen smoking pot and drinking beer in his Gold Coast bar back to a time when things seemed simpler for a brokeback man on a motorcycle. Dom introduced the concept of "gay bars as art galleries" when he premiered his murals inside the Gold Coast he and Chuck founded in 1958, four or five years after the world's most likely first leather bar, Cinema, as reported in Larry Townsend's 1972 *Leatherman's Handbook*, opened in 1953/4 on Melrose Avenue in Los Angeles.

Al Shapiro aka A. Jay (1932-1987), the art director of Clark Polak's *Drum* magazine (1964-1967) which Rex read, was also the founding New York art director of *Queens Quarterly* (1969). For the June 1974 cover of *QQ*—which likely helped trigger the *Village Voice* attack on Rex in 1975—Al published a rare color drawing by Rex just before Al quit *QQ* to move to San Francisco where I met him and his new lover Dick Kriegmont at the Barracks baths in late summer 1974. Three years later in a package deal, Al and I joined *Drummer* together as art director and editor-in-chief: March 17, 1977 to January 1, 1980.

While Rex was deadly serious about male representation, the good-natured Al satirized homomasculine sex, leather fetishes, and camp in his monthly cartoon strip, *The Adventures of Harry Chess*—which, beginning in Polak's *Drum* (10,000 circulation) before moving to *Drummer* (42,000 circulation), was the world's first ongoing gay comic strip. Almost in tandem, Rex's first *Drummer* cover was issue 10, November 1976. Al's first cover was issue 15, May 1977. Rex's gay gaze presented one kind of "leatherman look" on the cover and Al's quite another. In 1980, Al told me in his *Drummer* interview: "I marvel at Rex's technical aplomb and his sleazy male content."

Don Merrick (1929-1990) aka Domino was a New Jersey construction worker, lumberjack, and cab driver who, although their styles were different, drew the same type of men as Rex. Their gay gaze was fraternal and complementary. Domino's grafitti-like scratch-and-sniff scribble style created fantasy men sketchier than Rex's pointillist men. While Rex drew Rex men from his idealized imagination, Domino sketched realistic blue-collar Joes from his working life. Rex drew homomasculine men. Domino drew heteromasculine men. He told me about his Rex-like harvesting of seed-bearers in *Drummer* 29, May 1979: "Right now, I'm trying to instill in my memory the face and greasy work clothes of the manager of a certain New Jersey Amoco station. I'm determined to get him alone one of these days, so that I can memorize the rest of him." More verbal than Rex, Domino added the mixed dimension of graffiti-dialogue balloons—worthy of a Kilroy in a toilet stall in a bus station—inside his S&M frames to narrate his drawings. Rex, who did not speak until he was four years old, knew his pictures spoke volumes and were beautiful beyond words.

Rex had a special regard for his friend, San Francisco artist Chuck Arnett (1928-1988), a founder of the Tool Box (1962), whose mural on the Lascaux cement wall behind its bar had been published in *Life* magazine, June 26, 1964. At that culture-quake outing of gay masculinity, Rex, the new kid in New York, was twenty years old. Sixteen years later in 1981, he spoke of Arnett when after the Folsom fire, he was so desperate to get his drawings into gay rags to spur mail-order sales that he agreed to be interviewed for a feature I was writing about him for *Skin* magazine, volume 2, number 6.

Rex: I like Chuck Arnett very much. I think he's too strong for the mainstream of gay appreciation and he's probably best known for his Red Star Saloon poster [1972] as well as his works at the Ambush Bar.

For October 17, 1990, Rex drew the ad poster for the Lone Star Saloon's first Anniversary Earthquake Party celebrating the bar's destruction, survival, and move to a new location—from 1099 Howard Street at 7th Street to 1354 Harrison—because of the

October 17, 1989, Loma Prieta earthquake which also destroyed the *Drummer* office. Cued by the name of the Lone Star, he drew a red star (one of the few splashes of red in Rex's black-and-white drawings; often reproduced as a white star) raised high on the long arm and fist of a leatherman that was homage to Arnett's famous Red Star Saloon poster, and to the red, black, and white of the Nazi flag.

> **Rex:** I think Arnett is the only true American fine artist with any track record in the homoerotic world. That man can lay down pastels like Renoir and not compromise the strength and raw sexuality one bit. Very immediate stuff, never lets his technique get in the way to shortchange his content or, more important, his audience.

Later in our interview, he assayed Tom of Finland and offered his Rexian theories about gay art, entertainment, and class prejudice.

> **Rex:** Tom of Finland is the father of this business. There's never a sense of degradation or tawdriness in his characters. There's never anything sleazy about Tom's creations.

> **Jack:** Some critics consider your men sleazy.

> **Rex:** My men are working class. If critics see that as sleazy, perhaps they have a class hangup. My working-class heroes are sweaty real reflections of life. Gays confuse the definition of sleaze. Real men aren't sleazy. There's actually something rather pure about the dirt and sweat earned from honest labor. The stink of the working class is quite different from the self-indulgent stink of laying about in a bathtub in the backroom of a gay bar. The homosexual fascination with filth is based in part on a deep-seated conflict and fascination with the working-class background. In its origins, filth came from honest labor, hence honest emotions, hence honest people. As opposed to make-believe [bar] filth that is "applied" rather than "earned." Yet another fantasy of pretend sweat and dirt. Hence, pretend people.

Each of Rex's contemporary artists was a star with his own passionate fans. But no artist scares the horses the way Rex's intensity challenges the politically correct vanilla gay gaze. Some "artistes" are artists and some are entertainers. With *entertainment*, you get exactly what you bargained for. With *art*, something you might not have expected happens. The artist, like Rex, confronts you. You look. You see. Your way of seeing begins to change. You change. Your dick as a medium of magical thinking rises up like a wizard's wand that channels you forward into unexpected mindsets and sex trips you had no idea you were going to like so much. In Freudian terms, middle-class Super-Ego values taught by your parents slip another notch sideways toward your sex-driven Id and the strange men whose candy and rides you were warned about.

Jack: When you speak of other gay artists, what do you mean?

Rex: By the term *gay artist*, I don't mean the window dresser at Macy's creating flower pastels on weekends, or the tidy lesbian making abstract sculpture in her garage. I mean people who have directly undertaken the terribly difficult chore of portraying the human form engaged exclusively in homosexual acts or the homosexual lifestyle. These are the artists to whom I direct my criticism.

Jack: The marketplace here in New York, San Francisco, Los Angeles, Europe, seems suddenly flooded with these gay artists of whom you speak. Nude and copulating forms seem everywhere.

Rex: Yes. And I find most of them have everything going for them but one vital ingredient: no real sense of real male sexuality. Much of their work is heavy in technique and low on originality, content, and realism.

Jack: From years of artists submitting to *Drummer*, I've noticed that instead of drawing authentic pictures based on the sex they've actually had or seen, many of them base their pictures on other pictures. Like Tom's. Like yours.

Rex: *Ersatz* sex. Erotic art without sex is like light without heat. Porn needs sex. If an artist lacks the facility to communicate real sexuality, then he should go into interior decorating, or portrait work, where his skills—and feeling—can be put to better use.

Jack: You use the terms *erotic art* and *porn* interchangeably.

Rex: I prefer *porn*. There are no doubts as to its intention. It's like coining a four-letter Anglo-Saxon word from the Greek.

Jack: It is Greek which I studied for three years. In Greek, *pornē* means *whore* and *graphein* means *writing*.

Rex: Exactly. Sometimes I say *erotic art,* but I prefer *porn*. That makes you stand up and be counted. Also, fanatics don't attack *erotic art* with the same verve they'll censor *porn*. And, of course, the word *art* intimidates all Americans. We all know we're suppose to "revere" *art* and "hate" *porn*. Aren't labels convenient? People naturally get confused when one is the other so I like to interchange them frequently when discussing these things. It keeps people thinking.

Jack: As an artist, are you a pornographer?

Rex: I certainly hope so! Otherwise I've got a lot of explaining to do to myself as to where the 1970s went.

Still, porn—like beauty—is in the eye of the beholder. In reality, much of the sex in my drawings is more ritually suggested than actually portrayed. But the end result should cause a hardon for men who like men. Really like men.

To be clear about Rex, one of the main purposes of erotically-charged gay art from toilet walls to museums is masturbation. Tom of Finland and other one-handed artists like Laguna surfer Skipper aka Glen Davis (1944-?), who drew for *Drummer* 15 and 186, talked of their process in connecting their penis-to-pen hardons to their viewers' hardons. Tom said, "If I don't have an erection when I'm doing a drawing, I know it's no good." Skipper added, "My drawing starts in my dick and the drawing's done when I cum. This can take hours."

Rex explained on his website:

It's all about the penis. The penis in all its varied "states" grabs your attention as little else does in life, if only for the fleeting moment of recognition and revulsion it takes to turn away from it. So the penis as "image" really does have the potential to emotionally and physically fulfill the maxim that art should "move you." In the case of pornography, the artist is presented with the option to literally move his viewer with "physical" results that few other art forms can match, bang for the buck…. It's a win-win for both the artist who gets creative satisfaction from creating it, and an audience that often gets delirious "satisfaction" from viewing it.

Jack: You often load whole feature-length movies into the content of your single-frame drawings. Your realism, intensity, and content all turn some guys on and others off.

Rex: Yeah. Just like real life.

Jack: But aren't you possibly too tough…too masculine?

Rex: One can never be too masculine in my book. But make sure you've got the right definition to that word too.

Jack: Why have you so defiantly devoted your considerable talent to *porn* as opposed to *art*?

Rex: I wanted to contribute something I felt people needed. It seemed to me the world didn't need anymore portraits, still lifes, automobile ads, or clown faces. It seemed to me there was never enough porn. Then too, I like to think that porn separated the men from the boys. Art for me was too similar to entertainment, which in turn amuses you. Porn on the other hand—good porn that is—can shake you up, attract or repel you. True art has the ability to move, to change. But, on the whole, I think people dislike art because in reality they dislike being changed. Porn on the other hand asks nothing other than that you enjoy yourself—so powerfully that it actually changes a physical portion of your body from soft to hard. Perhaps porn is a kind of Super-Art. In my case too, porn allowed me to present a "type" of man who is perennially out of favor with the artistic "set" who find a nemesis in the hard-assed working-class hero.

Jack: How ironic because so may of them fancy "Marxism."

Rex: I think for gay men to have so underestimated the working-class male is very wrongheaded.

Unlike many published gay artists, Rex studied anatomy and was an intentional *flaneur* and voyeur of men on the streets. He was a Platonist in search of ideal body parts, making a fetish of classic chins, cocks, feet, and hands. Like Charles Atlas selling muscles in comic-book ads and Dr. Frank-N-Furter creating custom-made hunks in *The Rocky Horror Show*, in just seven days Rex could make you a man.

In 1984, during an afternoon picnic Mark Hemry and I hosted in our backyard for our friends David Hurles, Robert Mainardi, and Trent Dunphy, Rex, in an impromptu anatomy session asked me to put on my leather jacket to pose positioned with my wrist just-so, coming out of the sleeve, because he needed to make a Polaroid reference photo so he could sketch the exact angle of bone and flesh for the last tiny detail in his drawing "Pigsticker."

Reversing the camera on Rex to shoot him for a reference photo was farcical. His longtime friend, tattoo artist Robert Roberts, told me about Rex's reticence in terms of Roberts' photo "The Red Line": "As you know, Rex adamantly avoided being recognized. He did, however, let me photograph his hand holding my grandfather's plumb bob, then got all concerned that someone would recognize that it was his hand."

In Summer 1987, Rex wrote with charming candor about his work and his marketing.

Dear Jack, As a follow-up to our conversation the other day, I'm enclosing the following items. 1. A copy of my present brochure, which you may or may not want to send out to your [Palm Drive Video] customers... 2. Here are some new works I don't think you have. You may have seen them in censored versions in *Drummer* or *Inches*. It was just about a year ago [Summer 1984] I was up at your place with Bob and Trent and I made you pose with a leather "arm" for my "Pigsticker" drawing. So your arm has been drawn by Rex. Here's a print of the finished version.

Also, the "Cigar Face" [modeled on boxer Chuck Wepner] which I thought you'd like (another?) print of.... I've spent my whole year trying to develop these new "bum" faces—up to now it's been hit or miss, close but not perfect.

In these last two drawings [in his *Armageddon* series whose shocking "Rex Man with Pan, the Goat" on the cover had to be censored and replaced with a Rex man hovering over a skull with a knife in its mouth while the Rex man sets fire to $50 bills.]...I've finally hit the mark; got JUST what I wanted—no more, no less. I think the face on the cover art (burning the dollar bills) comes the closest to these new faces, but even he is not truly focused as are these new ones.

I always got good customers from David's [Hurles/Old Reliable Video] mailing list; his photographs seemed to appeal to a type that would also like my drawings. I think your people [Palm Drive Video customers], off the beaten path, would also find them interesting. Write and let me know, or phone to speed things up. Best wishes, Rex

Rex was a good writer, an astute critic, and an intriguing artist-in-residence with his patrons and friends in San Francisco where in 1985 Mayor Dianne Feinstein controversially named him as one of the City's one hundred most influential artists. In 2005 in our little on-again-off-again Bloomsbury, he wrote the introduction to

Speeding: The Old Reliable Photos of David Hurles. To his dying day, Rex complained that his erstwhile friend David (1944-2023)—who raked in a million in cash three times over and lost all three million to hustlers—never thanked him. Was Rex Shakespeare's green-eyed Iago? He knew how to carry a grudge—even after David three years later suffered a drug-induced stroke in his filthy slum apartment in 2008 and spent fifteen nightmare years disabled in assisted living. When David died on April 12, eleven months before Rex, the pointillist who kept an active frenemies blacklist, wrote, "My introduction to *Speeding* was eulogy enough for him to whom I haven't spoken in thirty years."

For twenty years from 1990 to 2011 when Rex made his escape to Amsterdam, Bob Mainardi, author of *Hard Boys: Gay Artist Harry Bush*, and art collector Trent Dunphy provided Rex with his own Larkin Street studio on the private second floor above their beautiful "olde curiosity shop" of their photo and magazine archive, where for fifty years they bought and sold collectible vintage erotica over the counter of their storefront, "The Magazine," at 920 Larkin in the Tenderloin. In 2016, as art patrons devoted to preservation and history, they donated their four-story building to house and archive the physique photography and art of the Bob Mizer Foundation. In 2012, Bob Mainardi (1946-2021) wrote:

> Rex is one of the foremost artists of forbidden and politically incorrect sexual activity among men. His is more than merely "Gay art." Rex the artist is a historian, a voyeur, a muckraker, and a trouble maker, a provocateur, a sensualist and a hedonist, the sensitive and observant portrayer of a secret world…. The world of leather and denim, steamy basements and grimy garages, anonymous sweaty tops and groveling sexpigs is perfectly suited to his black-and-white detailed and moody pointillistic renderings.

Rex, who had a mouth on him, told me Bob's favorite artist was the Hun whom Rex did not like because the Hun could draw in two days what would take Rex two years. "I've analyzed this," Rex said. "I'm jealous that the Hun can crank out the work so fast, really jealous of that. Then I justify it by saying the Hun's work isn't that good, but I don't think that is just. A lot of people like his work. It's very popular, more popular than my work today. He's worked very hard at it. It's work I've never liked. I think my work has a lot of taste. I've devoted my life to raising the standards of these things so that people will take it seriously. The Hun's comic-book mindlessness to my eye—it might seem catty—but in a nice academic sense, it is just mindless. I think he's a lunatic. So many young people are drinking him in and fashioning their fantasies around him. I see it as really detrimental. So many people prefer his work over mine, and I look at them and wonder.

"The Hun felt he was superior to me in language and everything. The weekend I was with him in Los Angeles, well, I'm very forthright and rowdy. I talk a lot and use gutter language. He doesn't talk like this. We drove around and whatever reaction I might have had to something, he would have just the opposite. It was like dragging a little old lady around. 'Can we go to Knott's Berry Farm?' and 'I can't go out in the sun.' And I'm thinking, this man is shoveling piles of piss on tortured campers? It just struck me as psychotic. I've had nothing to do with him since. He's always tried to be very friendly to me and I've been very cold toward him.

"Bob here at the store," Rex said, "is an intelligent man and sees it all, you know, but he's also very naive, had a very sheltered sex life, hasn't had the opportunity to do the things you and I did. He doesn't relate to my work. To him it is unrealistic. I've had many people come up to me and say, where do you get these wild ideas? Even those medical things? Things, real things, that have actually happened to people."

In 1981 I asked Rex, who so often drew from photographs, what photographers he admired.

Rex: There are two. Bob Mizer of Athletic Model Guild in Los Angeles has been photographing men for his AMG *Physique Pictorial* since about 1945. Nearly every man in America has come out on the subtlety of Mizer's catalog of young American toughies wrestling in oil and posing in jockstraps, hard hats, and bodybuilder briefs. I think the brutal honesty of his lens is devastating in its ability to capture the quintessential sexuality of males as they "present it" to one another. His photographs are as unadorned as a passport photo with an immediacy which belies the fact they even are photographs—we see rather only a slice of life. For that reason, and because these are not "pretty" pictures, he has been overlooked by the gay media in general.

Jack: And the second photographer you admire?

Rex: David Hurles who runs Old Reliable Tapes and Photos [and would expand from four-minute silent Super-8 movies, still photography, and audio-cassette sextapes of toxic masculinity to video production in January 1982]. He's a younger version of the Mizer School of Photography. Though documentary-like in tone, there is a subtle difference between Hurles and Mizer. The eye of Hurles works on more sophisticated content. His camera is totally unobtrusive, divested of any artifice whatsoever. Modesty prevails in these pictures and yet his photographs of young street hustlers and ex-cons vibrate with a straightforward vision of the world which most of us will never see or experience. These are the men you'd love to touch, but don't dare. Hurles is a genuine artist in this respect who, like Bob Mizer, seems to languish in the backwash of the gay media because the prerequisite "glamour" is not there.

Rex agreed when I recalled that when Bob Mizer who mentored Hurles died in 1992, David wrote one of the most touching and informative obituaries one friend has ever written for another.

Jack: Yes, it is odd that none of these men you've mentioned is really a popular hero in the gay media—raised to the stardom of Colt Studio or Fred Halsted.

Aggressively homomasculine Los Angeles film director Fred Halsted (1941-1989), the polar opposite of fashion designer Halston, was the *Drummer* columnist whose extremely Rexian leather movies,

L.A. Plays Itself and *Sex Garage,* were inducted into the permanent collection of the Museum of Modern Art in 1974. What Halsted intentionally made to be pornographic suddenly became avant-garde art. The hemorrhoidal reaction of the politically correct to Halsted's mainstream validation led not to an understanding of Rex's work, but to the damning of leather culture and art in the *Village Voice* in 1975.

> **Rex:** Yes, their total visions are, I think, just too heady for gay men generally. David Hurles, for instance, invests his photographs—by way of his street-hustler subjects—with a kind of terror a lot of time. Gays don't want terror anymore than they want real filth. Men, on the other hand, know terror and filth as simply more aspects of everyday life in the real world.

> **Jack:** You may know in 1981 when I summed up David [*Man2Man Quarterly* #8, 1981], I wrote a representational *National Enquirer* headline to make David sound exciting while proclaiming his truth: "Terror Is My Only Hardon."
>
> Maybe the configuration of jerking off to terror reduces the stress of terror. At this point in history, you seem like an artist working hard to maintain your vision and values in the midst of a gay paradise gone mad.

> **Rex:** Perhaps. Do I sound too severe?

> **Jack:** Probably. But how do you feel about being interviewed? Have you changed your mind about journalists?

> **Rex:** Well, at least you haven't asked me what's my astrological sign.

Always on the hunt, Rex cruised out of his studio to sketch reference notes on location of real-life faces, bodies, penises, and postures of men enjoying themselves in truck stops, pool halls, steam baths, and USO waiting rooms at bus stations and airports. Mark and I once ran into him at San Francisco International when we were flying off to Paris, and he was hanging out there in the air terminal outside the open door of the busy USO Lounge, doing military recognizance of the cruising kind once so popular in Greyhound bus stations near army and naval bases. He later wrote that he so liked the postcard we sent him from the Louvre that he was going to use the figure on it for something, "maybe with angels," saying he'd "never drawn angels, so it might be a sensuous bad angel."

Rex had a talent for memorizing men of all kinds whose sex appeal he synthesized and amplified turning life into art. He once told me, "You've got to make ugliness dazzling."

His Larkin Street studio was located, perfectly for him and his artist's eye, in the skid-row slum of the Tenderloin district, the Rex Riviera, still lurid from its post-Gold Rush provenance of dive bars, pool parlors, boxing gyms, steam baths, burlesque joints, and vagrant men. To hit the sidewalks, he exited his studio through the street-floor vintage-magazine shop where Trent and Bob gave him archival access to literally millions of stimulating images in straight men's adventure magazines like *Saga*, *Stag*, and *Man's Life* which he referenced the same way Mapplethorpe found inspiration in the photos in 1960s gay magazines like *Physique Pictorial* and *Tomorrow's Man* in 42nd Street adult bookstores.

One example of Rex using pop-culture magazines as sources for his portraiture explains his gift for transforming offbeat beauty into beat-off art. In "Cigar Face," dated 3-10-85, he pictured his dramatic black-and-white close-up portrait, a gorgeous gargoyle, of champion heavyweight boxer Chuck Wepner—who fought Muhammad Ali—based on a color photo of Wepner on the cover of *Sports Illustrated*, March 24, 1975.

That delighted me because I had saved and framed the Wepner cover of that issue when it arrived in my mailbox in 1975, and could instantly measure how Rex amplified sports reality into the sexual fantasy of erotic art. He dot-dot-dotted the intensity of Wepner's brutalist face and eyes, ingeniously adding a phallic stub of aggressive cigar to his mouth, like the tongue of a grimacing Maori mask, delivering to the homomasculine gaze all the sexual threat and pugnacious menace the ugly-beautiful beast Wepner had on offer. When I complimented him on transforming this cover, he blushed as if he'd been "found out," as if his borrowing were plagiarism, but he quickly recovered with a little lecture about the synthetic creativity of sourcing images. He said, "Picasso said, 'Art is theft.'"

Jack: Your drawings seem to feature these ordinary men—almost a kind of Everyman—in basically ordinary situations. They're rough-cut types—aggressive, obsessed.

Rex: They seem like normal men to me. Don't get me wrong. I enjoy beautiful people, but I'm suspect of beauty and its toll on the human condition. I've seen "beauty" close-up and it's not a pretty sight. So-called plain, ordinary, or even ugly people seem to have much nicer personalities in the long run.

Jack: Is that why you don't draw conventionally "beautiful" people?

Rex: Actually, I don't think my particular audience is interested in beautiful people. On the other hand, many of my supporters have often commented to me on the "beauty" of these characters. So it's all in the eye of the beholder and where you're coming from, not where I'm coming from, as to whether I draw beautiful people. I'm also a realist and I'm aware that 95% of all men in this world are not beautiful. I know this fact and my audience knows it. We never went into this hunt looking for beauty. We were after men.

Jack: Do you prefer ugly people?

Rex: The concept is almost unknown to me. What others call ugly I've often found quite beautiful. Beauty always announces itself to the eye from a great distance. I spot it, but it bores me. To be young and beautiful is the easiest thing in the world to be. What fascinates me is how people endure when nature turns against them, is no longer on their side. Here the plot thickens and the real beauty—if there is any—will shine through. That's the only beauty I truly appreciate.

If the Platonic Ideal of a real-life Rex model could pose repeatedly for Rex, or star in a movie treating Rex's work as a cohesive graphic novel, he would be heteromasculine British actor Tom Hardy who is the incarnate archetype of virtually all of Rex's rugged homomasculinity in his hard body and many faces tender to tough from his motorcycle outlaw in *Bike Riders* to his Mafia gangster in *Capone*, his prisoner in *Bronson*, his MMA fighter in *Warriors*, and his road-warrior outlaw in *Mad Max: Fury Road*.

Jack: How would you advise others to "judge" the appearance of other men?

Rex: First, forget about "pretty." The hard truth is men are not pretty. Pretty is a transient quality. Character endures. Men endure.

Jack: Do you wish there were more men featured in today's porn and fewer pretty boys?

Rex: No. I'm not that opposed because I know pretty is the beginning and end for so many others. Let them have their pleasure. I object more that so much of today's porn suffers from "staging." Poor America, she's so manipulated. In the old days, a camera filmed people having sex, and we called it porn. Today, people have sex in order to perform on camera, and we call that porn. Think that last line over again.

Jack: One is real. The other is acting.

Rex: You see what I'm saying is that the energy of today's porn is different, and as such I think audiences sense it with growing dissatisfaction. I've noticed how many men react instinctively when they view "old" vintage porn—black and white, unprofessional models doing it in some motel room and being badly photographed. They're rife with blemishes, don't have on a touch of leather, and have bad bodies. Oh, but somehow the "reality" really excites viewers. Today's gay porn consumer isn't entitled to one single mysterious shadow on face or body. In glamorizing porn we've also made it dull.

Jack: What do gays who buy *Drummer* and publications like
it end up with?

Rex: *Ersatz* men, I suppose.

3

MATTRESSES STAINED WITH THE
MEMORY-FOAM OF MANSEX

Rex draws for big boys grown up enough to face their fantasies that
must be fed. Like a toy machine gun, his Rapidograph pen rat-a-tats
the dots he shoots into his target images. Cameras shoot at the speed
of light. Drawing takes longer. He once told *Drummer* that he often
has to do sixty or seventy versions of something to get the final version right. Culling those versions with a big game hunter's eye, he
builds and captures an essence and accuracy the viewer's experience
confirms.

Who hasn't been to the baths and bars and after-hours clubs
and seen and felt, but been unable to capture in words or graphics,
exactly the *frisson* and soul which Rex communicates in his *Rexwerk*
drawing "Bathhouse"? That drawing was one of the five I published
in *Son of Drummer* (1978), helping readers get into his drawings
with expository titles like "21 Tongues" and "Mad Doctor."

His "Bathhouse" is a heptaptych of interconnected scenes like
six film frames of male sex circling around a Grecian urn, and very
like Edweard Muybridge's cabinet cards showing a sequence of six
images of *The Horse in Motion*. Rex shows cinematic brilliance about
the flow of serial sex romping, and deserves respect for capturing the
athletic joys of Dionysian promiscuity.

Rex was inspired by his experiences at both the original and
new St. Mark's Baths (6 St. Marks Place, 1965-1985) in New York
which as the largest gay bath in the world was a centripetal Xanadu
of spinning international DNA and divine decadence before politics
and plague destroyed the sanctuaries of bathhouse culture. Once
upon the Titanic 1970s, before the iceberg of AIDS, the St. Mark's
halls and cubicles as well as the venerable Everard Baths, 28 West
28th Street, offered the dedicated sex tourist, voyeur, and vagrant

cocksucker more peepholes and gloryholes per square inch of ply-wood than a grille in a priest's confessional.

When latter-day people shake their judgy heads and cluck out the bias of hindsight that leathermen didn't know what was lurking around the corner, well, who does?

"Bathhouse" is his nostalgic homage to the sexy, seedy glory of the tubs now gone with the wind. Each cubicle in the drawing sweats with Rex's S&M humidity: hairy, buzz-clipped and rough-shaved, muscular, tattooed men, tramps, thieves, vagabonds, kill-ers, decked in the stuff of fetish trips he makes you see, smell, and taste—armpits, toenails, smelly socks, pissy jocks, sweaty uniforms, dirty jackboots, and outhouse leathers. Cocks drip cheese through thick lips of hood-winking foreskins that were his signature body part. Nipples big as pencil erasers stand erect on hairy pecs. Rex's roustabouts live on the wrong side of the tracks in no-tell motels with mattresses stained with the memory foam of mansex.

In 1977, when I assigned Mapplethorpe to shoot the cover for *Drummer* 24, I asked him to use my friend and playmate Elliot Siegal, the manager of St. Mark's, as his model because Elliot looked like a human version of the kind of hard man *Drummer* iconized and Rex drew. Mapplethorpe so liked the scruffy biker-punk au-thenticity of Elliot that he shot him and his lover Dominick in 1979 for two pictures in his *X Portfolio* of thirteen signed gelatin silver prints in a black-cloth clamshell case which Sotheby's called "one of the most provocative ensembles of photographs in the history of art."

Linking Robert and Rex to equate them because Rex's portfo-lios were as important as Robert's, I published *Drummer* 24 with its Mapplethorpe cover simultaneously with my specially curated New York Art issue *Son of Drummer* in September 1978 placing my article "The Robert Mapplethorpe Gallery (Censored)" next to my article "Rex Revisited" to equate Rex with his star-studded peers in our *Drummer* Salon. Rex was saddle-stitched together with a cen-terfold by Tom of Finland, drawings by Etienne and Bill Ward and Harry Bush, and photographs by David Warner and Lou Thomas of Target Studio, and erotic fiction by poet Thom Gunn aka Sam

Browne. In those pages, I printed nine photos from Mapplethorpe's forthcoming *X Portfolio* alongside five drawings from Rex's portfolio magazine-books, *Icons* and *The Paladin File*, published by Trading Post Enterprises, 960 Folsom Street, in San Francisco.

Because of Rex and Robert, gay history took a legal step forward in 1979 to protect the rights of the people who create gay media. Immediately upon publication, my *Son of Drummer*, my passion project promoting my two friends, became involved in likely the first gay copyright infringement suit in the United States when *Blueboy* publisher Don Embinder aka Don Westbrook (1935-2017), infamous in American media for his business associations with the Mafia in gay bars, hotels, and publishing, bound several thousand copies of the copyrighted 62-page *Son*, most of which I'd written, inside an issue of the *Blueboy*-owned *Numbers* magazine.

Drummer attorney Steven Ames Brown said that Embinder in Florida thought it was a joke when *Drummer* dared file suit in the U.S. District Court in San Francisco; but Embinder lusting to include the stylish Rex and Robert in his gay vanilla lifestyle magazines, stopped laughing when, to avoid trial in 1981, Blueboy, Inc. settled to credit *Drummer* $20,000 of advertising space inside *Blueboy* over three years.

Back in Rex's day, the Mafia was always trying to get into the pockets of our gay pants. In 1979, a few months after the publication of *Son of Drummer*, Rex who knew the Mafia first hand, laughed when I told him that Don Embinder had telephoned to ask if he could hire me away to write for *Blueboy*, and I told him writing *Drummer* was quite enough.

Embinder coveted my "Rex Revisited" feature and captions because he wanted to exploit the Rex drawings.

> Rex has a new series called *The Paladin File*, a portfolio of quality 8x10 glossy photo reproductions of his latest work. Their quality insures the fidelity and minimum loss of detail which have made Rex drawings a hallmark.
>
> Set No. 1 is called "On the Road." Not a story, it is five different drawings never published before, set in the world of

truckers and transients along the highways of America. The men are brutal, primitive, fine.

Set No. 2 is titled "Leathermen." This is the world of black leather, bikes, bondage, and submission. Each set contains five 8x10 glossies suitable "as is" for framing and holding in one hand. Each set: eight bucks. Two sets: fifteen. All photos: super-hot! New sets are to come. Smart man.

Rex has located Rexwerk in San Francisco because in the coming 1980s, he predicts, San Francisco, particularly South of Market, SOMA, will be to erotic male artists what Hollywood was for film artists in the Golden 1930s. San Francisco is now the Dream Factory. For homomasculine men, South of Market is the Back Lot, and Rexwerk is the major erotic studio.

Rexwerk Gallery is open by appointment only on Saturdays and Sundays from 6 to 9 PM. Call for appointment: (415) 863-18XX. If you can't wait to get to the Source of It All, send a $4 check or money order made out to Drawings by Rex, Box 347, San Francisco, CA 94101. You'll get three glossy 8x10 prints on Kodak photographic stock insuring faithful reproduction and minimum loss of the fine detail to help you make it through the night.

Rex is our gay Ovid—the ancient Roman poet who changed people into animals in his *Metamorphoses*—because Rex always surrounds the metamorphoses of his homosurreal and amoral alpha beasts with the taboo iconography of bestiality: dogs, horses, goats, snakes, monkeys, and apes morphing into humans. His men themselves are a magical bestiary of sex dawgs and dogs, pigs, and bears who don't give a fuck and will fuck you up. The seductive adrenaline threat of his forbidden but irresistible animality is palpable: "Don't throw me into that briar patch." You don't want to look, but your gay gaze can't look away. You dare not risk inviting real-life hard men into your lovely home, but you can feed your hungry head while holding a Rex drawing of a magnificent manimal in one hand.

In drawing after drawing, like storyboard frames for a narrative film by Jean Cocteau, Jean Genet, or Kenneth Anger, Rex dots his dudes into existence as veterans of male initiation rites and rituals in factories, prisons, and the military. His men are a roll call of rough role play and rugged romance: sturdy blue-collars who suck, fuck, fight, drink, drug, and dominate in rooms of falling plaster, naked light bulbs, dripping washbasins, a shower down the hall, the floor littered with the macho refuse of their mondo-sleazo juke-joint pleasures: Budweiser beer cans, crushed Lucky Strike packs, guns in the glove box of a pickup truck, knives, drug syringes, and condom scumbags.

If war-baby Rex, who said he loved Europe from reading hundreds of grownup books as a boy, had a literary avatar, it was Genet mixed with his selfie character Querelle in his novel *Querelle de Brest* (1945) with illustrations by Cocteau. Genet's opening pages of exposition, all of them, are pure "Rex" who could also have illustrated the novel. The way Genet himself was the two maids (played by male actors) role-playing their mistress in his 1947 stage drama *The Maids*, Rex was both Genet and Genet's own avatar, the man Querelle, in his homosurreal drawings sleazing through waterfront saloons, dens of thieves and sailors and hustlers, and leather bars where serial fuckers, rough sex, drugs, sadomasochism, and sodomy measured manliness.

In Rainer Werner Fassbinder's 1982 film *Querelle*, the homomasculine actor Brad Davis (1949-1991)—who, small-boned at five-foot-nine, had the same lean physique and height as Rex—plays Querelle in this gay screen classic whose operatic leathery art direction overtly styled after the fashion of Tom of Finland could just as well have been styled on Rex. It's amusing that with Rex militantly hiding his birth information, the last shot of *Querelle* is a picture of Querelle/Genet's handwritten birth certificate with a voice-over saying, "Father unknown. Apart from his books we know nothing about him."

In 1978, Rex created a close-up drawing of a leatherman with his tongue licking out the mouth of an overflowing condom that Robert Opel used as an invitation to Rex's opening at Opel's

Fey-Way art gallery. Each mailed invitation arrived with an actual condom glued on by Rex himself. On the condom, the printing in tiny four-point black ink on the yellowish rubber read: "Rex Originals, Fey-Way Studios, 1287 Howard St., San Francisco, April 8-19 [1978]. Reception for the Artist. April 7, 8-11 PM. Admits 2." Prime among all the clever 1970s mixed-media pop-art objects, and invocative of Satanist Aleister Crowley's actual dots of sperm ejaculate reproduced across the cover of his book *White Stains* (1898), this rubbery archived invitation for *Rex at Fey-Way* is preciously fragile. With themes of Satanic hedonism, Rex, like Mapplethorpe, often pictured the face of the Devil Satyr Pan in his work.

Jack: Your drawings are intricately littered with working-class debris.

Rex: Yes. The exhaust of real life. No designer sheets.

Rex's men celebrate the independence of their physical bodies and sexual choices defying Mom's Apple Pie, the Golden Rule, and the American flag the anarchist artist wanted to burn. His hard men we can't keep our eyes off are the "trash" our parents warned us about, and the forbidden stranger danger makes us hard. His men are icons of the rugged gender identity that homomasculine men adore: an endangered erotic micro-orientation of virility we boys grow up protecting, against all odds, in our own secret Boy Scout hearts despite blowback from straight men and vanilla gay men who forget about the diversity and range and beauty of all the alternative masculinities on the Kinsey Scale from straight men to drag-queen men to knock-down-and-drag-out leathermen.

His homosurrealism in his drawings like his identical conjoined twins sharing two torsos and two dicks in *Sex-Freak Circus*, dated 7-30-91, reveals the *doppelgänger* truth of identity and psychology that his play-pal Thom Gunn offers in his Barracks bathhouse story "Star Clone" in *Son of Drummer* and in his three Barracks poems: "1975," "Saturday Night," and "In The Corridor." Gunn's morphing men are brothers to the men Rex renders.

4

**REX AND THOM GUNN:
PINBALL PICTURE AND POEM**

Thom Gunn (1929-2004) and Rex—the leather poet and the leather artist—were friends with benefits who met by chance on Friday, November 7, 1975, when Gunn flew from San Francisco to New York, and headed out to cruise the Ramrod bar at 394 West Street in Greenwich Village. The British immigrant Gunn, at forty-seven, was the internationally famous San Francisco author of the leathery *My Sad Captains* (1961) and, later, *The Man with Night Sweats* (1992). Rex and I never had sex, but we had Thom in common as a playmate.

New Yorker Rex, at thirty, was suddenly famous because only four months before he and his art had been profiled in that scandalous anti-S&M feature article in the July *Village Voice*. Gunn wrote in his diary the following November 7: "I go out, & in Rr [Ramrod bar, one minute from Rex's apartment] meet Rex, of the drawings [*Village Voice*], & go home w/him for nite, nice long & mental." In December 1980, Rex gave Thom the "Rex Calendar 81" inscribed: "Thom: Good Luck in 81.—Rex."

Rex was proud of his best-selling series of three Mineshaft calendars. On New Year's Eve, 1982, he posed for Mineshaft photographer George Dudley who shot Rex smiling and holding his 1983 "Miner with a Pickaxe" calendar, standing with manager Wally Wallace next to the Mineshaft's main bar. There's a more famous "Rex" photo by Richard Young showing Freddie Mercury partying at Legends Nightclub in London, 1979, wearing a white T-shirt with one of Rex's silk-screened Mineshaft drawings on his chest. Mercury who read *Drummer* also wore a Rex T-shirt under his leather jacket in Queen's 1978 music video "Don't Stop Me Now."

On March 1, 1981, Gunn wrote: "I am invited to opening of Rex's show [at his new studio] on Hallam Alley. I take Allen Day [1941-1987, the S&M pen-and-ink artist aka 'Strider' whom Gunn helped move from Boston to San Francisco in 1977]. Afterward, we go to Brig for a short while."

Rex had drawn a poster, "The Liberating Experience," for the Brig, now the Powerhouse, at 1347 Folsom Street, that was owned from 1978-1983 by German immigrant Hank Diethelm. He fascinated Rex who was erotically envious because at fourteen Hank had been drafted into the Hitler Youth before he was rescued by American soldiers in 1945 when Rex was one year old. In 1983, a trick from the Brig murdered Hank in an S&M bondage scene in his home which was set on fire.

Back in that day when just walking in the door of an anything-goes leather bar was considered permission enough, gladiators in the consensual arena, just for kicks, played at public sex in plain sight as part of the do-it-yourself floor shows in the bars and baths because if you want something to happen at the high-school dance, you have to make it happen. The difference between a straight whorehouse and a gay bath is that the bath patrons are the whores.

When Rex learned the German word for such horseplay, he titled his 1976 portfolio *Männespeilen*. On July 11, 1985, ten years into their friendship, Gunn wrote: "Tied up Rex's cock in the Ambush. & an awful sissy brt me home but soon left."

Their simpatico S&M bond was enduring, nurturing, and productive. On Christmas Day in 1996, Gunn was invited to Christmas dinner at a friend's apartment: "About 14 there, inc Rex, with whom I arrange for [San Francisco journalist-historian-curator] R[obert] Prager [died 2014] to interview.

The pointillist and the poet worked our milieu of bars studying the "Nighthawk" faces, poses, and postures of male leathersex in SOMA. Both hung out at the Ambush bar on Harrison Street where artist Chuck Arnett tended bar, and the colorful pinball machine stationed to the right of the door as you entered welcomed you into the dark bar. The social life around that pinball was so popular I think it may have been that exact pinball machine that Gunn and Rex iconized in their work—although it could be any pinball in any bar.

I paid attention to such cultural convergences, because to me, as editor-in-chief of *Drummer* living the life and seeking new content for a hungry monthly magazine, both artists were documenting specifics of our SOMA sex culture we all knew even then before AIDS could not last forever. In *Drummer* 24, September 1978, at the same time I published the feature on Rex, I wrote the leather satire "Castro Street Blues" with the admonitory tag line: "Years from now when you read this—and you will read this—remember The Way We Were (1978 Style)." Which is what we are doing now.

In 1979, Gunn and Rex, possibly triggering each other trading bar gossip over coffee, simultaneously created matching pinball art. Gunn produced a graphic of his pinball poem "Bally *Power Play*" as carefully as Rex drew the spermy pinball picture he completed January 26, 1979, picturing rough beasts hanging around the pinball machine in the Ambush bar where artist Lou Rudolph [1951-1992] also often sat sketching the "cabaret" scene on location like Toulouse-Lautrec and Otto Dix drawing the nocturnal underworlds of Paris in the 1890s and Berlin in the 1930s.

Observing the choreography of postures and "bodily gestures" in gay bars, Thom and Rex realized that pinball machines brightened up the dark with their big attractive windshields of flashing painted glass that rang up the score and lit the action-packed faces and torsos of the players and gamers. In fact, negotiating the playing field of the noisy pinball machine without going "tilt" is akin to negotiating the playing field of the bar itself reflected in the pinball's Freudian array of lights, noise, spring-loaded plunger rod, banana flippers, bumpers, rollovers, free balls, captive balls, kick-out holes, and the drain at the bottom where balls are lost.

In the pop culture of fisting, the pelvic thrusts of crotch and belt buckle thrown by the player leaning into the pinball machine call attention to the performance of his powerful forearms and hands fit for fisting, and undulating butt suitable for rimming and fisting. As American artists, Gunn and Rex—whose drawings would be perfect for the lit back-glass of a Bally pinball machine—both felt the pop-art call of the game the same as the painter Wayne Thiebaud with his "Four Pinball Machines" and Warhol with his Polaroid photograph "Pinball." Is it any wonder Mapplethorpe had a pinball machine in his studio?

So, being cool in an age of mixed media and collage, Gunn, to help raise money for social justice, allowed his "Bally *Power Play*" words to be designed into a small graphic poster by the Massey

Press who published his "Bally" as a single-poem broadsheet of four leaves, in a small folio, limited edition, of ninety with thirty-five signed, on handmade paper, 10x15, hand-printed by David Brooks of Massey Press, illustrated by Mary Harman (not by Rex) and sold to benefit the Body Politic Defense Fund.

At the same moment, Rex was selling prints of his four brutalist leather pinballers (plus one manspreading knee) grinding into the Ambush pinball machine to his own list of clients, and through *Drummer* mail-order to thousands of readers. Mary Harman's polite depiction of Gunn's pinball machine may have suited the straight fundraiser, which, loosening its modesty, could have tripled its money at a leather-bar fundraiser if Gunn had insisted on a second very impolite version illustrated with Rex's pinballers. In that charmed 1970s-1980s circle of friends, Rex in the round robin of peers was to Gunn what Gunn was to Mapplethorpe and Mapplethorpe was to Rex and Rex was to Tom of Finland.

Ranking Rex and Tom, French editor Ralf Marsault in 1986 described the unique Rex as "One in a Century" in *Rexwerk*, his book of fifty drawings (1975-1985) with its blood-red cover emblazoned with Rex's stark black-and-white drawing "Phoenix."

The ever-mysterious Rex dedicated *Rexwerk*: "For Jim [who is "Jim"?] who is so much a part of these drawings."

Rex gave me a copy of this limited edition *Rexwerk* hand-stamped number "0572." About the art of Rex and his Rapidograph pen, Ralf Marsault wrote in *Rexwerk*:

> Enter into this arena of exclusively male violence. [Too often writers, critics, and scholars analyzing the S&M kink scene use the word *violence* which is non-consensual action when what they are describing is consensual *action* which is the true word to use.] But in order to face the Ringmaster of this superbly insolent danger, we will have to grovel. For to be like Rex is to renounce our ideas, abdicate our origins and to accept in silence, kneeling in communion before The Dot…. Rex is unique in this century.

Rex who knew art history engaged with ideas and psychology
to relate to his audience in his black-and-white tenebrism not unlike
Caravaggio who in rich dark colors also depicted visceral groups of
languorous, almost lewd, S&M men going at each other, top and
bottom, in chiaroscuro scenes of homoerotic action. Rex drew his
pictures from an insistent masochistic voyeur point of view because
most people looking at porn choose a bottom's psychology in their
sensual search for domination and worship.

Drawing alpha men to conjure orgasm was good business. In
the magic world of recreational sex fantasies, bottoms search for tops
so the top can, in all the coded roles of Master/Coach/Cop/Dad/
DI/Trainer, work/beat the shit out of the bottom; get the bottom's
shit/act together; and basically save/transfigure the bottom from the
graceless impotence of his worthy/unworthy self washed clean in a
baptism of piss and a shower of sperm.

A porn fan loves porn that scratches his masochistic itch for
bottoming because he gets to be forced to be bad so it's not his
fault. *Drummer* courted this guilty pleasure, cultivated this masochistic gay gaze, so successfully that thousands of men sent us money
demanding more so that by 1978 we were printing 42,000 copies
of each monthly issue. During its twenty-four years of 214 issues,
Drummer presented artists like Rex to millions of international
readers.

5

REX, RELIGION, AND RIMBAUD'S *SEASON IN HELL*: PREDICTING FASCISM IN AMERICA

Some guys have a favorite Rex drawing that gets them off while
dismissing another Rex work they "can't stand because it's, well,
too heavy!" To each his own. *Heavy*, like *beauty*, is in the eye of the
beholder. Does anyone like all the work of any one artist? *Drummer*
12 warned: "He draws his icons from his own world. The world of
Rex excludes you or draws you in, at your own risk."

Rex had warned the *Village Voice* about his politically incorrect
yet inclusive gay gaze which was, especially in New York, an erotic
ethnic attraction not unique to him. "Young Puerto Ricans," he

said, "are born into sex and they're tough. They're gonna murder someone in a few years—and they're like the 'Mona Lisa' to me."

Rex cornered this niche fetish market for danger in tandem with our mutual friend David Hurles who said of his own Old Reliable street hustler models, "I would rather sniff the armpits of a tough young Mexican boxer after a fight than climb between clean sheets with a Colt model."

How perfect if over the years when I bought David tattoos for two of his birthdays in 1977 and 1982, we'd only thought to ink him with a Rex original after the fashion of the illustrated tattoo artist in Rex's drawing "Tattoo Works." But that was years before Rex began designing tattoos for clients.

In 2018, Robert "Mad Dog" Roberts wrote in his autobiography *Mad Dogs and Queer Tattoos: Tattooing the San Francisco Queer Revolution*:

> After I got my first tattoo… I got another tattoo which I asked my friend, porn-noir artist Rex, to design. It was two hearts connected by a lock, with flowers and the phrase "True Love."…[When I started tattooing], business for me really jumped thanks to my friend Rex, who did an interview of me for *Drummer* magazine [issue 112, 1988] titled "Prick the Skin," putting me in an international spotlight. [With Rex freelancing tattoo designs as a side hustle, Roberts recalled inking a client's] …abdomen and pubic area with a tattoo designed for him by Rex.
>
> Had he wished, Rex could have been a great tattooer. The designs on his figures [the tattoos he drew on his Rex men] aren't just hasty representations of any old piece of ink. They are immaculate little gems, some interpretive, others quite original, and they glow with the best qualities of tattoo conception: tight design perfectly balancing elements of dark and light, as well as provocative body placement.
>
> Rex's style of pointillism, sometimes called "stipple," is in the tradition of the great pen-and-ink illustrators such as Virgil Finlay, Wallace Wood, and Berni Wrightson. The use

of dots to build form is readily adaptable to tattooing and works well in combination with standard techniques.

In the autumn of 2005, Roberts began tattooing Rex's friend, Clyde Wildes, with Rex tattoos. He inked Wildes' arms, but time and tide canceled a shield-size full-back tattoo that—reproducing the sex-gangster cover of Rex's *Armageddon*—would also have nestled the face of a tongue-flicking sinister Satan chin deep into the top of Wildes' callipygian cleft. The image fully completed on his left shoulder and biceps replicated Rex's drawing of boxer Chuck Wepner that Rex based on the cover of *Sports Illustrated*. If any one face-portrait represents signature Rex, it's Wepner.

In his 2018 book, Roberts was being kind even though Rex, his Brutus, had wounded him deeply. Clyde Wildes noted, "For years, Rex and Mad Dog were inseparable. When Mad Dog's partner Tim died in 2007, he decided to leave San Francisco and move to Palm Springs. Rex took the news of Robert leaving San Francisco very hard and never forgave him." In the way Rex dumped his friend David Hurles, he dumped Roberts who was born April 19, 1947, and died of cancer eight months after Rex on November 5, 2024.

Rex dreamed up his drawings to please himself, but he welcomed patrons who kept the starving artist afloat by buying his tattoo designs, T-shirts, and portfolio books. The first drawing in *Rexwerk* is a kneeling leatherman, 10-30-83, inviting you, rather like a Rex Selfie, into the book he's holding with a raised forefinger beckoning, "Come here. I dare you." Some ideas work too well not to repeat.

In 1994, the Leslie-Lohman Gay Art Foundation, a new museum making news at 127 Prince Street in New York, titled its October 25 to November 26 exhibition *Rex: Persona Non Grata* and sent out glossy limited-edition postcard invitations like the 2-16-92 drawing of a Rex Man tattooed with "USMC" and "Tiger" while horsing around with his friend tattooed with the horsey name "Flicka." A second postcard featured a tight close-up of fingertips pulling apart a foreskin revealing the glans of a cock head inked with the word *REX* drawn in script as his legal signature.

His drawing, "21 Tongues," 8-15-76, was commissioned by one of Rex's close patrons. The title, he told me, was a personal joke between them because there are not twenty-one tongues in the drawing. Perhaps the client was a priest satirizing the traditional Catholic hymn, "Pange, Lingua" ["Sing, My Tongue"] written by theologian Saint Thomas Aquinas (1225-1274) to celebrate men bonding with the perfect Body of Christ. Various composers have created musical fantasies of the homoerotic hymn. Why couldn't Rex who delighted in drawing sacrilegious pictures of S&M monks and priests draw one?

As if pointing out the sacred, *Drummer* 12 reported in 1977 that Rex titled his 1976 book of "sex worship" and "rugged communion," *Icons*. Rex, a nonsmoker, whom I never saw under the influence of any substance, seemed to be white English-Irish-French stock whose work, like Mapplethorpe's, smacked of cultural, if not personal, Catholicism in the religious iconography of several drawings like his exquisite monks of the Inquisition.

Kinksters thrive on gay codes of double entendre and ritual worship. Aquinas' text of Transubstantiation trembles with homoerotic desire to become One with the Alpha-and-Omega Man, Christ, with carnal lyrics that could caption "21 Tongues" about *flesh* and *blood* and *seed* and *hand* and *man with man* and *adoration* and *newer rites*.

Whatever the sacrilegious joke, this specific drawing has universal appeal to consumers of fetish pornography seeking domination, submission, and worship. In his work, Rex is an empath who feels their needy lust and feeds it with his gods and monsters like the vampire in the drawing dated 10-3-82. He is a sideshow barker who attracts them into his carnival tent to give them what they want or what he, also a mind reader, thinks they need so he can sell their sex thrills back to them via mail-order.

"21 Tongues" with its own "theme song/hymn" is also a "holy picture" in the gay religion of Eros and Priapus. Rex's design here evokes religious art in its placement of its figures. It's all about worship of the ritual kind acted out nightly in the sanctuaries of backroom bars, bathhouses, and the Church of Saint Priapus founded, with its confessional gloryholes, in San Francisco in 1973. Viewers identify with the naked thirst of his groundling acolytes kneeling along the Communion Rail of the Piss Trough eager to receive and worship the elevated alpha male who streams a powerful flood of piss down on them, dick in one hand, and one hand on his heart, in the way the elevated Christ streams rays of grace down from his bleeding Sacred Heart on thronging worshipers in centuries of traditional religious paintings of the God-man, such as Raphael's *Transfiguration* in which unworthy humans kiss the feet of Godhead.

In a kind of 1950s Hollywood sci-fi drawing dated 9-20-82, Rex channeled gay German Symbolist Sascha Schneider's 1904 "Hypnosis" to create his solo leather Superhero—whose Superpower is the Gay Gaze itself—with long, force-projecting laser beams shooting out of his eyes like Superman's X-ray Vision.

Rex's worship is men. Rex's religion is anticlericalism at its best. In several drawings, he reduces worship, and religion itself, and Catholicism especially, down to orgies of depraved priests, blasphemous monks, and debauched altar boys in his bawdy Chaucerian scenes that could have illustrated Maria Monk's 1836 famously anti-Catholic book *Awful Disclosures of Maria Monk, or, The Hidden Secrets of a Nun's Life in a Convent*. Going way beyond the pietistic sadomasochism so beloved by Fundamentalist Christians cuming in their popcorn boxes at Mel Gibson's bloody S&M fetish movie *The Passion of the Christ*, Rex could make his "Passion of the Christ" irresistible to gay sadomasochists with a taste for blasphemy.

On January 3, 1991, Kevin Davis in the *Bay Area Reporter* interviewed Rex in his essay "Power in the Forbidden: Pornographic Artist Rex Looks at the Reality We Call Human Existence" in which Rex placed himself in the context of religious hypocrisy and art history.

> I think as a child I wanted to grow up and become an Anarchist because I was so repelled by the perpetual venality on which American society operates—all doxied up in the U.S. flag, crucifixes clanking ominously whenever a new thought appears in the room. All the great museums and universities of the world, including the Vatican, contain their prized

collections of Pornographic Art. Nearly every great artist from Michelangelo to Picasso has tried his hand at Pornographic Art.

The artist exists to make waves. You have to take chances. Do whatever people don't want you to say or do or be. The forbidden has power.

You'll note that Pornography has only two real critics: the Church and the State.

Everyone else seems to know where babies come from and what goes on in the real world when the lights go out.

And what goes on is that during sex—and thoughts about sex—Church and State lose their suffocating control over our minds. For those precious minutes they cease to exist in our lives.

At the same moment the scandalous Mapplethorpe obscenity trial raged in Ohio in September 1990, my friend and collaborator, former *Drummer* editor John Rowberry who had become editor of *Uncut* magazine, reviewed Rex's new publication, *Rexland*, with the sardonic warning of gay self-censorship: "We can only show you one drawing in this 'family magazine'… [and] only hint at the subject matter of the other eleven."

In 1995, when Rex, the profane theologian, was proposing a series of erotic drawings based on the Bible, he told me: "You once were Catholic. You must know your Bible backwards and forwards. I don't. I have no religious training whatsoever of any kind. I'm very lucky which is one reason I think I've always been so open-minded. I didn't have to overcome any guilt or anything. The downside though is, outside of the movies, I never learned anything about some of the great sadistic sexual stories of the Bible. The Bible always struck me as one of the most barbarous and obscene and earthy books. It's been re-written so many times, even by gay guys [the gay King James I of England self-published his bespoke King James Bible in 1611], why not draw *The Bible According to Rex*?

"The punishments," he said, "are so cruel and so out of proportion and everything is so black and white. Good and evil are on a preposterous level. In that sense, it is such a wonderful piece of literature. The fact that I've always hated it, it is time for me to come to grips with it and make something aesthetically out of it in my own art life. The male 'Dance of the Seven Veils.' Magnificent biblical faces. I think the sexual aspect lends itself to a perfect S&M script. I don't want to do it as a joke. I want it to look so serious that it will move religious people.

"I must tell you," he prophesied, "I don't approve of religion. I think it is the cause of all evil because it politicizes it, like nationalism. All the religions come to the same kind of nastiness. The world is in desperate need of spiritual awakening. Not a religious awakening. Everyone is searching and instead of looking into our own abilities we have to constantly fall back on these tenth-rate religions. All the religions right now are on the offensive and they're all growing, whether it's Jehovah's Witnesses or Billy Graham or Islam or the Catholics or the Mormons, they are all just going nuts, all over the planet. In Russia, religion is booming.

"It's 1995," he said, "and I'm thinking about the next century. Am I going to put ten years into my Bible project, or my *Peter Pan* project? In *Peter Pan: The Lost Episode*, I want to tackle something we all think we know: death. I'll make the whole thing happen at night in the dark in eleven sex scenes, and a cover, with filthy sailors.

"I don't want to clash with any other Peter Pan concepts. I want to make it as nasty as I have ever done in a room, like a dungeon, full of candles to give it a religious quality and a sinister quality. Details make my pictures work for masochists."

Living near San Francisco's waterfront Barbary Coast, the historic vice district next to the Tenderloin, Rex hoisted the Jolly Roger of sex pirates targeting established authority. "Captain Hook," he said, "is a natural for this, already sinister. I looked for him for a long time and finally found him, a wonderful rat-faced character in a comic book. He's one of the ugliest characters I've ever drawn. Incredible detail. Every vein. Every pockmark. His skin is like leather. Every crease. The bone structure. His broken and chipped teeth. A sneer. Very sexy. Very hard to do. Made even more fabulous by my lighting. If I get his eye right, it would be in the Louvre. Very few artists in this country would take ten years to work on twelve drawings."

"But in ten years," he asked, "where will the audience be? What will the world be like? I think that by 2030, there will be such a fundamental rethinking of religion that religion will take over. It will be church and state together in all the countries. It won't be happy. The laws are going to be changed. We are going to go through years of a real hellish rediscovery of religion in the name of benefiting society. All this censorship and hypocrisy about art is just an excuse to arrest everyone in the country and take away civil rights and suspend the Constitution. Right now, the austere bad guys have control and are just terrorizing us.

"I'm mentioning this dreadful future to you, Jack, because you could be of help to me, if you're not appalled by me. I know I've appalled you on occasion."

I kept quiet. To get the story, I had learned never to rise to his bait. I tactically listened to keep him talking about his *Peter Pan* that was his lewd *Lord of the Flies*.

"The Puritans who came here," he said, "were all insane. And intolerant. They hanged a teenage boy [Thomas Granger] for having sex with animals. We've had 200 years to develop these religious nut cases. I've always wanted to draw a Tijuana donkey act, go back to my roots, but if these people had their way, nobody would be going to the bathroom. This is what gay political correctness is about. They're afraid of their shadow. Government is criminalizing every conceivable thing. This is coming out of a fear of the new technology that no one understands and the immense poverty of the social system.

"None of the religions is going to pan out. Religions have only survived because of geographic isolation. They could all delude themselves for millennia that they were 'It.' And the tragedy now is that they are finding that they are butting their heads up against another God and another God and another God and none of them agree. So after a certain point it is the Tower of Babel and we have to live in this world of media babble. That's why the educated countries are the first ones to get suspicious of God, because when you see

25,000 religions cutting off the genitals of their women and slicing the dicks of their men, your love of their grandeur really fades. But up to now this has never been talked about."

Like Mapplethorpe using the tropes of religion to illustrate transformational sexual desire, Rex could have drawn and sold inspirational calendars of hot young male martyrs suffering in Rexstasy to Pentecostal Christians, Catholic priests, and altar boys. In our homomartyrology from Saint Sebastian to Pier Paolo Pasolini to Derek Jarman, Rex was heart and soul a free-thinker re-conceiving gay incarnations of male flesh, and sanctifying male rituals, profane and depraved. For all his underground versatility, snotty gay gatekeepers kept him out of their establishment art loop when he had, like Mapplethorpe, the cheeky buzz of Beelzebub in the devil-may-care faces in his art in which, because he said he liked to read books about Satanism, the face of Satan and his minions frequently recur thematically.

When the Limited Editions Club commissioned Mapplethorpe to illustrate Rimbaud's *A Season in Hell* with eight photographs in 1986, it could just as suitably have commissioned Rex—who like the teenage Rimbaud ran away from home for the sake of art—to contribute eight drawings to pair perfectly with Robert's eight images in that deluxe Quarto edition of 1000 numbered copies.

During one of our years of occasional meals together, a certain time over hamburgers, fries, and a microcassette tape recorder in the Blue Muse diner where he was a regular, Rex said, "I'd love to do a version of the Bible, twelve scenes, because the Bible is so sadistic. Religious paintings are almost all obscene, clothing ripped to shreds. Samson at the mill. All I have to do is rip the loincloth off. Brothers selling brothers as slaves. Jesus being taken naked down from the Cross by rough Roman soldiers.

"I think *The Last Supper* painting would be a natural for me. Everyone would get the reference. We know that supper table. You can show it and those languid male postures in many ways. Also for a good artist like myself, it would be an honor and a challenge to learn from Leonardo. I wouldn't want to debase it in any way.

I would want to transpose it. Sort of like taking a symphony and making a masterful transposition to a piano piece.

"I have a magnificent German etching, an amazing sexual one of Jesus being taken down from the Cross by all these men. It's very erotic, everyone's naked and sexual. It's all there. All I would have to do is buff up those bodies, add those dicks. That's the way life really was. This is a case where you don't want to change anything. I've never done anything where I've outright copied. By just changing a few elements, I want to show how you can absolutely rewrite history.

"This will drive religious people crazy. But I don't want to do it as a joke. I want it to look so serious that it will genuinely move religious people."

And get leathermen off.

6
COLLABORATING WITH REX ON PAGE AND SCREEN

Rex was always avant-garde by years and decades. So writing about him in *Drummer* before he introduced himself in his January 1978 letter, I've both read him and listened intently as a proper first-responder journalist to the rarity of his every word spoken in person and in telephone conversations. I never cared if he was playing me. As a Catholic seminarian studying ten years for the priesthood in the 1950s, I'd learned how to shut up and hear confessions using critical thinking. From the first day I saw his astonishing work, I knew he was a young talent to watch.

As an academic writing about gay popular culture, I took years of "Rex notes" and filed them in my archive because I did not want him or any emerging gay artist I met through *Drummer* to become lost to history. Perhaps his reluctance to be written about or photographed was a primal survival reaction he adopted as a youngster reacting to the boyhood of homophobia he described to the Tom of Finland Foundation. Nevertheless, we worked together professionally on page and screen. Depending on his mood and his need for free publicity, the private person he was sometimes let writers profile his public work in various magazines. I'm grateful he allowed me to shoot several archival black-and-white 35mm pictures of him who thought his letters once read should be destroyed—even though people who received them can remember what he wrote.

Deflecting publicity may be a great strategy to ignite a cult around one's work, but it also disrupted communication, scholarship, publicity, business, and history around him who once was miffed because an art dealer told him he wasn't famous enough in celebrity culture to sell at higher prices. Or in Japan.

Whose fault was that? His mystique hurt him. The reverse psychology of silence as a publicity gimmick may have worked for Greta Garbo, but I can't forget how Rex fumed in the early 1990s when those new next-gen gay magazines in New York blew him off because they'd never heard of him, or perhaps because they had heard he bragged he was troublesome and they didn't need the grief from him and his poison-pen letters.

Maybe the contrarian talked or didn't talk to be quoted, but talk he did to be provocative because acting up he was hooked on the rush of endorphins he got watching people watching him "performing Rex." He liked that he was known for bursting forth to speak his mind publicly with aggressive opinions about his work and the world. Venting is social maneuvering as entertainment. He was one of those incorrigible artists who is so eccentric you hope to sit next to him at a dinner party.

What a relief on August 22, 1986, when the dysfunctional *Drummer* publisher John Embry sold the magazine he'd never really understood to Anthony DeBlase, PhD (1942-2000) and his lover psychiatrist Andrew Charles, MD (1939-2006). To celebrate the historic transition, Rex and Trent Dunphy and Bob Mainardi immediately announced their intimate "*Drummer* Restoration Dinner Party," Folsom Fair weekend, September 28, 1986, 2:30 PM, to welcome the new publishers upon their move from Chicago.

In preparation for the party, Rex set a perfect tone when he drew a customized invitation of a "Greaser Leatherman" for the gentlemen's soiree. If ever a *Drummer* Salon dinner party for eight gay men was ripe for a screenplay, this sit-down summit had characters, wit, and intrigue enough for a Merchant-Ivory production. Celebrating the exit of the old regime of Embry, the longtime *Drummer* creators around the table in the photography-filled Dunphy-Mainardi Victorian included the three hosts, art director Al Shapiro and his partner Dick Kriegmont, photographer Mark I. Chester (born 1950), Mark Hemry (born 1950), and me.

Rex was a raffishly attractive tablemate keeping the conversation moving even as DeBlase launched into an emotional monolog about their first two months of owning *Drummer.* Tony said they thought they had purchased *Drummer* free of any encumbrances, until they were immediately besieged by creditors and vendors hoping the new owners would pay them what Embry still owed them.

Rex sort of laughed. I sort of laughed. All of us who were owed money by Embry sort of laughed when DeBlase cracked a nervous joke hoping that none of us would ask him to pay what Embry owed us. At that moment, Tony invited Rex to draw the cover illustration and me to write a cover story for the historic special issue *Drummer* 100, November 1986. DeBlase, giving Rex this second cover, later gave Tom of Finland his first and only *Drummer* cover, issue 113, February 1988. DeBlase's anointing of Rex was as significantly important as DeBlase's creation of the Leather Flag (1989) and his founding of the Leather Archives & Museum (1991). But he didn't pay us either.

Rex then, later, and always, reckoned his insights meant to be quotable were too important to gay art history not to be leaked privately to friends and journalists who could pass his words along like publisher John Dagion who as Rex's designated press agent printed personal scoops about Rex in his *Trash* magazine. My grail as a gay historian was always to sit Rex down to speak his mind into my video camera as he did for my audiotape recorder. But he would not give face.

In May 1995, regularly updating each other, he sent me reproductions of two drawings with a hand-written note on a yellow Post-It saying, "New stuff for your files. Not to be copied under pain of death." Over the years, our work in tandem was published in magazines like *Drummer* and *Skin,* Volume 1, Number 6, 1981. Together we collaborated on the matched story and drawing, "Tele-Fuck," dated 2-20-83, for a phone-sex feature in *Just Men,* Volume

2, Issue 2, January 1984. We teamed again for the drawing "Officer Mike: San Francisco's Finest," dated 6-13-83, in *Just Men*, Volume 2, Number 4, May-June 1984.

That same year, publisher Winston Leyland commissioned a Rex original, dated 4-22-84, for the cover of my novel *Leather Blues* for Leyland's Gay Sunshine Press. What a cover to judge a book by. The requested drawing of a smoldering leatherman was so perfectly Rex that Rex re-purposed it regularly and posted it as the opening image on his website Rexwerk.com. Winston also hired Rex to draw the cover of *A Sand Fortress*, a reprint of the 1968 novel by prolific novelist John Coriolan who wrote so much about gay sex during World War II. Rex re-purposed that drawing when he pasted it into a sleek commercial display ad for my Palm Drive Video studio in *Adult Video Magazine*.

Collectors and Onanists know Rex from the dozens of magazines that did dare to publish some of his selected drawings: *Drummer, Honcho, The Advocate, Folsom, Toy, Just Men, Inches, Torso, Stroke, Uncut, In Touch for Men, Instigator, Straight to Hell, Manifest Reader, Mach,* and *Trash*.

7

THE REX VIDEO: REX MEN WILL LEAVE
A STAIN ON YOUR BIG SCREEN

In 1987, at the height of AIDS, and because there was no inexpensive way to produce coffee-table photobooks to gather, publish, and preserve endangered erotic artists during the plague, I decided to do on video the archival work we did in *Drummer* to save art history. In a sense, I put *Drummer* on screen with my series of erotic artist galleries featuring *Drummer* artists like Rex, Domino, the Hun, A. Jay, Skipper, and Etienne who died just as we began working together.

Rex had mentioned his interest in making a Rex video as a fresh way of publishing and marketing his work more widely into gay popular culture because people bought more video cassettes than books or magazines. So I took him at his word, and shot a sample reel which I sent and pitched to him in a letter five years before the internet became available to the public on April 30, 1993.

On April 5, 1988, I wrote:

Dear Rex. Having once talked with you about you expanding your palette into the video medium, both because you
were interested, and I said I would….included with this
letter is a working print, a rough cut. Actually the finest
compliment I can pay your *oeuvre*, as friend, fan, and fellow
artist, is to move my graphic "video eye" over your single-
frame graphic concept.

I sought, as a writer, to pull out the characters, the drama,
the detail, the tension by making sometimes six pictures out
of your one frame. Your style is very filmic. You often draw
in storyboards [where] within the frame various action/emo-
tion occurs, and inside a single frame as in the six separate
panels of sex action in the six separate cubicles inside your
single "Everard" [St. Mark's] bath drawing [published ten
years before on the first page of the Rex review in *Son of
Drummer*].

You translate beautifully from page to screen. The graphic
artist on video! From stasis to movement! From drawings
spread out on a table to drawings thundering across screens!
Taping your drawings is a fresh rebirth of your past work.

Through this introduction through a new medium,
your audience, now a video audience, can buy you, in fact,
re-buy you, because you are now in their new medium of
choice—while at the same time presenting you to men who
buy videos but never buy books or packets of drawings.

The probing macro-lens gave me an even greater appreciation of your art in both form and content: from the stylized execution of details in the tin ceilings in the blue-collar
hotels to the contents of an open glove compartment. In
short, I tried to pull out the drama and detail of your drawings which typical American viewers, unguided, with no
critical ability, may miss when presented with your single
frames, not knowing consciously where to look, or not per-
ceiving how you finesse and focus your graphic, emotional,
erotic power.

The Rapidograph style never looked so loomingly, dottily impressive. ("Sunday in the Park with Rex.") The video leads viewers into a cumulative Impressionist experience. As frame after frame, sequence after sequence of your drawing spins across the screen, the accelerating effect is mesmerizing, potent, dirty, lascivious, magical. Action! Adventure! Pages of drawings stream by handlessly. Your men keep coming, insistent in eye contact with the viewer, one after the other, like increasingly magnificent contestants in a bodybuilding competition.

Effortlessly, the viewer sits, watching, "hands free" for stroking, carried along by Rex in motion. The video turns the pages of all your work for the viewer. If you have created, say, a 1000 single-frame drawings in your career, the video camera can multiply each of those drawings at least five times, increasing the visuals of your work to 5000, expanding both the time-code length and the design field of the single frame, showcasing your art with all the detail of a private tour through an erotic gallery.

I was amazed, watching the finished sample edit, to be swept along by the sheer force of your 8x10 images coming, boom-boom, staccato, at me on the 40-inch screen. What an expansion! What a discovery! I hope this surprise package pleases you. I can pay your work and your art no greater compliment....

If, as you said to me, you wanted to make a video, perhaps this is the first one. If you like the concept, it's yours. I think the time has come at this century's end for Rex to be showcased, marketed, and appreciated as a video artist. Garbo talks! Rex moves! Let me know what you think of this little experiment. When it come to drawing men masculine for men who like men masculine, nobody comes close to you. As ever, Jack

So in 1989, Rex brought fifty-some images, some priceless originals and some excellent copies of originals, to my studio rostrum camera to be sorted on my easel into a storyboard narrative for the

65-minute film-*noir* feature *The Rex Video Gallery: Corrupt Beyond Innocence.*

I recognized the challenge set up in *Drummer* 12.

Rex never sets up a narrative series. All the story is there in one flash, telescoped into a single moment and isolated on the page. These are drawings you look at one at a time. In each one, Rex distills the actions we have all seen, done or imagined, but which we get to bring off only rarely and never do so well.

My job was to create a streaming loose narrative while remaining faithful to Rex's eye to which I was sensitive because, translating media, I wanted to be absolutely true to his gaze. I tried to climb into what Rex might do with a video camera, and treated every drawing as a single frame in a movie montage unreeling *Rexwerk*. I took my cue from the coiled kinetic energy in his single-frame drawings and translated his energy into the actual kinetics of film through the use of panning and zooming and editing of the kind Ken Burns uses to give life to vintage photos.

I set each drawing on my easel, and shot five or ten minutes of each picture, Take One to Take Ten, starting and stopping a dozen times from a dozen different points of view as if each drawing were a real room, a real set on a real soundstage. I treated Rex's men entering stage left and stage right as real human actors waiting to hear the director shout, "Action!"

My goal was to lift the silent hands-on haptic experience of Rex from static page to moving-picture screen using camera movement, depth of field, tracking shots, zooms, and editing juxtapositions to inject movement, rhythm, time, and sound that were implicit in his dynamic still drawings.

If Character A was looking at Character B, I focused into Rex's 8x10 picture with a close-up of A's face and eyes and then panned across the small drawing to the face of B at whom A was staring to catch the double-take reaction in B's face.

Then I'd pull back to a wide shot establishing the context of the two men in the room; then an insert close-up of a crumpled pack of cigarettes; a fast zoom shot in on a dick; a foreshadowing insert of the face of a new Character C who would not appear in another separate drawing until ten minutes later in the narrative; then a return to a three-quarter shot of Character A looking at B.

All this lens work and editing, that took two months to create a 65-minute video, was to add the emotional movement of erotic rhythm and pacing to the still drawings. All the cumulative technique was to drag the viewer's gay gaze and critical thinking into the sum total of the drawing, directing him, tutoring him, to look at details he might have missed looking at the whole. With Rex's work the devil truly is in the details. Typically, timing the beat, I'd shoot straight on into a drawing, my video frame framing his frame, for an establishing shot to expand the perfect moment of one single drawing into a ninety-second montage of images investigating that drawing.

Oftentimes, shooting around Character A and Character B, I'd focus on a detail, and then pan the camera from a tasty detail in Drawing A to a tastier detail in Drawing B fusing the two separate Rex pictures into one streaming organic graphic created by juxtaposition to guide the viewer like a museum docent leading the public walking through an exhibit.

The pre-digital VHS format itself added a certain vivid electronic pulsation to his static images. Rex himself did the art direction for the dramatic finale in which he summed up his indelible pointillist images into one Big Dot that, as it fades back into the dots of the first drawing shown in the video, evokes audience movie memories of the big dots of circular planets and moons made dramatic by the pounding chords of *Thus Spoke Zarathustra* in *2001: A Space Odyssey.*

So what does a Rex drawing sound like? To create the distinctive erotic audio design of Rex's murmuring world, we chose not to use "found music" like *Zarathustra.* Instead, Mark Hemry who edited and produced the video engineered a hypnotic slow-jacking house beat on one audio track—as if it were music from another room down the wet, dirty hallway at the Waiting Arms Hotel, a fisting palace that existed briefly on Folsom Street in the 1970s.

Over that muffled thump, he mixed and reversed a variety of sex-pit sounds in a lowdown act of performance art. He built his soundtrack directing his Foley artists (us two) to pour water from a pitcher into a bucket of water to mimic piss in toilets escalating from teasing trickle to streaming force. To suggest flophouse halls, we stomped out footsteps, zipped and unzipped our leather jackets, stroked our chaps for the hot creak of leather, flicked lighters, coughed, spoke ruzza-buzza whispers, crumpled paper, slapped our thighs, scraped our boots on floors, flushed toilets, jangled chains, and rattled keys to capture Rex's world.

On April 5, 1990, I sent him the first copy of the finished video.

Dear Rex,

Congratulations! Here's the *Rex Video Gallery*. Thank you for your patience. Life is short. Art takes longer. We're very pleased with the look and sound of the video. We're sure it will sell nicely based on how well *The Hun Video Gallery* is selling. To that end, because, as we told you, one hundred percent of all the income from the retail price goes directly to you, we're enclosing a $200.00 advance against your first royalties to help tide you over. Thanks for not pressuring us while we worked to translate your art to video with great care. Thanks also for giving us the latitude to interpret your drawings. You've always known how much we appreciate your work. Hope you are enjoying *Some Dance to Remember* which we sent off to you some time ago. All the best, Jack Fritscher and Mark Hemry

On April 10, 1990, Rex, who was a mad perfectionist about duplication of his drawings, wrote a letter revealing both his kindness and his analytical mind in his own words.

Dear Jack: It works! I'm very pleased with the *Rex Video Gallery*. I can't think of a single thing I'd change. I want you to know—especially—that I think the soundtrack you're created is SUPERIOR to the one [sample] I submitted. You've really "captured" the essence of what I was trying to create.

Also the "voice" is excellent and as a "performance" is much more orchestrated to the visuals on screen than mine could have been. Every pause, sigh, and sink-drain gurgle falls in the appropriate place—like a [Bernard] Herrmann score for a Hitchcock film. I think this soundtrack is a real trend-setter—a new form of soundtrack design for the porn film.

I was aware when turning the sound off how "ordinary" the pictures became, and yet how seamless and dynamic they become when the "narrative' sound is on, unobtrusive. It really makes the whole thing work. I can clearly see the care and work you guys have lavished on it. I dare say it's lovingly done. It sure looks like the film I planned.

As emphatic as I am about my ideas, I'm never so foolish or vain to assume it's the only point of view possible. Apparently, you were able to work with my concept. Unreal.

The only spot I caught a change that you made was at the very end when the BIG DOT fades back to the beginning picture, and that was right and correct and better to do so. I'm very impressed with the camerawork.

It's a shame no one can appreciate what a technical tour de force the miniature camerawork in that film is; the pans are so smooth and confident that the drawings appear to be as if they were giant tapestries that you could pan for yards across. Little do people realize, you're panning for thirty seconds across a scene that's only two inches in length! Between the sinister soundtrack and the power of the close-up photography, it's amazing how [H. R.] Geiger-like the drawings appear to be. They become almost like paintings.

Yes, I was very impressed with myself thanks to you. Again, many heartfelt thanks to you and Mark for the work you've done on my behalf. I appreciate it. And all Best Wishes for your new book which I see everywhere and which I hope is doing well.—Rex

Five years later, on May 1, 1995, Rex, still riding high on the rush of the video, sent this letter.

Dear Jack. This is still a great video and will be a collector's classic, but it's in the wrong place [home video screens]. From the very first I've had the gut feeling that this really belongs up on a big screen—in a theater—without distraction, to be fully appreciated. You should pay money, sit in a darkened theater and see and hear this thing on a hundred-foot screen. If I had the money, I wouldn't hesitate to rent something like the Castro Theater and show it for a weekend myself. It's a film you want to SEE.

He was correct about small versus big screen. In 1990, our Rex video had debuted on a small screen as a "Best in Show" video installation, credited to Rex, Mark Hemry, and me at the New Langton Arts Gallery, San Francisco. By 1995, Rex had forgot that in 1992, Mark Hemry and I had premiered the video to great applause at the alternative 9th Olympia Film Festival in Olympia, Washington. It was a one-night lecture event which Rex did not attend. So he missed that first big-screen experience and the champagne kick of the Olympia Theater marquee spelling out our double bill of *The Rex Video Gallery* and *The Hun Video Gallery* as "Rough Night in Sodom and Gomorrah."

In 2016, German curator Bernd Althans gave our *Rex* video its European premiere as a gallery installation in his *Rex Verboten* exhibit which I co-sponsored at Galerie/TheBallery, Schöneberg, Berlin, where all funds from the DVD sales of the *Rex Video Gallery* went directly to Rex—as they always had from every sale from the first. That exhibit like the 1990 Palm Drive Video brochure inviting the curious to step right up to Rex double-dared fans to look at Rex's art as a way to look inside their own hearts, minds, and orgasms. "See life through the eyes of Rex, because, like Rex, you may be 'corrupt beyond innocence!'"

8

TOUCH-ACTIVATED ART
TURNS NAZI TABOO INTO TOTEM

Rex knew the territory on which he pissed ink. He drew each authentic *mise-en-scène* on white paper with his Rapidograph pen that tapped out his drawings that have no straight lines in them. He drew in seclusion with a bottomless jar of jelly beans and a package of Red Vines licorice sitting on his desk next to his small television monitor playing video cassettes of Leni Riefenstahl's *Triumph of the Will* (1935) and *Olympia* (1938) and videos of goose-stepping Nazi parades with Stormtrooper music because like Tom of Finland and Hollywood Rex liked the erotic aesthetics of Nazi style, uniforms, and discipline.

War-baby Rex, like postwar boomer punk rockers reshaping culture alongside him in the 1970s, created art and anti-art around the Eros and politics of fascist imagery to co-opt it, and make the point that Nazis were about control, and that punk, like leather culture, was about freedom. Staying in provocative character during Christmas of 2023, with three months to live, Rex told Trent Dunphy that while confined to a wheelchair after months "incommunicado" in an Amsterdam nursing home, he passed the time in his "terminal isolation and periodic depression" with "my Nazi recordings, Winston Churchill tapes, Wi-Fi, and Netflix." He added:

> I've had a remarkable life and cannot complain that I missed anything it had to offer. Our generation lived in the best of times. I look forward now to death which cannot be far off. "Existing" alone like this is not something I'm looking forward to in the long run. I'm ready to go whenever the iceman cometh. Given the way the world is going, I'm kind of glad I won't be around for what's coming towards us in the next decade.

Romancing the Nazis, Rex reflected his times better than the cringing *Village Voice* that cried a river over leather culture. In the mid-1970s, leather bars like the Ramrod in San Francisco were on slow midweek Movie Nights regularly screening a four-minute 16mm clip of the camp musical number "Springtime for Hitler" from comedian Mel Brooks' *The Producers* (1967). In pop culture, the cautionary Liza/Nazi/Fosse *Cabaret* (1972), and Liliana Cavani's sadomasochistic *The Night Porter* (1974) used Nazi chic that in Cavani's so-called "Nazisploitation" film equated sexual obsession with fascism, so said the BBC whose poll of critics listed *The Night Porter*, for which Rex could have been art director, as number 32 on the "100 Greatest Films Directed by Women."

Even so, soon after being hired as editor of *Drummer*, I told publisher Embry I'd quit if he did not stop printing a monthly display ad for the Gay Nazi Party, the gay "National Socialist League," with its Nazi insignia of "Winged Eagle and Swastika" that he began running in the very first issue of *Drummer*. Even as the now 94-year-old novelist John Rechy decided he did not like Tom of Finland using Nazi symbols, I decided Tom's aesthetic use was one thing, and Rex's psychodramatic referential use was another.

Born in the USA in 1939 before Hitler invaded Poland, I grew up during the war which Rex born in 1944 did not, and I could not abide Nazis literally *recruiting* in *Drummer*. That was a bridge too far.

The Gay Nazi ad had the nerve to take the song title "Tomorrow Belongs to Me" from *Cabaret* and pervert it into the Nazi tag line "Tomorrow Belongs to You!" When Embry dropped the display ad, the National Socialist League, claiming it a violation of free speech, sued him, and he lost, case closed. The point was made and the ad quietly disappeared.

In 1939, Christopher Isherwood who knew a thing or two about Nazis warned in *Goodbye to Berlin*: "People laugh at them, right up to the last moment."

I wasn't laughing. Pushed by the *Anschluss* of the Moral Majority of the Republican Christian Right, and by the anti-gay Anita Bryant in 1977, I wrote a militant essay reviewing Pasolini's radically gutsy and perfectly Rex-like anti-fascist film *Salo or the 120 Days of Sodom* in *Drummer* 20, January 1978. To warn readers about the clear and present danger of American fascism, I cited Nobel Prize winner Sinclair Lewis' 1935 novel, *It Can't Happen Here*, a cautionary tale about a dictator taking over American politics, in which Lewis sounded the warning: "When fascism comes to America, it will be wrapped in the flag and carrying a cross."

On February 6, 1975, five months before the *Village Voice* shamed Rex in July, Susan Sontag, wondering how in the world repressive Nazis became eroticized, wrote in her essay "Fascinating Fascism" in *The New York Review of Books* that the gay attraction to the Nazi aesthetic is "no more than a variant of camp…which is unfettered by the scruples of high seriousness." She added spot-on: "The color is black, the material is leather, the seduction is beauty, the justification is honesty, the aim is ecstasy, the fantasy is death."

Both Rex and Tom—worshiping athletic bodies just like both the Nazi Party and Muscular Christianity—remind us of the politically-incorrect Freudian pleasures we sometimes think we should cancel in our "moral" selves when we feel we're too "nice" to allow our "porn" selves to play around transgressively with taboos. One of leather culture's seminal films, Kenneth Anger's *Scorpio Rising* (1964), was a Jesus-and-Nazi-biker inflected gay sequel to Marlon Brando's stylish outlaw film *The Wild One* (1953) directed by László Benedek who was a seminal influence on Rex. Rex often let the *The Wild One* play silently on his studio monitor. He misted himself in a realtime rush of grainy dots of black-and-white motion pictures while he sat stippling black dots on white paper for his still pictures. Some of his drawings unreel like alternative scenes omitted from the "straight" final cut of *The Wild One*. Benedek carried a political message when he fled Hungary as the Nazi Kradfahrer on motorcycles came to power like a really bad biker gang. When he arrived in Hollywood, he turned the Nazi bikers, as if in warning, into Brando's fascist bike gang in a classic film that shaped a generation out for kicks.

Rex's "Black Socks" strikes some as a somber heavy drawing. The sailor being serviced is a cynical hard-ass: aloof, tattooed, uncut, hairy, muscular, and dominant. The tattooed biker who sucks the sailor's foot through his black sock kneels, booted, in the ritual litter of porn mags, liquor bottles, and used yellow-mesh popper capsules that fuel restless nights of men following their cocks around. A third man stands reflected in the mirror. A fourth peers his big eye, focuses his gay gaze through the viewfinder of a gloryhole in the wall.

Who are these two extra men? Why do two toothbrushes stand in the dirty glass? The drawing's strong voyeuristic sexuality and its high technical skill reflect what the curious critic might suspect is subtle clue to the artist's personal gloryhole vision of ideal male life—that is, if it is fair play to seek autobiography in an artist's fictional work. Rex did say, "My drawings define who I became. There are no other 'truths' out there."

Maya Angelou wrote: "The idea is to write it so that people hear it and it slides through the brain and goes straight to the heart." Rex was likewise into drawing to make guys open their eyes and their brains and their fanatic hearts, and work from their dicks up to their heads.

I once asked him, "Do you think art can put thoughts into people's minds?"

He answered, "That's true. Jane Austen could. Ayn Rand could. Why can't we? I do porn to bust people's balloons."

Men are often most susceptible to subliminal new ideas when tumescence opens them to transcendence. In his touch-activated drawings, Rex was not afraid to push his subject matter past taboo into totem to teach the joy of fetish sex. His through-the-looking-glass point of view so fascinates and seduces the viewer that the stoned voyeur forgets he was at first socially or morally repulsed by the raw human scene that's making him hard.

Men coming out of the closet of family, church, and state are often simultaneously shocked and thrilled that gay life offers so many alternative physical, intellectual, and psychic contradictions that liberate the soul. Tennessee Williams said, "Nothing human disgusts me…. I am a deeper and warmer and kinder man for my deviations." Through the visual and emotional geometries of his canny draftsmanship, Rex with his associative thinking as an autistic anarchist uses the pulsating teaching moments inside the mind-opening magical thinking of masturbation to transfrom and liberate the viewer's linear thinking and conservative sex fears into self acceptance and erotic liberation where outlaw sex feeds the Dionysian soul that is not afraid to dance even though it means being torn to pieces.

Once you've cum to a taboo fetish, you've taken another bite from Eden's forbidden apple of carnal knowledge. And you can't go back to Kansas.

9

EDWARD HOPPER, WALT WHITMAN, AND GAY AMNESIA

The way Leonardo da Vinci told the entire story of the New Testament inside the single frame of *The Last Supper*, Rex dumped more character, setting, conflict, plot, and theme into a single frame than most filmmakers shoot in a full-length feature. If masturbation is magical, Rex was a magician with ink, purposing his work to cause erections and orgasm. His dots had the power to make men cum.

"Mad Doctor," 11-15-76, for instance, dramatizes a counterphobic Nazi medical fantasy not offered by other artists who did not dig deep like Rex into gay men's fears of, for instance, forced institutionalization for psychiatric gay-conversion therapies whose tortures were as late as the 1970s still a constant mid-century threat that he spun into a healing thrill of stress relief. A cheer went up in gay bars in 1973 when the American Psychiatric Association declassified homosexuality as a mental disorder.

That's why I published "Mad Doctor" as a full page in *Son of Drummer* to offer subscribers a sample of his latest book, *Icons*. Most of his work stems from contemporary real life, but his "Mad Doctor" fetish pictures—one dated 11-15-76; a second 12-31-77—were occasioned by fans, most of whom age thirty-something in gay bars in the 1970s were impressionable young boys during World War II. Their Nazi fears and sadomasochistic fantasies and divine orgasms were anchored in Third Reich medical sex experiments on captured males. In 1975, war babies and postwar babies high on pot and poppers were zoning out in theaters on the high camp of the Nazisploitation film *Ilsa: She-Wolf of the SS* while mashing *Ilsa* up in their heads with Rex's theatrical Men of the SS.

Truth be told, Rex, if you study his drawings, was a brilliant still-life artist depicting and arranging everyday objects of characteristic male debris within his frames into which he then inserted his Rex men among the atmospheric objects he intended to add dramatic backstory to the men.

He who did commissions to buy lunch and pay rent preferred not to work with a client's detailed script, but more with a man's general concept. He was quite willing to develop the real guts of someone else's fantasy, because, he told me, "Drawing the sex comes easy." He laughed. "I spend more time drawing the lampshade lighting the sex. I figure I average out working at $5.37 an hour."

So to support himself between commissions and bartending, he sometimes hired out as an interior house painter.

Imagine having your bedroom painted by Rex.

No matter what he did to survive, he lived to squeeze the ink out of Eros to fill his pen.

At the opposite extreme from "Mad Doctor" is "Jack Off," a quiet study Edward Hopper might appreciate with its Hopper-like window curtains billowing to show breezy movement within still paintings like "Hotel by a Railroad" and "Evening Wind." "Jack Off" is exquisite early Rex. Its romantic YMCA isolation of solitary love on a bored summer afternoon has made it a favorite of Onanists everywhere.

Here the hunk is alone, independent, a Rousseauian noble savage, an American archetype, a cowboy on the Kerouac road in Marlboro Country, not necessarily queer, yet invitational, self-reliant, available, laid back like one of Walt Whitman's luscious common men. Rex and Walt were a pair of comrades. Rex's world of brokeback bromance contains Whitman's multitudes of errant men, aggressive, promiscuously anonymous, alone and in groups, that Whitman, himself a lover of bus drivers, and soldiers, and comrades assayed in his queer "Calamus" poems in *Leaves of Grass*:

> Whoever you are holding me [my art] now in hand....The way is suspicious, the result uncertain, perhaps destructive... The whole past theory of your life and all conformity to the lives around you would have to be abandon'd....

As a brilliant finale to his career, Rex could have canonized his American reputation by creating a dozen drawings, a *Whitman*

Portfolio, illustrating select lines like the following from America's greatest poet who hung out at Pfaff's gayish bar in Greenwich Village in the 1860s. In 1975, a hundred years and a mile from Rex's studio, that location so revered in gay history became the disco "Infinity" at 653 Broadway.

Whitman's lines of poetry often read like picture-perfect captions for Rex's drawings.

"Twenty-eight young men bathe by the shore, Twenty-eight young men and all so friendly...the homeliest of them is beautiful."

"All this I swallow, it tastes good, I like it well, it becomes mine, I am the man, I suffer'd, I was there."

"If you want me again, look for me under your boot-soles."

"To cotton-field drudge or cleaner of privies I lean."

"I go with fishermen and seamen and love them."

"I mind how once we lay such a transparent summer morning, How you settled your head athwart my hips and gently turn'd over upon me, And parted the shirt from my bosom-bone, and plunged your tongue to my bare-stript heart, And reach'd till you felt my beard, and reach'd till you held my feet."

10

REX AT THE BLUE MUSE CAFÉ

From 1995-2000, Rex rode his bicycle through the debris of Tenderloin streets to eat breakfast almost daily at 10:30 at the Blue Muse Restaurant and Bar, 409 Gough Street at Hayes, near City Hall Civic Center, a mile from his Larkin Street studio where the 29-year-old artist and singer Cynthia Louise (Lloyd), one of those female servers gay men love, began kidding with him sitting, 50-something, at his usual table over his usual omelet and fruit.

Voyeur Rex liked the Blue Muse for its morning quiet and its noisy weekend cabaret performances because no matter the time of day it was a sex-circus parade of neighborhood leathermen, artists, fetish freaks, and drag stars running for "Empress of San Francisco."

Cynthia told me on June 6, 2024, "I waited on Rex five days a week. I always worked the morning shift. The owner Sydney Wong said not to bug him too much while he was eating and reading the newspaper and checking the stock market. We all thought he was East Coast Money."

This was around the time his mother had died leaving him the nest egg he put into stocks and lost.

"He had an odor," Cynthia recalled. "He smelled of men, leather, and sex."

Rex smelled like his drawings.

"That smell was wonderful to me. I love gay men very much."

Living that sensibility, Cynthia, known as "Ciel," became one of the dedicated caretakers for Rumi Missabu, the disabled Cockettes founder and global star of *Elevator Girls in Bondage*, who died age 76, April 2, 2024, five days after Rex's death.

"I feel I'm a gay man in a woman's body, but I'm not trapped there. I'm a free agent. Rex always had great respect for my gender. I later became a dominant mistress for fifteen years so I understood his work which influenced me.

"I liked the way he smelled which was sexy to me. I could smell what he was into. I knew what he was doing."

"When did you find out that Rex was REX? Did he tell you he was an artist?"

"He was somewhat mysterious. He was quite like a sex-magic warlock. Sometimes he'd disappear for six months, but we never worried because he always came back. He talked more after he came to one of my openings and saw some of my paintings. We had a vibe of two artists connecting. One day when I served him his Coca-Cola, he showed me a box of about thirty pieces of jewelry, all, he said, from the women in his family. From his mother. He said he didn't want to sell it. He wanted me to have it. Some very good costume jewelry plus a gold-and-amethyst ring and a gold wedding band. I was quite moved. He told me he didn't care if I sold it which I didn't because I knew he really wanted me to keep it."

"Did you two keep in touch after you left Blue Muse?"

"Three or four years later [2004/5], I ran into him at Folsom Fair. He was a handsome man, but by then [age 60] he looked less muscular, drawn, like he'd been ill, but he seemed grander wearing a white shirt and jeans. He was still so charming and friendly. He invited me to go with him to an after-Fair party at Stompers."

Rex confirmed his respect for Cynthia when he squired her into the ongoing leather salon at Stompers Boots, 323 10th Street, which was a boot-fetish oasis owned for fifteen years by the leatherman and local KRON 4 televison news photographer Mike McNamee (1939-2018). McNamee, our mutual longtime friend, was the raw-boned six-foot-five Irishman, Harley biker, and filmmaker who had dared shoot 35mm erotic crucifixion movies outdoors on the roof of the Slot bathhouse, 979 Folsom Street, in the 1970s.

In 2016, Mike donated the pair of Stompers boots used to cast each bronze boot print set in cement honoring our leather dead—including Thom Gunn, Tony DeBlase, Chuck Arnett, Hank Diethelm, Robert Opel—in the "San Francisco South of Market Leather History Alley" on Ringold Street where, as an advisor to the original concept, I've suggested new bronze boot prints be added to include Rex and Mike whom Rex eulogized from Amsterdam in the *Bay Area Reporter*.

"I remember," Cynthia said, "there were about forty men hang-ing out in Stompers shop and garden and Rex introduced me as his 'Secret Wife' which I thought was such a very sweet dear thing to do and I loved him for it. That afternoon, he finally came out and told me who he was as an artist and how he'd worked with the Mafia. He trusted me. He truly influenced the erotic side of my work. We exchanged phone numbers and addresses, but we lost touch. And still, I remember him tenderly."

11

MOST CENSORED GAY AMERICAN ARTIST

More than Mapplethorpe was at first, Rex was the gay American artist most censored by the gay press until Robert's art pictures were busted and put on trial as porn in Cincinnati in 1990. Vanilla critics who dislike Rex's work object not because of his gorgeous technique, but more out of a misunderstanding of his challenging subject matter, his sexual psychology, and his homosurreal gaze and intellect.

From the first, the vanilla objections ran to cliche and to truth. "Faces aren't pretty. Bodies too muscular. Too rough. Too dirty. Too old. Too young. No smiles. No blonds." I leave it to others to assess his use of disability (*Sex-Freak Circus*) and bestiality (dogs and horses everywhere) and young lords of the flies who are a tad too cherubic in many of his drawings, and in his *Peter Pan* portfolio which, from what he told me about the drawings I've never seen, may be beyond the pale of current legality. For many reasons, I subtitled *The Rex Video Gallery: Corrupt Beyond Innocence*.

Two months after the anti-gay indignity of the Mapplethorpe censorship trial in Cincinnati, the angry and disruptive Rex took on censorship in Kevin Davis' *Bay Area Reporter* interview, January 3, 1991, in which Rex proclaimed his bare-knuckle Declaration of Independence from censorship. Davis wrote:

> The first thing you should know is that Rex doesn't care what you think about smoking, IV drug use, pederasty, or bestiality.... He says: "Censorship is a desecration of the artist's idea. So drawing Dirty Pictures is very much an act of Civil Disobedience, much more satisfying and probably more productive than burning the flag... So I decided to become a Pornographic Artist... I think when Pornographic Art is well done, it does come close to Anarchy. But it has to be very well done, and that's very rare. But it's what I strive for—to really get their juices flowing till they lose control: That's Anarchy.
>
> "Throughout history the greats in every art form have shared one ingredient, and that is a passionate appreciation of the earthy—not always pretty—aspect of the reality we call human existence....Gay publishing was once the radical outlaw. Now we're just giving away our hard-won freedoms.
>
> "After the historical precedent of the past, the gay community has drawn a blank. [Still smarting from the lashing

he got from the *Village Voice,* he continued] The gay press is going through a conservative time. There is a conspiracy of silence. They're frightened and intimidated.

"At first, I put up with it. I left out cum and fucking... [Now] I'm only drawing what can't be published. Magazine distributors don't fight. They're a business now."

Drawings cause quandries because it can be difficult to judge the exact age of a person in a drawing, but Rex did not take kindly to any cautions about age in his pictures. Did gay editors suspicious about the legal age of his *putti* simply decide to play it safe and boycott his work in his lifetime? Time will tell if his representations of youth will cancel his reputation and the entirety of his art.

Even after his sixty-year career, Rex in America remains deeply controversial. And still too *outré* to publish. The prim continue to priss out at his raw masculinity, and yet some hide their spank-bank of his scary art under their mattresses, not wanting socialite friends to know their fetish taste for leather and the rough trade of a walk on the wild side.

No wonder Rex moved to Amsterdam in 2011. He was already working long distance with editors Stephan Niederwieser and Simeon Morales at Bruno Gmünder Verlag in Berlin who published his work as part of the gay art canon in the unflinching 2012 collector's book *Rex Verboten.*

Feeling new vigor in Holland, Rex introduced his revived online mail-order business with a press-release autobiography quoted here with permission for archival permanence and study from his website which may disappear. Rex, the lifelong fabulist, role-playing in sex and life, wrote his story in the third person like a treatment for a biographical screenplay to satisfy fans' need for a dramatic answer to endless questions of how he became Rex. As Thelma Ritter said in *All About Eve,* "What a story! Everything but the bloodhounds snappin' at her [his] rear end."

"Who am I?" Entering this world without parents, a name, a place of birth, and—most of all—without a history will launch this child on a life apart from others.... Free from the mental baggage imposed upon others by nationality and religion this child begins life with an open mind and a clean slate… This child will grow up to become Rex.… Diagnosed with autism as a toddler, the child was adopted by a farmer at the age of three to go live on a New England tobacco farm… He did not learn to speak until the age of four.…

At the age of eight, he was in the fields working among the men, fetching water.… shirtless men sitting in the shade drinking beer, playing cards, singing and joking… These first indelible images of men planted a seed for a life-long attraction to working-class men…

When he turned ten, the farm burned to the ground.… [and] in the fifth grade, he was punished for reading Dostoevsky's *Crime and Punishment*.… He sought refuge in the local library where he was certain no other children would find him… when [he was] not contemplating suicide… tough working class bullies beat him up after school… Television taught him New York was an exciting place.… [So] he played hooky from school, stole some money, and bought a train ticket to New York [where on 42nd Street and Times Square he] …found used magazines [showing Tom of Finland] in adult bookstores that convinced him New York City was his destiny…

At the age of twelve, it was as if he were boycotting childhood… He was cranking out 1,000-page novels… reflecting his own gloomy life.… [while] reading books on burlesque, slavery, adultery, white supremacy, incest, divorce, rape, infanticide, lynching, Satanism, and Marxism.

At fourteen, the boy ran away to become a Beatnik in Greenwich Village.…where the underage boy was quickly seduced… and took to it like a Duck to Water.…

At sixteen, he was earning his own living [first as typist; then as kept boy] in New York City… He first learned about homosexual sex from straight men…in sleazy Bowery straight bars.

12

THE EYE OF THE ARTIST: AGING AND LEGACY

Rembrandt, Goya, and Degas had bad eyesight. Monet suffered from cataracts and his paintings of his water-lily garden pond at Giverny show how cataracts creating a kind of blurry "Impression-ism" affected his work.

I remember Rex reacting when our dear mutual friend, the artist Al Shapiro who created the world's first gay comic strip *Harry Chess* for Clark Polak's *Drum* magazine in 1964, went blind from AIDS in the last year of his life. Soon after Al died, Rex and I were talking about artists and eyes.

Jack: With all your close work, how do you take care of your eyes?

Rex: Years ago they were getting bad, but they seem to have gotten better. I've trained them.

Jack: Second sight often comes after first sight is lost.

Rex: The poor cannot afford good eyeglasses. I have a good pair of glasses. The cost was awful, a lot of money. One of my eyes has astigmatism and the godsend was these cheap drugstore glasses. They're wonderful. I buy packs of them. I use a lower-power glass during the day and a higher-power one when I'm working at night.

I had a bad eye infection for about five years. It was a stye and it was very disfiguring. I went to an ophthalmologist. He said, there's nothing wrong with your eyes. You have very healthy, strong eyes. I said, what's with this stye thing? He said, that comes from eye strain. It's sort of like a volcano, a big zit. It has to run its course.

But I said it's been going on for five years. He couldn't give me anything for it. And I had paid a fortune for that visit. It eventually went away. But I do eye exercises. Kind of train my eyes. I thought positively about it. Now I limit my drawing very strictly. I experimented with natural daylight

light bulbs. I started paying attention to glare on paper. And I limit my working hours. It's worked out great.

Jack: How old are you, actually? In terms of…

Rex: Oh, in terms of my eyes? I'm a thousand years old.

Jack: I know, but when you tell a doctor how old you are…

Rex: Oh, I'm not telling you what I tell the doctor. I told him whatever age I was at the time. You know, they just want to get you onto the table and cut out your cataracts. It's all a racket. They don't tell you that diet and exercise can bring your eyes back a long way. I think the retina gets less flexible as you get older. Our eyes don't adjust to light so easily. That's an age thing. I'm working slower and slower what with my eyesight use reduced, and taking time off to earn money, and the world is getting more and more expensive and my audience is shrinking and shrinking.

I said to myself: Rex, you're not going to live forever. You might live a long time, but at the rate you work, it's taken you ten years to do twelve drawings. As soon as you get older, it's going to slow down. Maybe twelve to fifteen years to do the next twelve and then you're into your 70s. What are you going to do with the rest of your career? Just where do you see it going?

It came as a shock to realize that my career is already over [1988] in the sense that the volume of work already exists.

Then I thought, what do great Hollywood stars do when they get into their 50s and 60s? Then you can play the role of the Great Man. You have nothing more to prove. If you've survived that long, obviously your reputation is kind of made and, what I think you should do in your old age is take the kind of chances that you couldn't take when you were younger when you were trying to become famous.

Obviously, when you pass out of the limelight, you're free to do what you want. You know how to do it and you can really enjoy the art which you couldn't do when you were younger and were pleasing people. Getting people to think you could do it.

That's why even more I want these last projects to add up to bodies of work. They might be the only things I am remembered for. People can say, "Here is Rex's *Sex-Freak Circus*. Here is his *Peter Pan*. Here is his *Bible*." The rest [of the individual original drawings] will get kind of disseminated and buried into private collections.

Up to now, I've never given that added dimension of taking on a whole storyboard or plot or theme or subject. Up to now what stories I've told are each in one picture—and magnificently so, I must say. It can be done.

I can tell the whole Bible in one picture. I have the skill to pull it off. But, in hindsight, I think I have done that one picture, that one plot, mastered that, and now in these last years I'd like to dwell on all the things I haven't been able to do. Like "water," for instance, for *Peter Pan*. I'm studying now how to draw water.

Drawing sex is now a minor thing with me. I do that in the first three seconds and then, like I told you, spend ten months on the lampshades and getting the light just right. That didn't use to be the case.

13
A ROOM OF ONE'S OWN-PETARD

Rex's longtime Amsterdam friend and gallerist Marcel Sluiman curated *Rex Uncensored*, the first European public exhibition of all of Rex's existing work, in Sluiman's CNCPT13 Gallery in 2014. On August 13, 2024, Marcel and I chatted about his tender eyewitness memory of Rex who called Marcel, "Son."

Losing Rex feels like losing more than a friend. We met in 2013 in my gallery CNCPT13 during Amsterdam Gay Pride. He just walked in and introduced himself. I did not know him, nor recognize his name until he pointed at my guest bookshelf hosted by the gay bookstore Vrolijk. About fifty of his *Rex Verboten* books were for sale right in front of me, and that's when I realized who he was. Like many people, I assumed Rex had died years ago, but here he was.

We met several times soon after to discuss his dream to exhibit in my gallery. We worked it out in weekly meetings that made us friends. We had dinners, walked for hours, visited gay bars, got high nightly in Amsterdam, and traveled a lot over the years. Rex loved Amsterdam by night. To him, Amsterdam and Berlin were the last places left on earth where you could find the magic of the gay fetishes he showed in his work: "For at least," he said, "as long as it will last." Rex was not an optimist.

When he lost his room in the Amsterdam Anco hotel, he rented a room in my house in the Jordaan district in Amsterdam centre, and during that time we spent six months in Thionne, France, where he created several art works far away from the fetish scene. After that, he finally got his very own apartment that he painted totally black just like his apartment in San Francisco and just like the black in his work.

Rex did not want me to make photographs. So even though I shot many private photos during our adventures, I never published them. He said his looks and surname were irrelevant and would just disturb "the fantasy of my fans."

We organized his exhibition *Rex Uncensored* in my gallery April 4-May 1, 2014. In September 2016, we traveled together with our CNCPT13 exhibit to Folsom Berlin because Rex had been invited for a major "Rex" gallery exhibit [Galerie/The Ballerie, Schöneberg] with streets, a hotel, and several parties decorated with Rex art. We did the same two years later in Antwerp at Darklands. Sales were always a bit disappointing, but he got the attention for his work and name and that was all he really wanted. He loved the fact that nobody knew who he was, let alone that he was still alive.

[From February 23-25, 2018, the Darklands Festival, Europe's biggest annual fetish event, hosted Rex's last exhibit before he died: *Rex World 1968-2018: Back to the Future,*

50 Years of Creating Art; The Rex Retrospective. The Festival showcased over 200 Rex images, most never exhibited because of censorship and gay politics.

Alphatribe magazine celebrated the exhibit in issue 7, January-March 2018, with, on the cover, a Rex drawing of a black-and-white Leather Dog Face with the big word REX in red on its snout. The drawing also suggests in its Rorschach ink dots and blots a homosurreal leatherman's torso with elbows rampant.]

Rex was an observer. He was autistic, and basically lived sober. He ate the same pasta almost everyday except when we went out for our weekly dinner in a restaurant when he ate pizza with red wine or Coca-Cola. In the evenings, he'd sit down to draw, millions of dots year after year, and always with a joint and poppers on his desk, ready for action. "The best way to experience my work is high on a joint and sniffing a popper," he explained. While drawing, he listened to recorded speeches [Hitler and Goebbels] and European and American news from the first half of the 20th century. He owned thousands of recordings.

He lived from a few sales per year of originals and commissions and sales of Mineshaft T-shirts. He stopped drawing in 2019. His last drawing was a logo for a gay bar in Amsterdam.

His biggest frustration was losing so much original work in America due to a fire, and to theft, and the fact that about fifteen of his drawings went missing late in life. He found some peace knowing his work would show online forever. For good reason, he subtitled his exhibition in my gallery: *Rex Uncensored: Surviving Is the Best Revenge.*

While caring for my mother during her final illness, I did not see Rex in his final months. Not that I didn't try. He refused to see me because he did not want me to see him in his final days. He wanted me to remember him as the strong man he was: able to move, walk, talk, eat, debate and drink with. He always started his emails to me with "Hey, Son!" I never had a father. Rex came near.

Rex chose his own death.

He stopped eating.

He passed on March 28, 2024.

14

JEALOUSY IS SELF-INFLICTED MASOCHISM

In Berlin on June 6, 2016, Marcel Sluiman, interviewed Rex in an unpublished audio recording that I transcribed in which Rex talked candidly about hating Robert Mapplethorpe, worshiping Tom of Finland, and dealing with his own personal struggle with old age and fame.

> One night at a club in New York, Robert was annoying me and the hot guys in my group. Really hot and all different. No one liked Robert. He wasn't a warm guy. Very calculating. Patti Smith was becoming famous [1975]. I was becoming famous. He wasn't. This [annoyance] went on for about six months or a year. He was an enormous pest. One night, my friends all went into the bathroom together, and I was all alone at the bar. So I said, "ROBERT! What do you want from me?"
>
> He was drunk and I was drunk.
>
> He lost control and slammed his fist down on the bar and said, "I want the fucking respect you get."
>
> That was a great moment of truth for him. A very revealing moment.
>
> He said to me, "With your talent, you could be a millionaire. Why don't you do something with your talent?"
>
> I had a fabulous career in fashion as a teenager in London, Paris, and New York. I said, "Robert, I've been where you want to be and it's not a place you want to go."
>
> He said, "Oh, Mister Know It All, you're such a fool."
>
> I guess I did know it all because he's dead and I'm alive.
>
> When he became really famous, I was envious of him. He used the leather scene because he could find creeps to

photograph. Leather was a spectacle for him. He never got involved in those people's lives.

When I saw him in San Francisco after the fire [1981] when I was very poor, living on the street, and working in a warehouse for fifteen dollars a day, he was coming down the street. He'd been giving lectures all around the world on photography at universities, flying to Europe getting two to three-thousand dollars for them. He was two years younger than me, but his hair had turned white. He looked like an old man. He looked so unhappy. He saw me across the street and he ran through the traffic and grabbed me like a long-lost friend.

That's what fame does to you. It isolates you. You can never belong to the human race again.

That's why I so guard that no one sees me. Because once someone sees me, I have no life. When I ask people not to photograph me or introduce me to people, it's so I can go to backroom bars [to avoid starfuckers, and have anonymous sex].

When I left New York, I was so famous everyone pointed me out, and I learned from that when I went to California. The reason I did this—that no one understands—is that people so enjoy imagining who drew this work that I could never live up to that. What's wrong with having this mystery that lets people have this image about a wonderful magical person somewhere out there who does this stuff? Once they see I'm mortal and an old man, well, the mystery's gone. I was pretty good-looking when I was younger. I looked like a Rex drawing.

It's time I confronted this [aging] part of myself. I am kind of a legend. I've been doing this stuff for fifty years. So you only have to do the numbers and you're not going to expect a young man.

Tom of Finland told me, "You are so smart not to be photographed. I regret that I allowed it."

Tom was a god and a mystery to people. But that was before selfies and cell phones and cameras everywhere. So now I try to be as attractive and guarded as I can be. I've got to get rid of my stomach. I can do it. I must make the best presentation in the most sympathetic atmosphere that I can.

I'm sorry I'm vain. I've worked out all my life because I draw the male body and I have to learn about it, study it. In the old days, I had to pose for myself as my own model in mirrors.

At my openings, it's a freak show. That's why I present myself wearing a suit. I'm the only one who looks like a normal person. Like I came out of a fine hotel. I'm in control. I have to stand out. Because the people who come to my shows are fabulous. Rubber. Drag queens. They come in Swan Boats [spinning Björk's iconic swan dress worn at the Academy Awards 2001], or sealed up in leather with crucifixes and swastikas. It's party time at my shows. They're all young and gorgeous. So I play against type as the only one in a suit. I worked in fashion. So I know how to wear clothes. I should do more rubber drawings because they're very popular now. I consider leather *passé* actually. In America, not here in Germany.

15
EXIT PURSUED BY A BEAR

Six weeks before Rex passed, he circulated a grand-finale email about changing his will. On February 16, 2024, he declared he was "fading fast" and was "too weak to write" a new will and would need help from Amsterdam locals to do it. But if he did it, was the new will signed, witnessed, dated, and filed? Was he in his right mind? He who loved drama got so much satisfaction from the chaos of social estrangements in his daily life that it seems he wanted to continue his roguery beyond the grave.

His email threw his estate into disarray, which may have been the avowed anarchist's purpose, because he wrote he intended to delete as executors longtime American friends who on news of his death were left seeking his final will in order to determine how their legal responsibilities may have changed regarding the curation and preservation of the mercurial artist's archive of drawings and copyrights.

"My being dead will only increase the frenzy around my art…. Potentially," he wrote as the personification of his own famous Rex man with $50 bills to burn, "there is art worth about €400,000 at current estimated value which will automatically double in value upon my death."

16
REX HAS LEFT THE BUILDING

As an artist, Rex's vision of homomasculine men, prowling under the full moon of macho, still seems appropriate for humanist gender balance in a feminist-inclined era. Friendly with women and denigrating no gender, Rex was a champion of masculine-identified gender: a *suum quique* artist pursuing the romance of stoic American manhood in its hard-edged rebellion against the diktats of politics and religion and corporations. Like Brando in *The Wild One*, the establishment was his enemy. Watching that 1950s leather-biker movie, the teenage Rex came out as a rebel with a cause when Brando was asked, "What are you rebelling against?" and he sneered back: "Watcha got?"

"I've always felt," the swashbuckling artist of his own radioactive *Peter Pan* pirate series told me, "that pornography is a sword to lance society's boils." He went to his X-rated grave raging against the state of American civilization that like his mother, father, and gay mainstream culture he felt had rejected him.

Rex offers agency and ecstasy to men who like men masculine. *Art is a harsh mistress.* Love Rex, or hate Rex, no one, fan or friend, is unmoved by Rex who, it pains me as a mindful eyewitness of nearly fifty years to say, depended on the kindness of strangers and then bit the hands that fed him. *Art asks everything of the artist.* Free from his autism, anger, Nazis, and the *Village Voice*, may the lonely Rex, the loneliest man of the solitary Rex men, rest in peace with his art ascendant, dot, dot, dot, for the ages. Let him live beyond his death. Think of him. Honor him. If need be, forgive him. *Art keeps the artist alive until all that is left of the artist is the art.* Look at a Rex drawing. Pour a glass of tea and sympathy and spill a drop for lost brothers.

—Text by Jack Fritscher including all conversations with Rex and all interviews of Rex ©2025 Jack Fritscher

* * * *

The Rex Video Gallery: Corrupt Beyond Innocence, Palm Drive Video, Rex Drawings, Original Soundtrack, 65 minutes, 1992. Approved by Rex; directed and photographed by Jack Fritscher; edited and produced by Mark Hemry

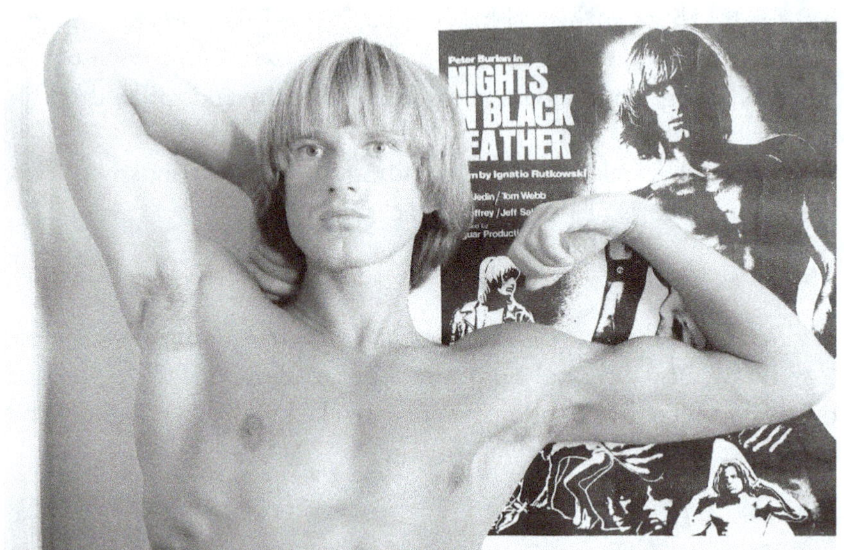

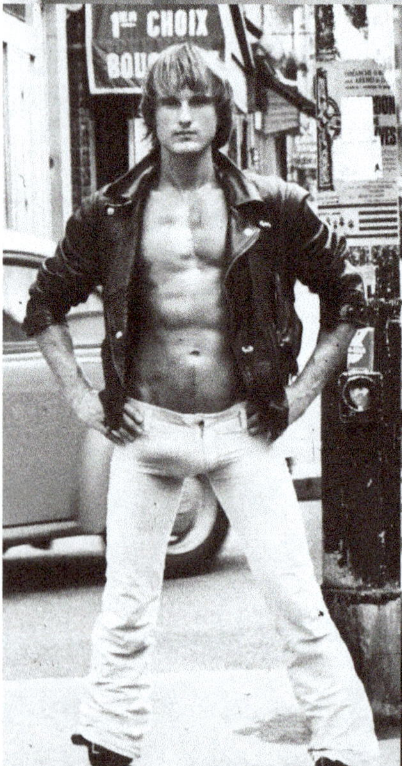

Peter Berlin, San Francisco, 1973, and Peter Berlin, Paris, 1990, courtesy Peter Berlin. Berlin and Fritscher after speaking together on stage for the audience Q&A following the premiere of Randy Barbato and Fenton Bailey's HBO documentary *Mapplethorpe:Look at the Pictures*, Castro Theater, San Francisco, March 20, 2016. Photograph by Mark Hemry

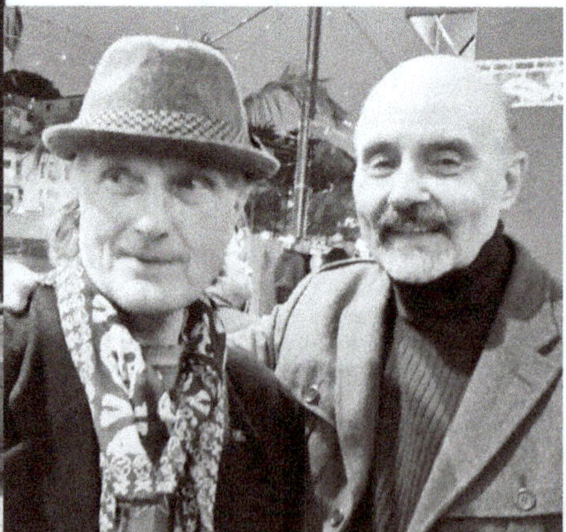

PETER BERLIN

AFTERNOON TEA WITH
"THE LION IN WINTER"

**Celebrating the 80th Birthday
of Artist and Icon Peter Berlin, the Avatar of
Armin Hagen Freiherr von Hoyningen-Huene
in Conversation with Jack Fritscher
San Francisco
November 11, 2022**

**A Treatment for a Screenplay
*The Peter Berlin Story***

Jack Fritscher: Hello, Armin Hagen Freiherr von Hoyningen-Huene. Is Peter Berlin available?

Peter Berlin: Peter Berlin is not.

Jack Fritscher: Mr. Berlin has left the country?

Peter Berlin: [Laughs] Yes. He left about twenty years ago.

Jack Fritscher: He left twenty years ago? Your avatar left?

Peter Berlin: What is left of my dream lover is me, Armin.

Jack Fritscher: Sorry. Could you please speak a little louder?

Peter Berlin: Oh. Oh. Now, yeah, you see I'm frail and old. Right?

Jack Fritscher: That makes a pair of us. You're three years younger. That's why I'm calling because your seniority perhaps frees you to say new things you've never said before. I wish we could meet in person as we have so often, but I'm now entering my fourth year of strict Covid quarantine. You're probably reclined on that lovely bed in your apartment you've photographed so perfectly. There are many interviews of Peter Berlin. I would like to interview Armin Heune.

Peter Berlin: Yes. I'm only doing this interview because I realize you are such a good writer. I'm not saying it to flatter you, but I guess you would give your work high grades. Right?

Jack Fritscher: [Laughs] Well, in the way you appreciate your work, I understand mine.

Peter Berlin: Of course, of course. What I feel about my own work, which I don't even call work, I was just shooting pictures of myself.

> Shooting on location in the 1970s, Peter lensed his modernist "Self-Portrait in Painter's Cover-Alls" and his nude "Self-Portrait on the Roof of the Ansonia Hotel" while the Ansonia housed the orgiastic Continental Baths in its basement where Bette Midler sang with Barry Manilow on piano to gay audiences in white towels.

Peter Berlin: It was for no other reason than just, you know, capturing my daily sort of life. I must confess that I never owned a motorcycle. You know Buena Vista Park the way it was when cars could drive to the top and there was motorcycle parking? Well, I just climbed on one of the parked bikes and took my picture and left.

Jack Fritscher: To thine own selfie be true. Your transition into Peter Berlin created a foundational gay character that captured the gay imagination just after Stonewall. In fact, you arrived in America in 1969. In the 1960s when you were creating "Peter Berlin" on your body, John Waters was creating "Divine" on the body of Glenn Milstead, and Andy Warhol was creating "Little Joe" on the body of Joe Dallesandro.

Peter Berlin: The Swinging Sixties. "Divine" had Waters. "Peter" had me. Everything is timing, yes? I wish I had the time and talent to write, to sing, to make music. I haven't done any work for years. I'm not proud of it. The direction of the human race distresses me. Who cares about Peter Berlin? The planet is sending messages that something bad is happening, and no one cares about it. That's on my mind. Why should Peter make another photograph?

Jack Fritscher: In a toxic world.

Peter Berlin: I nearly called you to cancel because sometimes I have these episodes of really feeling not good.

Jack Fritscher: I'm sorry to hear that and happy you didn't cancel. You're a trooper.

Peter Berlin: For years, doctors have looked at my heart and poked this and tested that, and other things, and never could really diagnose anything. Then it sort of subsided. So now, once in a while, I have these odd feelings of lightheadedness and nausea.

Jack Fritscher: We've lived through AIDS and Covid and the collapse of San Francisco and shades of Sondheim's ladies who lunch: "We're still here." Even though neither of us has AIDS or coronavirus, we're still "Black Leather Swans" with mileage from the last mid-century. And we're moulting.

Peter Berlin: [Laughs] Now I'm feeling fine.

Jack Fritscher: You're celebrating your 80th birthday coming up on December 28th, aren't you?

Peter Berlin: Did you look it up? There's a lot online with the many interviews I've given over the years for magazines.

Jack Fritscher: I did look up your date of birth. Actually, I first wrote about you forty-two years ago in *Skin* magazine.

If you recall, we've been acquainted since the early 1970s on Polk Street, plus while I was editor of *Drummer* and Robert Mapplethorpe shot you on Fire Island [1977] and me in New York [1978].

Peter Berlin: That's right.

> *Drummer* 123, September 1988: With AIDS deaths raging, I
> wrote the "Solo Sex" feature to introduce readers to the safe
> sex of masturbation while watching actors perform solo on
> screen. "In the 1970s, I met Peter Berlin... a perfect Nar-
> cissus of Solo Sex practice. For years, the reclusive, blond,
> sylphlike Berlin has sold Solo Sex movies and videos of
> himself, shot by himself, featuring himself jerking off with/
> against himself on screen. Berlin has rarely shot another
> model, and has turned his own image, with his own camera,
> into an aesthetically, and one hopes, financially successful
> cottage industry of mail-order Solo Sex. Peter Berlin, in...
> his tour-de-force films, *Nights in Black Leather* (1973) and
> *That Boy* (1974), is the perfect symbol of the high-flying Solo
> Sex Act of Man Alone, of Man as Island, of Man Sexually
> Self-Satisfied."

Jack Fritscher: Last night I re-watched all of *Nights in Black Leather* and *That Boy*.

Peter Berlin: You did? You did your homework.

Jack Fritscher: To be prepared to chat with you. In my archives, there is my Peter Berlin folder. I must tell you how much I like Jim Tushinski's documentary [*That Man: Peter Berlin*, 2005]. Perhaps this afternoon we can go beyond all those interviews and films to dig into something fresh about you—Armin—the artist at eighty who at twenty created his avatar Peter Berlin.

Peter Berlin: Right, right. People think they know Peter, but what they know is rarely about me, the person behind Peter. Peter Berlin is my stage name. [Armin Huene lives his life as an artist in pursuit of his muse who was Peter Berlin.] I'm a photographer, but I am not known like Robert Mapplethorpe or Marcus Leatherdale.

Jack Fritscher: May I say that just as there are now feature films about Mapplethorpe and Tom of Finland and Basquiat, there should be a Peter Berlin biopic.

Peter Berlin: There would have to be three actors playing me as a boy, as Peter Berlin, and then as the old man I am now.

Jack Fritscher: Have you seen Harry Styles in *My Policeman*? That movie has two actors playing the same character, one as young, one as old. And there's Timothée Chalamet. He's androgynous, award-winning, and a fashion icon who could channel the Peter Berlin Look.

Peter Berlin: I like Harry Styles. I think he could play Peter Berlin. While we talk, are you taking notes?

Jack Fritscher: Here at the beginning is where I ask your permission to record this.

Peter Berlin: Yeah, yeah, yeah, yeah, yeah. I think this is a good thing. I wish I would be able to record it too. I wish I could have saved all my recorded phone messages I got over the years. I would love to have all the messages Mapplethorpe left in the 70s and 80s.

Jack Fritscher: Me too.

Peter Berlin: Did you make a lot of notes?

Jack Fritscher: I started keeping a journal when I was fourteen. From my journal notes in the 1970s, I wrote my novel *Some Dance to Remember* which is about the 1970s on Castro Street and Folsom.

Peter Berlin: I would encourage everybody to keep notes.

Jack Fritscher: I would too. Sam Steward kept his *Stud File* on every trick he ever had. Each on an index card.

Peter Berlin: I know about Sam. There's a book, right?

Jack Fritscher: Justin Spring's bio. It's called *Secret Historian*. It too should be a feature film.

Peter Berlin: My friend Eric Smith gave me the book, but I don't read much and I just sort of paged through it. But what I would give to have a Polaroid picture of all my tricks, thousands and thousands of tricks I had over the years.

Jack Fritscher: How many?

Peter Berlin: Thousands. Because I was—not to brag—collecting tricks. Sex was my thing. My photography was a sideshow.

Jack Fritscher: That's the way we were. We were all like John Rechy collecting tricks aka "numbers" in his [1967] novel *Numbers*. Would you say 10,000?

Peter Berlin: I have to think about that. But at least 10,000. When I came out in the 60s, I had been living in Berlin for ten years, and going out every night. I was never looking for a relationship. I got off on getting people off. Sometimes without even touching. Just the idea of seeing a man standing opposite to me, existing in ecstasy. I could have maybe two, three, four men a night. I did that for ten years, twenty years, thirty years. I wish I would have a journal and could give you the number of 20,000.

Jack Fritscher: We're all Rita Hayworth in *Fire Down Below* when she said, "Armies have marched over me." I think our sex lives like our daily lives are essential, especially for those of us who rode the merry-go-round of that first decade after Stonewall.

Peter Berlin: That's what I mean. Armies. I'm so glad that your timing and my timing of being born was brilliant. I was born in 1942.

Jack Fritscher: I agree. I was born in 1939. People today who didn't live through the war and its aftermath, and the 60s and 70s may not understand that we were lucky to have met so many men so intimately.

Peter Berlin: The war in Germany.

Jack Fritscher: Right. My first memories are of that war. I was in grade school when it ended, and we all went downtown to celebrate in the streets. You and I are the unique generation of gay war babies.

Peter Berlin: I was too young to remember the war itself, but I think the 1920s and 30s must have been great in Berlin.

Jack Fritscher: Think of how much the wild Weimar Republic in the 1930s was like the 1970s.

Peter Berlin: Great in Hollywood too, right?

Jack Fritscher: *Cabaret* made the connection and with all its Academy Awards taught us something in the 1970s about Weimar bisexuality popular at places like Studio 54.

Peter Berlin: There was so much sexual freedom. Our time was really very special. Didn't you think in those days after Stonewall that life would get better? Back then, I said, "Oh, this is really nice." In my mind, in my fantasy, I always felt it could get even better. I thought the World War would be the last war ever. I was sure, first of all, that the Church would die out, all that nonsense about God and Jesus. Well! I was wrong in that—and I was wrong about things getting, [chuckles] you know, getting better. With AIDS and all. My grandmother was a Catholic, but my mother left the Church. When she was twelve, she asked a priest to explain the Immaculate Conception, and he said, "Marion, there are things we can't explain," and she said, "Okay, enough."

Jack Fritscher: We were born lucky. We were very lucky to have been young and active in the window between the invention of penicillin and the arrival of HIV. We had great sex in a wonderful time. I also thought things were getting better during that time until Anita Bryant and AIDS and the politically correct raised their ugly heads.

Peter Berlin: I must explain I was never politically interested or active. When I came to America, I knew there was a war going on in, you know, the war...

Jack Fritscher: Vietnam.

Peter Berlin: Vietnam.

Jack Fritscher: Right. People forget that Vietnam dominated the 1970s. Men, including gay men, were still being drafted, some right off the streets of the Castro. Vietnam didn't end till 1975 the year *Drummer* was founded.

Peter Berlin: I didn't read the papers. I was always going out to have a good time. Anita Bryant, I read about her, but nothing of that affected me. See, when I came here I talked to younger guys, and heard the horror stories of being born in Texas, or being born into Catholic guilt. They had to get out because of gay bashing and religion. That never happened to me.

Jack Fritscher: So that American bigotry seemed like American fascism even to you who were born in Nazi-occupied Poland?

Peter Berlin: Yeah. Horrible. I was impressionable, but I was too young a boy to experience the Nazi occupation, but I remember the American occupation of Berlin.

Jack Fritscher: You were lucky. Tom of Finland was nineteen when the Nazis bombed Finland in 1939. He was born twenty years before us. He told me one night at supper, without flinching, that as a young man he was turned on by the uniforms of the Nazis who were occupying Finland. Look at his drawings. The fetish influence is there.

Peter Berlin: You see, I was protected. My poor mother, my poor dear mother, had three children. She had to flee from the Baltics to Berlin. Her husband, my father [1915-1945] died, was shot dead in the last days of the war [when Armin was three]. But me as a child? I was out playing in the sand in one of the big holes of a bomb, uh, you know, when a bomb goes off, what is it?

Jack Fritscher: A crater?

Peter Berlin: Crater of a bomb. That's where we were playing in Berlin. So, I just had a ball.

To experience the context of the wrecked world of children playing in the rubble of postwar Berlin, see director Fred Zinnemann's film, *The Search* (1948) shot on location in the city ruins, starring the beautiful gay Montgomery Clift and the marvelous Czechoslovakian child star Ivan Jandl who won a special Academy Award. Some of the film's official screenings were hosted by the National Society for the Prevention of Cruelty to Children.

Peter Berlin: When I arrived in America, I was very surprised at how much drama people here in this country went through during the war.

Jack Fritscher: My first memories are of food and gas rationing. Nightly blackouts. Air raid wardens. Men leaving for the war. Women building tanks and bombs. Nothing compared to you, but until the war ended, I feared the Nazis and Tojo were going to kill me. My parents helped me a lot when we gathered up good pieces of our clothing, like my mother's fur coat, and sent them off to displaced persons in "DP" camps, as we called them, in Germany.

Peter Berlin: I grew up okay about cops in Berlin. It was only when I arrived here and started cruising that I first had to run away from the police in the park.

Jack Fritscher: Right. In 1978, the San Francisco police raided my office at *Drummer* and tossed all our drawers and filing cabinets. Just like the Gestapo. Maybe you remember the night of the White Night Riot [May 21, 1979], the cops stormed the crowds on Castro Street and drove us down the street beating people with batons.

Peter Berlin: I knew about White Night. But Peter Berlin stayed outside of politics. I would only have read about it, right? It didn't affect me, right? What's the word in English? I sort of was unaware and not interested.

Jack Fritscher: Aloof, aloof.

In the opening monologue of *That Boy*, the voice-over exposition is a thumbnail of what it was like to see Peter walking down the street. The narrator says about Peter: "I used to watch him on Polk Street everyday and wonder what he was looking at as he'd walk by a window, stare into it like mirror, and leave. Parading down the street in his tight white pants showing off his huge organ of pleasure. Everyone would stare at him. Weird people. Boys. Girls. Young men. Freaks. Everyone staring at his cock. Doing anything to get attention. Still he ignored everyone….I suppose he knew they would follow him. Anywhere. Everywhere. Just to get one more look at his cock."

Jack Fritscher: In an age of San Francisco hippies, you were kind of like that other German, the Pied Piper of Hamlin, walking down Polk Street gathering up the Flower Children, but the pipe you played, displayed, was the most famous uncut cock of the 1970s.

Peter Berlin: [Laughs] Now I think I was then sort of a stupid person, just not aware of his surroundings.

Jack Fritscher: Armin! You were never a dizzy blond.

Peter Berlin: No, no. But I was sort of out of it. My father died because of politics. Lies and fake news. People would ask: "Do you know about this book or that film?" There was a person once at a party talking to me and he asked me, "Do you read?" And, I said, "No, I don't read." He looked at me and said he felt sorry for me. He said, "In school in Germany you had to read, right?" Reading was part of my education, but I didn't read. I was so, so *visual*. That was a big negative for that person.

Jack Fritscher: John Waters says if you go home with a guy and he has no books, don't fuck him.

Peter Berlin: Let me tell you. As an artist from postwar Germany, I was tired of politics that ruined everything.

Jack Fritscher: Politics can cause PTSD.

Peter Berlin: I wasn't politically active. I knew there was a Harvey Milk—and could have cared less. I didn't vote for him or anyone else. I wasn't trying to change things in San Francisco. I was changing myself in America.

Jack Fritscher: Inventing your self?

Peter Berlin: Inventing Peter Berlin.

Jack Fritscher: Your performance art. Your street theater. You were a rebel whose cause was knowing your self.

Peter Berlin: My days were spent at the beach, at Land's End [at the west end of Golden Gate Park], oiled up, and looking good, and high. Okay? I saw I could create attention. So when I went home, I said, "Okay, take a camera and make a picture."

I tried to capture the image I was creating. That was my life. That's so completely different from Mapplethorpe and Leatherdale who were trying to achieve their own certain vision, especially Robert, and all the other photographers who saw their photography as a career to be successful and make money. I never had money in my mind. That's why I'm poor.

Jack Fritscher: It's hard to make money from art.

Peter Berlin: With all the books you've written, you couldn't live on those?

Jack Fritscher: Oh, no, no, no. My God, no. As a gay writer for sixty years, I've earned about a penny a day. If that. Some books take ten years. Plus since the internet started [early 1990s], I've posted my books free to all online. Like you, I don't create for money. I write to document gay experiences. Even while I edited *Drummer* on the side for three years, I've always had a straight job. So on weekend afternoons I'd see you cruising Polk Street, and as a writer, I'd observe you from afar because your act was too fascinating to interrupt.

When Peter strolled down Polkstrasse in 1972, even before releasing his first film which would have made a great music video, I could hear Lou Reed singing his new song, "Walk on the Wild Side." When people mention a sighting of Peter Berlin, they always remember where and when they first saw him on the street—and what they thought. Like a Hollywood star, Peter's hand, foot, and dick prints should be cast in the cement in front of what's left of the Alhambra Theater on Polk Street.

Jack Fritscher: I liked watching you—just like the guy you cast as a character, the voyeur, watching you, the exhibitionist, from across that Polk Street intersection in *That Boy*. I studied you because I was taking mental notes of the rise of Polk Street and Castro Street and Folsom Street.

Peter Berlin: In my documentary [*That Man*], Armistead [Maupin, author of *Tales of the City*] said he saw me at the beach and he came up to me and said that he figured that, like him, I didn't want to be approached and have to talk to so many people and hear them saying things repeated over the years. "I saw you on Polk Street," or "I saw you in Provincetown," or "I saw you in New York," you know, always from afar, because that was my thing. [Four minutes into *Nights in Black Leather*, Peter talks on screen about these kinds of fan questions.] To save my privacy in public which was Peter Berlin's stage, I gave the impression: "Please don't come up and try to talk to me."

Jack Fritscher: You are Armin. They wanted to talk to Peter. I never approached you then because I dug your vibe. I thought of you as the Gay Garbo. I would no more have talked to you while you were performing "Peter" than I would've talked to an actor on a Broadway stage.

Peter Berlin: Now, looking back, I like saying, "I played the role of Peter Berlin."

Jack Fritscher: Yes.

Peter Berlin: And I played it very well. Right? It *was* like I was on stage. And the people who realize that, like you, said, "Okay, that's what he's doing. So I'll just watch him."

Jack Fritscher: I saw what you had to offer in your tight clothes and your Saran Wrap white tights [which, according to the *New York Times*, inspired Freddie Mercury to "shrink-wrap his junk."] I appreciated your exhibitionism. Your show on the road. I went on my way thinking how well you captured your street image and distilled it into all the pictures and ads you ran in papers and magazines to sell your movies.

Peter Berlin: There was not one political thing in my films.

Jack Fritscher: That's radical. Has any gay filmmaker ever said that? Your movies, like Leni Riefenstahl's, were about beauty which transcends politics.

Peter Berlin: Whenever people talk to me about my films, I always say they're nothing to write home about. Now, years later, I'd love to re-edit the films to make them better.

Jack Fritscher: As I told you, last night for the second time in fifty years, I watched both of your movies, *Black Leather* and *That Boy*, and really enjoyed them both.

Peter Berlin: So you prepared yourself.

Jack Fritscher: Of course. Out of respect. I've been preparing for you for three days. I've got five pages of notes to ask you.

Peter Berlin: I'm so flattered because, you know, back when you published that *Drummer* article on Tom of Finland, I always felt that I was not included as part of that *Drummer* leather art scene.

Jack Fritscher: No, you weren't. You were thought of, and then purposely excluded. At first, homomasculine leathermen did not know what to make of your leatherish androgyny. When I interviewed the director Roger Earl [in 1997], he told me on the record that when he was casting *Born to Raise Hell* in 1975, he thought "Peter Berlin would be perfect as the lead." But the producer [Terry LeGrand] wanted a more standard-looking leatherman like Ledermeister, the brawny hairy Colt model who was the lifelong erotic avatar of

San Francisco actor Paul Garrior. Paul looked the part, but he was not really a leather player. So they cast Val Martin, our first "Mr. Drummer," a leatherman immigrant from Brazil, in the role you would have played. Like us, Ledermeister, who just died, lived into his eighties, but Val died young of AIDS.

> The Peter Berlin character is a vivid example that gender is construction and performance. In *Drummer* 66, July 1983, when Peter got his only mention on the contents page, the shameless publisher John Embry reductively compared Peter to the campy Chippendale dancers.

Peter Berlin: I did not know all those details, but being directed by someone else? Ugh. So difficult in my first film. I always felt I was not into that "Leather Thing" even though I wore some of it. I was not part of the so-called fetish scene because I was shy, and I didn't want all that "leather fraternity" stuff of parties and dinners and orgies. I only wanted to get laid.

Jack Fritscher: Like Erica Jong, you were in search of a zipless fuck.

Peter Berlin: What's that?

Jack Fritscher: Casual, spontaneous, anonymous sex with strangers.

Peter Berlin: Exactly.

Jack Fritscher: So, instead, you played at the baths, like the Barracks on Folsom, to get your kink on?

Peter Berlin: The Barracks? I loved it. There was the [Red Star Saloon] bar downstairs, and then behind it and upstairs the Barracks bathhouse. It was the best.

Jack Fritscher: I agree. [Leather poet] Thom Gunn wrote lyrics about it. I spent hundreds of nights and weekends there. Third floor. Room 326. First door left top of stairs.

Peter Berlin: I liked to go to the Barracks after cruising the streets after the bars closed.

Jack Fritscher: The Barracks had a lot of rough and creative S&M action, hundreds of men orgying in pig piles, but it wasn't solely leather because the Barracks was a kind of three-story theater with lots of exhibitionists and lots of voyeurs. It was a three-ring circus. You didn't have to play S&M games or even touch anyone to have a good time.

Peter Berlin: You're right. I liked walking up and down the hallways and posing under one of the spotlights at ends of the halls. Men who like looking liked my exhibitionism.

Jack Fritscher: Peter Berlin was obvious, obscene, and hot. You were your own art exhibit, a voyeur's dream.

Peter Berlin: I didn't get involved like Mapplethorpe did.

Jack Fritscher: Peter Berlin never shoved a whip up his ass.

Peter Berlin: I heard about the games Robert played from my friend, Jochen Labriola [1942-1988, German-American painter]. Jochen was an artist and my best friend and my patron in those days. I never had to work again. Thanks to him. He taught me how to paint. He was the one who actually got me out of Germany—and that's why I ended up in America. Jochen had a fling with Robert, and told me, uh, how you sometimes sit and say, "Oh, you know, uh, the games Robert was playing." His trips were never, never my thing. You see, I met Robert when he approached me because I was Peter Berlin. He liked my fame.

Jack Fritscher: He introduced himself to me because I was the editor-in-chief of *Drummer* and he needed publicity.

Peter Berlin: He was always very impressed that people recognized me, and he liked that. So I only know Robert from talking and hanging out with him, but I never had sex with him. It never occurred to me that I even wanted it. Right? The same with Marcus Leatherdale. You know, one thing that really surprised me in the *Mapplethorpe* [HBO] documentary was when you read into the camera the letter

Robert wrote to you about Leatherdale—that he found Marcus basically naïve. That surprised me.

On September 12, 1978, Robert wrote me a letter complaining about some wannabe who was bugging him. "The 'punk' leather boy from San Francisco is getting more and more on my nerves. I hate naïve people. He just left wearing his motorcycle jacket. I feel as though he shouldn't be allowed to wear it as he just doesn't have a sophisticated sense of sex. I hate happy, naïve people." I never asked Robert the guy's name. I didn't pry. I never knew who he was. However, in 2015 when Randy Barbato and Fenton Bailey came to my home to interview me for *Mapplethorpe: Look at the Pictures*, I read into their camera several letters Robert had written to me, including the one about the anonymous troublesome punk leather guy.

Creating a perfect made-for-TV moment, the genius directors, the producers of *RuPaul's Drag Race*, who know their business shot a close-up of Marcus Leatherdale while they played for him the recording of me reading Robert's letter. It hit him like a punch in the face. I felt sorry for him caught on camera. Had I known the unnamed guy was identifiable and alive, I would never have read the letter out loud. I debated over and over about contacting him and apologizing for the weird concurrence, but I didn't want to make matters worse because he may not have known that it was my voice reading the letter. And why bring up a sore subject with someone I never met? After having a stroke in 2021, he committed suicide in 2022.

Jack Fritscher: Well, Robert and Marcus kissed and made up after he wrote that letter to me.

Peter Berlin: Then they hung out for quite a while, huh?

Jack Fritscher: They did. They ran around Manhattan like twin boyfriends. Robert hired Marcus to work as an office manager in his studio. And then competition reared its head.

Peter Berlin: Because they both were photographers.

Jack Fritscher: Some say they were fighting over models. Marcus beat Robert to Madonna. And Leatherdale's photographs often looked too much like Mapplethorpe pictures, plus Robert, you know, in the early 80s was moving away from white guys to black guys.

Peter Berlin: I remember Robert telling me he only had sex with black guys.

Jack Fritscher: Robert had an interracial eye even as a student at Pratt that evolved while he and I were romantically involved in the late 1970s. In the 1980s, he turned his gaze from white guys to black men on and off camera.

Peter Berlin: When I was in his loft [24 Bond Street], he showed me some of his pictures. The Warhol portrait of him was hanging on the wall, right? And the cocaine was always there. So I asked, "Robert, no more nice white guys?" He said, "No, only black guys." It sort of surprised me. "Over the years," he said, "I realized I basically was attracted to black guys." I also realized for myself there's something about black men or the black soul, not only beautiful, but there's something so, so, authentic. I've had two black roommates, one several years ago, Bryce White, who had been in jail, and one now, Reggie. I think of the bodies of those guys. White guys can go to the gym for twenty years and will never will look like this black perfection.

Jack Fritscher: Race, sex, gender. Welcome to America. Can you tell me about your father? I know you were only three, but can you describe the postwar Berlin scene growing up fatherless, what you and your mother felt, what your mother later told you about the last days of the war when he was shot dead?

Peter Berlin: One of his comrades who was with him when he died told us that at that time the *Wehrmacht* was rationing guns and ammunition, and sending unarmed soldiers who had no protection to the Eastern Front.

Jack Fritscher: Like Putin in Ukraine.

Peter Berlin: Yes. Like Putin. So my father was in the situation where the Russians were close, but he was unarmed. He was a sitting duck and he was shot dead. My mother only knew it because, at some point, she got a postcard from Dr. Weiss, a soldier who was a doctor, but she never got any sort of confirmation from the German government. My father was about thirty years old when he died.

Jack Fritscher: Was he drafted into the German army?

> A number of gay men in the U.S. in the 1970s had escaped Nazi Germany after being forcibly ordered as Hitler Youth to the Eastern Front in the last days of the war. As fourteen and fifteen year-old boys, like Hank Diethelm, the jolly immigrant owner of the Brig leather bar on Folsom Street in San Francisco, they disobeyed the order, ditched their uniforms, and fled West into the arms of Allied troops who rescued the teen boys, and brought them to the U.S. In a tragic irony of murder on April 10, 1983, Hank who—to deal with his postwar PTSD had made a counterphobic sex fetish of Nazi S&M—was tied up, tortured, and strangled in a dentist's chair in the basement playroom of his home where his body was set on fire destroying his house.

Peter Berlin: Yes. He had to go to war. I was a baby. Because I have no memory of that time, just before my mother died two years ago, I asked her to write what happened in his last days. You remember that they tried to kill Hitler with a suitcase bomb under his desk, but he survived. When my father heard that, he got so upset. "How could you," you know, "kill the *Führer*?" He believed the propaganda they were fighting for the fatherland. And then in the last letters my mother got from him, he started to suddenly realize what was happening. You see this idea when the Germans say they didn't understand what was happening. There was truth to it. I was born in Litzmannstadt, Poland, while it was occupied by Hitler, and what I even didn't know, there was a concentration camp. Right? In Litzmannstadt. Right? I had no idea. I only know my mother told me one day years later, "Do you know that one of the inmates escaped from the concentration camp and knocked on our door and asked for help?" And my father gave him a horse to get away and he said, "I can't do more because it's too dangerous for my family. I could get killed." I mean, all these stories, what my mother told me, so awful. Maybe that's why I'm not so much interested in my own history.

Jack Fritscher: So your father as a young man was swept up into the politics of the times and believed the fake news until he realized what he believed was not what was happening.

Peter Berlin: Like me, he was not very much following the nitty-gritty of politics. So I'd like to think he knew nothing about the killing of the Jews. I know that my Hoyningen-Huene family is a big tribe. Still is. I had one cousin who was a very big Nazi. My mother said when he was at our dinner table that he spent time criticizing her for being too, um, yeah, too beautiful and too sexy, you know? And she told him, "Shut the fuck up. I know who you are."

Jack Fritscher: A Nazi relative at a dinner table? Worse than a crazy MAGA uncle at Thanksgiving. Your mother was not a Nazi.

Peter Berlin: No. In the circle of my parents' and grandparents' friends, there were so many Jewish people. I only knew their names. I had no idea who was a Jew or not a Jew. Later on, I was thankful that my family had no feelings of antisemitism, just like I'm color blind about race.

Jack Fritscher: Yeah. One might think your father didn't read and the consequences of that killed him.

Peter Berlin: I know. My father was a *Landwirt*, a farmer. We had land. I have pictures. We raised horses and pigs. He was just a country boy when he came from the farm and met my mother in Berlin. I remember her telling me the first thing she thought was, "Oh, he's so arrogant." But he had that Hoyningen-Huene name and there was a title and this and that, you know. So they married and she was widowed, and she and I and my brother and sister fled to Berlin where I grew up and came out while the East Germans [under Soviet Russia] were building the Berlin Wall.

Jack Fritscher: You were outed the day they started building the Berlin Wall? Yes? [Sunday, 13 August 1961]

Peter Berlin: No, I was out already. I had just come out. I was nineteen. But my mother didn't know it. It was a weekend, just another gay weekend, with all the East German boys coming over to West Berlin because that's where the fun was, and the clubs. I was picked up on a Saturday night by an East German guy and he took me home to East Germany. To East Berlin. Right? And the next day when I wanted to go back, the S-Bahn train we'd crossed over on was not running. I realized the trains were not going. I said, "What's happening? What's happening?" So I remember I had to walk back home passing through the Brandenburg Gate where I saw what were now East German soldiers rolling out this wire fencing thing, and I just stepped over it from East Berlin to West Berlin. And then I realized what was happening.

The reason I was outed that weekend when this all happened was because it was in the television news. Everybody understood the danger of what was happening. My mother realized: "Oh, Armin is not here. Where's Armin?" Right? And then I, yeah, was, yeah, outed. To her.

Jack Fritscher: Like your father, you were swept up into history. How were you outed?

Peter Berlin: Like I said, I was out before, but I always was very private. I never said anything. I seemed only a little bit out of the norm because of the way I dressed in tight pants I ran up on a sewing machine. Because I was gone all night in East Berlin, and because the news of the Wall was so frightening, my mother worried herself into a state. She asked me where I was, what I was doing. I was never into lying or anything, you know. And I never felt, "Oh, my God, I do something wrong." So right then I came right out with it. I came out to her because of the televison news. I said to her "This is what I do." She was horrified because homosexuality was something basically sick. My dear mother didn't understand. My whole family didn't understand. Then I found out my mother had found a letter I'd written about sex. All that happened on one day. I had to move out of my home and I was happy to move out to a rooming house. I finally felt very free, right? But then afterwards, my mother and my family adjusted. My sister had a lot of gay friends. My nephews, I have three of them, are now grown men who are completely good with it, right? But they are all straight. My nephew Martin always said he was very proud of me because every family needs a black sheep.

Jack Fritscher: Was your trick in East Berlin young or older?

Peter Berlin: No, no, no, no. I went with German boys. Young. I never went with older men. I never looked for older men. I never looked for my daddy. I've always looked for my age and younger.

In scenes in *That Man*, Peter has sex with the types of young black and blond ephebes he prefers. His contemporary Fred Halsted also romanced chicken born yesterday in his lover Joey Yale, his blond co-star in *LA Plays Itself* and *Sextool*, for whom writer-director Halsted said he coined the term *twink*.

Peter Berlin: I remember everybody seemed over twenty when I was seventeen—already too old for me, right? So that trick from East Berlin was my age. A teenager. He was nineteen. I remember he wore a suit which was never my cup of tea. But somehow we hooked up and we went to his place in East Berlin.

Jack Fritscher: Now I understand how it happened when your mother asked, "Where's Armin?"

Peter Berlin: Unfortunately, my exact memory fails me. I only remember my mother looking at me with disgust, you know? Because she looked at my tight pants and she was horrified. I completely understood that. I never, never, never had one negative thought about my mother, or my misguided stepfather. I realized at that moment that some people don't understand things. And one can't blame them for that. And I never blamed my mother. I never blamed my stepfather. She was a very traditional woman in those days. Now she's dead I can say this. She only had three men—compared to you and me. My father was her first. Years later, she admitted, "Oh, once at a party there was this beautiful man." Later she said, "Oh, my god, I should have."

Not long after my father died, she met Herr Kittel, my stepfather, a sort of a typical German. But nice, you know. I always had a good time with him. After the war, he moved in and was trying to make a living for us. He started to work for Daimler Benz, the Mercedes Benz company. And he worked himself up to a very good position and was a bit bourgeois which embarrassed my mother a little bit because he was always kind of showing off. My family is from a very aristocratic background. We never talked about money. That was something one just doesn't discuss.

Jack Fritscher: So he was your mother's live-in lover.

Peter Berlin: He thought that the man was the boss and the woman was in the kitchen. But my mother considered us lucky. She said, "My God, he stood by me and took on three little children." My mother always felt grateful because survival was very hard at that time. We had lost everything.

Jack Fritscher: So, Herr Kittel lived with your mother and you and your two siblings?

Peter Berlin: Yeah. At some point, he moved in with us when we lived with my grandmother who never accepted Herr Kittel. My grandmother was this woman who behaved like a queen. She wasn't bad, but she believed the servants were downstairs and we Hoyningen-Huene were upstairs. Is *upstairs* right? There was that feeling Herr Kittel is not one of us. There was always that thing about class. Now, you see, now I can talk about it openly. My mother is dead. Herr Kittel is dead. I always saw him from the outside, but I always felt good with Herr Kittel. When we were children, he helped us build little toys, like a little sailing boat. He took time for us and I always felt good. My sister's completely different because she felt completely negative about him, and that made life very difficult for my poor mother. My mother was always caught in between the two. She had to appease my sister and she had to appease him. I always felt sorry for my poor mother who worked so hard to feed us and keep us together.

Jack Fritscher: The grandmother you lived with. Was she born in Russia?

Peter Berlin: In Saint Petersburg. On the Baltic Sea. She spoke fluent Russian and she loved the Russians. See, this is the trouble. We think of Russia today as the enemy because that idiot Putin has made it so terrible now with his invasion of Ukraine. The Russian people are good, the way the people of any nation are good, until politics ruins them. Are American people bad because of what's now happening here in America with the percentage of right-wing nuts who are running the show?

Jack Fritscher: Right.

Peter Berlin: Americans mostly are good to Germans. German people are nice people, but back then there were some before the war who said, "Okay, let's find some scapegoat for our troubles. Let's find a scapegoat for the economy. Somebody has to pay." The Jews had to pay. I remember when my mother was hiding a Jewish man and woman who were our friends. I know about this from my mother's stories. She wrote so much beautiful stuff. All in German.

Jack Fritscher: She kept notes.

Peter Berlin: Yes. I've always had the idea of writing my autobiography. I have her writings. My family story is actually a very, very good story about my upbringing and my family. What I was like during the first part of my life before the second part of my life: the Peter Berlin thing. And the third part, me as Armin who is an old man, right? The old man telling the story.

Jack Fritscher: The Lion in Winter.

Peter Berlin: I always said, "Oh, my God, I wish I had money." I could make a film with the best talent of Hollywood. There's a German guy, a musician who writes film music. Hans Zimmer. I would hire people like him. Academy Award winners. I'd put out a casting call for some actor to play Peter Berlin. I can't think of one famous young person who could play me. I think it would be an unknown.

Jack Fritscher: We've mentioned Harry Styles who is famous, talented, and still young.

Peter Berlin: Yes. If a film were made, the actor playing Peter Berlin in the 1970s would become a star, or an even bigger star. He'd be one of three actors playing Armin as a boy, Peter Berlin as a young man, and then me as the old storyteller. Only I can tell you movie scenes that are real like one time in Paris I saw a beautiful man in a shop window and thought "Look at that guy!" Then realized it was me. It was like a shot of me on screen. I had found one of my dream lovers. Me. I wish it had been someone else. I would have liked to have met him. My other dream lover is a robot. My camera.

> In the first two minutes of Peter's first movie, *That Boy*, Peter's star face debuted on screen in a mirror like the introduction of Barbra Streisand's star face in a mirror at the beginning of *Funny Girl*. It's not narcissism. It a human moment of spring awakening when a young man first truly sees himself. With Pachelbel's *Canon in D* playing on the soundtrack, Peter identifies himself as a satyr among the wood nymphs. The opening edenic garden-park scene is his "Afternoon of a Faun" sequence.

Peter Berlin: A Hollywood movie of me is a dream that will never be realized. It would be the crowning glory of my life. I'm losing my memory. I'm ready to go. I had my life and I'd just like to go to sleep and not wake up. But I think that my double life as a person and as the persona of Peter Berlin would make an interesting movie digging into the essence of Peter Berlin who is a very in-your-face erotic character, like the Tom of Finland characters.

Jack Fritscher: What did you think of the *Tom of Finland* movie?

Peter Berlin: I loved it. I was impressed by its production values. I would have to watch it again. It seemed authentic. I wish there was less emphasis on the war scenes and killing than there was on scenes revealing the soul of what I felt Tom the person was. I really must watch it again. I liked the production, but I would have done it a little different. I always look at any film now as a filmmaker, as an editor. When I was a child, I watched movies for the story. As a filmmaker, I look at movies from a different perspective. Is the *Tom* movie still playing?

Jack Fritscher: It's streaming online.

All comparisons are odious especially when it comes to Origin Stories, but I think the lavender roots of a common gay history call for some comparison, contrast, and consideration of the interlocutory DNA of the generational and geographical male gaze. Tom of Finland (born 1920) and Peter Berlin (born 1942) were European artists working at the same time in the 1960s and 1970s. With a head start in the 1920s, Tom in Finland was in his forties and in print when Armin in his twenties in Germany in the 1960s began creating Peter Berlin. It's as if both visionary artists were coincidentally drinking from the same homomasculine well. So many of Tom's drawings of men in tight pants, cocks rampant, legs spread, torsos angled, resemble Peter's poses in his photos.

Both artists may object, but it's as if two men—like two generations of older and younger leather brothers—dialed into the same European homomasculine archetype and each made that platonic ideal of gay masculinity uniquely his own. Tom drew men like Peter posed, and Peter posed like men Tom drew. You say *Tomato*. I say *Toronto*. One's critical thinking must not make the logical fallacy, "Post hoc, ergo propter hoc," that because B follows A, B must have been caused by A .Armin said his life and work are simply "coincidental" with Tom's.

Queer scholarship has yet to notice that the artist whose 1970s drawings also resembled Peter Berlin and his look was Frederick L. "Toby" Bluth (July 11, 1940-October 31, 2013). He whose porn signature was "Toby" was a longtime and very important Walt Disney artist and stage producer who also had a gay underground career creating in 1970 his sexy-go-lucky cartoon drawings of his young blond avatar, "Toby," his own platonic ideal of a juicy teen piece of veal, not yet beef, with Dutch Boy blond hair, a button nose, a bubble butt, and a big cock.

Even though gay scholars have yet to notice the *zeitgeist* connection between Berlin and Bluth, the "Toby" drawings were everywhere in the gay press from *The Advocate* to *After Dark* because "Toby," whose succulent flesh looked pumped with sperm was the dripping epitome of the "young, dumb, and full of cum" blond look that dominated gay vanilla culture before grown men yanked the gay gaze from ephebes toward adult men in leather like Peter Berlin. Just so, those two magazines that liked "Toby" were the first publications to pay important media attention to Peter Berlin.

If ever any artist might have created a series of animation cells to present the *Cartoon Adventures of Peter Berlin*, it would have been Bluth who knew a thing or two at Disney about creating animated characters. While not cartoons, Tom of Finland's selected storyboard drawings also seem ready-made to be rounded up, maybe by artificial intelligence, to illustrate a curated graphic novel about Peter Berlin and his leather pals the way Tom created his *Kake* series of comic books.

For one of its ads appealing for subscriptions, *The Advocate*, skimming close to the popular Peter Berlin look, used a drawing of "Toby" reclined like a satyr in a field of flowers and butterflies (like Peter in the opening of *Nights in Black Leather*), stripped to the waist, pecs ahoy, wearing fringed bellbottoms, a cocked knee hiding a promised hardon. In the way that Peter Berlin of San Francisco advertised himself and his films insistently in the gay press, Toby of Los Angeles was also the come-and-get-it advertising image for businesses like the Key Club baths, the Fallen Angel bar, the Closet bar, the Coronet Theater, the Metropolitan Community Church, and the musical, *"Love: As You Like It*, A Male Musical. Shakespeare Transmogrified by TOBY. Previews start April 12, 1972 [when Peter was shooting *Nights in Black Leather*]. Tiffany Theater, 8534 Sunset Strip. All Male Cast of 25. Limited to L.A. run prior to S. F. and N. Y."

One can only wonder what kind of erotic convergence might have exploded on stage if Peter Berlin had auditioned for director Toby/Bluth to be cast in the role of Jaques for whom "All the world's a stage." Just like Polk Street.

"I never wanted to be on stage," Peter told me, "even if I could sing and dance. I wouldn't want to be that kind of product in front of a crowd. Peter Berlin only had one admirer at a time. Even two people would be too much."

Peter Berlin: In the late 1970s [1978], I approached Tom of Finland who was signing books in a San Francisco store. Tom said, "Hello," but he was distracted, like, he didn't say, "Oh, my God, Peter Berlin," or anything like that. He was kind of cold. I wasn't a collector of his work, but I liked the idea of having a Tom of Finland original. The meeting was not an earthshaking encounter. He said yes, he'd draw me. So I sent him photos and he made four drawings of me at $300 a piece.

Ultimately, Tom of Finland drew Peter six times. After the first commercial meeting in 1978, Tom on his own dime went on to draw Peter Berlin and Jochen Labriola as two cruising studs walking together down the street. The MOMA exhibited the drawing. About Jochen, Peter said: "There's a German word: *comrade*; it can mean friend or lover. It doesn't necessarily have to do with sex, just great fun, great humor, great understanding. When Jochen died, my life went from color to black and white."

Jack Fritscher: I have a clipping here I'd like to share with you. John Waters, who often works the same pop-culture beat as I, wrote in *The New York Times Style Magazine* that "Peter Berlin, Kenneth Anger, Joe Dallesandro, Jeff Stryker, Jim Morrison, James Bidgood, John Rechy, even Elvis and James Dean. None of them could have existed without Tom of Finland's art coming first."

Peter Berlin: John Waters is an interesting man, but this comment is stupid and inaccurate. If I had never seen a drawing by Tom of Finland, I'd still have become Peter Berlin. I see myself as the living expression of Tom's fantasy, but he did not create me. Tom created drawings. I created a live person. We were sort of coincidental. Tom is a good artist. Don't get me wrong. I like his work, and I like the Tom of Finland Foundation and Durk Dehner, but if Durk with his business head had not decided to become Tom's champion and turn him into a Foundation [in 1984], his drawings would never have moved from the small sex magazines to galleries and museums. Durk broke the porn ceiling and got him in museums.

> Tom of Finland and Peter Berlin, each in his own way, like the iconic fashion designer Rob of Amsterdam, were, alongside the power of *Drummer* magazine, the first "influencers" who helped create international leather culture.

Jack Fritscher: Does resembling Tom's men mean cause and effect or common sources? From before Tom and you hit it big in pop culture, gay leathermen cloning their image in the first leather bars in the 50s stood, posed, and dressed like straight 1940s bike gangs [Hollister] and 1960s biker movies after Brando and James Dean defined leather posturing in *The Wild One* [1953] and *Rebel without a Cause* [1955].

Peter Berlin: That all took awhile.

Jack Fritscher: Actually, when I was editor and at odds with the publisher, I managed to publish Tom's work as a *Drummer* first for Tom in my special arts issue called *Son of Drummer* [September 1978 featuring Tom and Mapplethorpe and the leather artist Rex].

Because publisher John Embry had a black list that included Tom for demanding payment for his work, Tom wasn't even mentioned again after my 1978 notice until four years later in *Drummer* 61, February 1982. After Embry sold *Drummer* to Anthony DeBlase in 1986, it took six years from that 1982 mention—and four years after Durk started the Foundation—for Tom to be published in *Drummer* on the cover of issue 113, February 1988.

Jack Fritscher: As I said, I watched your two films online. Your long and short films are very popular with lots of late-night hits on pornsites. Thousands of viewers watching for free just like I watched *Nights in Black Leather.*

Peter Berlin: Then I will watch it again. This is the problem with me. My memory was always bad. It's not the recreational drugs we all took. I remember in school for English lessons, the teacher was reading a story and writing new vocabulary words on the blackboard so we could all repeat them over and over. I had to make little notes to keep up. The same with mathematics. In English and mathematics, you have to remember the rules. Reading and writing were always so hard for me. That's why I asked you, "Did you make any notes?" I wish I would have written a diary or shot little Polaroids of all their faces.

Jack Fritscher: Like Mapplethorpe shot Polaroids of you.

Peter Berlin: Yes, because I have very few clear images in my mind of the thousands of boys I had. I do have lot of notes I wrote when I was stoned at the beach, oiled up, early in the morning when it was quiet. I was usually the first one there. And then I had my little "garage marijuana" to smoke and that always helped me focus my mind. Grass is fantastic, right? I don't do grass anymore.

Jack Fritscher: In pursuit of the origin of Peter Berlin, may we return to your family DNA in Saint Petersburg out of whose "Peter" maybe subliminally came your "Peter" Berlin—the way your famous relative, George Hoyningen-Huene [1900-1968] came out of the

Russian Revolution and became Chief of Photography of French *Vogue* [in the 1920s before meeting, in 1930, fashion photographer Horst P. Horst who was both his lover and model].

Peter Berlin: Many of the Germans living in Russia, like my grandfather, were working for the Tsar who hired German aristocrats to teach upper-class manners to Russian aristocrats.

> The Tsarina Alexandra was a German princess who married Tsar Nicholas in 1894 and ran a German-inflected Imperial Court until they were murdered during the Russian Revolution in 1918.

Jack Fritscher: How did your family become aristocratic? How did you get the baron title?

Peter Berlin: My family tree goes back to 1500 or so. It's a German title given by the *König* [king], and then passed to each generation. You inherit it. That all stopped in 1918 [with the fall of the German Empire at the end for the First World War].

Jack Fritscher: Was your father a baron?

Peter Berlin: Yes.

Jack Fritscher: Are you a baron?

Peter Berlin: Yeah. But it's no longer a title. Barons no longer exist, but the title became part of the name. My cousin in Berlin, who is old and sick, said she always felt like, "Yes! I'm a Baronin, a baroness." She married a scientist who was an earthquake expert, but she didn't take his name. She was always the Baroness von Hoyningen-Huene. I deleted myself from all that. I like that Touko [Laaksonen] called himself "Tom of Finland," but I purposely called myself "Peter Berlin," not "Peter of Berlin."

Jack Fritscher: Good branding.

Peter Berlin: So, the *von* and the *baron*, I never used because I never think in those royal terms, although I do, as myself Armin, appreciate certain behavior towards me, where I feel that somebody should give me respect. Maybe that's because when I was Peter Berlin, I was treated like a dumb blond. "Oh, he must be stupid!" So I'd immediately put the brakes on, and sometimes offended people who thought Peter Berlin was an arrogant asshole.

Jack Fritscher: Do you think that Peter Berlin is an extension of the baron? Is Peter Berlin more aristocratic than Armin?

Peter Berlin: Yes. Unlike little me, Peter Berlin has a commanding presence. The image I created is a very stylized expression of male masculinity without being overly butch. I'm not really a hard-core leather guy, right? Peter Berlin has always straddled a certain androgynous quality. He has gay and straight appeal. I have now a woman in my life. She's from Canada. She wrote to me after she saw my documentary. What was surprising, she thought, looking at my picture, that I was straight. Okay. On one hand, I look gay. On the other, straight. Art is in the eye of the beholder. I'm not any of those labels, those boxes, gay, straight, up and down, black and white. I don't go there because labels are just a made-up thing to put people in their place. I like the idea of straight appearance, you know? I just do. About homosexuality, I had so much to think about because homosexuality is so completely misunderstood in our stupid society. I think there is, I don't know, was it Mr. Jung said about some kind of scale, you know, really gay or really straight?

Jack Fritscher: The Kinsey Scale?

Peter Berlin: Yeah, Doctor Kinsey. Not Jung. You see my memory? Thank God, you know, I am definitely, definitely, definitely gay. I've never had an experience with a woman. It wouldn't even occur to me.

Jack Fritscher: We're Gold Star Gays.

Peter Berlin: Many of my friends have had experiences with a woman, and I say, "Rah! Rah! Rah!" because they all stayed gay. I did consider women. Why in the world do I eliminate half of the population? Wouldn't it be more intelligent to have sex with boys and girls? But I made my decision. It's not gender *so* much as beauty. I'm such a great admirer of male beauty and beautiful men. That word *beauty* is very important to me because it's a free word. Like *art*. You don't find it in the American Constitution, in no law book. It's really only in poetry. I always felt that beautiful people have different laws. Think about that.

Jack Fritscher: I have. I've lived it. I wrote a novel about the privilege of the bad and the beautiful in San Francisco. Beautiful men think they can get away with murder and your checkbook and your heart.

Peter Berlin: Romeo and Juliet never interested me because of Juliet. Love between a man and woman was not interesting to me as a boy. Nowadays homosexuality is really a mainstream thing on screen. Still there is no Hollywood movie of Peter Berlin who, it makes perfect sense, is still mysteriously taboo, like when my mother looked at me with genuine disgust. Magazines still censor my frontal nude shots.

Jack Fritscher: The most frightening thing in the world is a photo of a penis. Ask Mapplethorpe.

Peter Berlin: I'm constantly shocked when I see nasty news about gays in the political arena. I'm shocked. I'm shocked. A shock should only last split seconds, but when I'm shocked for three days, I say, "Oh, fuck you." Peter Berlin not fitting into that world makes perfect sense. So I don't go out. I live very much private. Like you, right?

Jack Fritscher: San Francisco is for the young. I retired to the woods north of the Golden Gate.

Peter Berlin: When I read your book on Mapplethorpe [1994] describing the whole scene of New York and Studio 54 and the Mineshaft in the 1970s, it seems now just like a dream, no?

> I think it's almost impossible for anyone who did not expe-
> rience the 1970s to understand how wild was that first
> decade after Stonewall. In 1975, the year *Drummer* began
> publication to report on the rising new gay leather culture,

New York City was a 24/7 sex party celebrating the "divine decadence" of *Cabaret* (1972) with thousands of newly liberated men coming from around the world to cruise streets, bars, baths, piers, parks, and clubs like Studio 54 and the Mineshaft. As we rose to heights of gay sex not seen since orgies in ancient Rome, we creatures of the night—unlike politically correct gay puritan censors, like Richard Goldstein condemning leather culture as akin to Nazism in the *Village Voice* in 1975—did not care that Manhattan was a dangerous bankrupt garbage dump where we felt safe and encouraged because the city was as lawless as the wild west and every cowboy knew the lyrics to "Anything Goes." The blighted urban context we had to walk through to get to our pleasure domes shows up in its full glory in Martin Scorsese's *Taxi Driver* and William Friedkin's *Cruising.*

Jack Fritscher: Oh, yes. In fact, I even call it "The Dream Time." It's all gone with the wind.

Peter Berlin: It was bliss. Back then, I liked live sex more than I liked porn. When I was in the bathhouses that showed porn in their lounge, it took me always two or three seconds to be immediately bored because what I saw is not what I wanted to see. I have a very limited erotic window. I'm not at all versatile. I could be the worst lay if I wasn't careful. So I had to reject people who didn't want what I want. When I was cruising the piers in New York, a guy followed me and started making small talk and ruined his chances. I said, "Talking is not the way it works for me. I have to start the minute we lay eyes on each other." He said, "What do you mean?" He said, "Can we redo it? "I said, "Okay, I'll stay here and you go to the other side of the street and start watching me."

Jack Fritscher: *The Peter Berlin Story*: Scene 1. Take 2. You directed the scene and acted it out.

Peter Berlin: Then it worked for me. And he liked it. That's what I would like a Peter Berlin movie to show. That kind of excitement without being X-rated. Especially now because of politics and censorship. There's five million hot scenarios possible that aren't X-rated. *Brokeback Mountain* was good, but not good enough.

Jack Fritscher: To timeline a film about you, when was Peter Berlin born?

Peter Berlin: The Peter Berlin character?

Jack Fritscher: Yes. [Laughs]

Peter Berlin: Peter Berlin was born in 1972 when I made my film *Nights in Black Leather* [released 1973]. I had to title it and put my name on it. I first put "Peter Burian" on it because there was a gay guy I thought beautiful who was named that in Berlin. Then suddenly this big envelope arrived from a lawyer in New York who accused me of stealing the name of Peter Burian who was a legitimate New York model. I was summoned to the office of that lawyer, and I said, "I'm sorry. I will change my name." And then I thought of Berlin, and chose Peter Berlin.

Jack Fritscher: Warhol couldn't have given you a better superstar name. It matches his superstar Brigid Berlin. You said Peter Berlin left the building about twenty years ago. So around the year 2000?

Peter Berlin: Yeah, it was a slow-motion exit, a shutting of a door. One night, I was cruising in Central Park. I was high and horny and feeling great. I looked up at the skyline, the buildings, Manhattan, and I said, "My God, I'm well over fifty. How long can this go on?" Peter Berlin was thirty when he was born. He was never young. He was never old. Peter Berlin is always thirty.

Jack Fritscher: You, Oscar Wilde, and Dorian Gray. The average age of a leading man in Hollywood has always been thirty-five.

Peter Berlin: People have always asked, "You do porno. What will you do when you are old?" I tell them I started when I was old, when I was thirty. Then I started just getting off by myself. I have a lot of unpublished videos of me getting off by myself. Do you get off by yourself?

Jack Fritscher: What? Quit the self-care act of gay magical thinking?

Peter Berlin: So then around 2000, I wasn't going to the bars anymore. I was cruising Folsom Street and Ringold Alley for hours, and I'd be the last one on the street. I found myself rather alone. Standing in the dark under a streetlight. I thought "What is this?" Having sex was my career. One night, around three or four in the morning, I met Reggie who I've had sex with for twenty years. In my iPhone, I have lots of pictures of him and the dates we had sex.

Jack Fritscher: Finally, you're taking notes.

Peter Berlin: The night we met, I looked at Reggie and thought, "Okay, Peter Berlin will meet Peter Berlin." I was still sort of Peter Berlin, aging out of young Peter, and I thought maybe Reggie could also be Peter Berlin. He had a body like mine that I could dress up in Peter Berlin clothes. So I started dressing him as Peter Berlin and shooting pictures.

Jack Fritscher: You were already casting an actor in a Peter Berlin movie.

Peter Berlin: With a black man. When I met Reggie, I still had Bryce, this guy who was living with me. My lovers were Jochen [Labriola] until he died, then James [Stagner who was white] for twenty years until he died, and then Bryce [White who was black] until he died in 2005. Then Reggie moved in and I stopped going out. I only have sex with Reggie. I wash his clothes, shop for our groceries, and cook for him. I told Eric I live like an old housewife in bed with my cat drinking tea.

When James was extremely ill for a long time and I was caring for him in my apartment, it was a very touching scene. One day, he was so weak, he said, "Can you make the pudding?" I knew what he meant. So I said, "Vanilla or chocolate?" So I made the pudding and gave it to him, and he poured his whole bottle of morphine into the pudding and ate it. I told him to lie down. He said, "You're always telling me what to do." He fell asleep, slept for hours, and then he was gone. And then Bryce who was so sick died during heart surgery. When Reggie moved in, he said, "You're not going to try to kill me too, are you?"

Jack Fritscher: Thank you for sharing that intimacy. What human scenes for your movie. But may I re-wind a bit? As a boy in Berlin, when did you first start dressing up?

Peter Berlin: I was in school where we all played sports. My grandmother had a sewing machine and I was tightening my shorts. I made them so tight that my sister said that people were talking behind my back. I did this very early on as a teenager. I found excitement in the sensation of tight clothing. Not only the look of it but the fit like a second skin. The feel of it. The constant vibration between skin and shorts.

Jack Fritscher: Peter Berlin wins the Battle of the Bulge. What a great mirror-fucking scene for your movie. A montage of how you evolved your look.

Peter Berlin: I always related to Marlene Dietrich and Marilyn Monroe. Miss Dietrich, you know, had this very tight see-through thing, and she wanted to have it sort of sparkling like it was electric. And Marilyn Monroe, when you think of her, you think not only of the blond hair and the face, but you think of her body that is so intriguing.

> In any feature film about Peter, this character-defining scene is an early necessity. In 1962, when Peter was twenty, he watched Marilyn Monroe on television singing "Happy Birthday, Mr. President" to Jack Kennedy. The moment is both scandalous and iconic. The world gasped and gaped. Her famous blond figure had been sewn into a skintight shimmering see-through gown designed by Bob Mackie who was famous for dressing Carol Burnett, Judy Garland, Liza Minnelli, Cher, and Bette Midler.

Peter Berlin: When you think about Peter Berlin, the character, you think about him done up from head to toe.

Jack Fritscher: Yes, the whole body. Were you about ten years old when you started this?

Peter Berlin: Maybe not ten, because it happened around puberty. So maybe twelve or thirteen. A fetish even though I was not aware of fetish. I knew tight pants were a must for me to get out of the house as Peter Berlin. Right? I mean, when I was Peter Berlin, everything had to really be pulled together. So I leave the house and I become that character. Whenever I left the house, I was "Peter Berlin." I played that character and I played him very well. I realized very quickly that I had to separate Armin from "Peter" because all that caused two kinds of reactions. I got a lot of negative reactions. I was aware that I was being looked at, but I didn't want to be looked at by a family with children, right? I didn't do my thing to be admired by the so-called public. That was not my thing.

I wasn't, you know, courageous. I just was never in the closet. I wanted to get laid. I wanted to have someone who saw me start to follow me down the street which was the positive reaction that happened many times. In San Francisco, I usually wouldn't go downtown to Union Square full of straight tourists. No. When you saw me on Polk, it was a gay street. At that time, I was living on Filbert Street and Polk Street. I would walk down to the Golden Gate YMCA past people who saw me every day. But I wouldn't walk like that in some straight area. I always played on the gay field. At that time, I remember always seeing the hustlers standing on corners on Polk Street. I always was intrigued by hustlers. I always liked that scene. And, of course, I was basically seen as a hustler.

Jack Fritscher: Did you ever hustle? Mapplethorpe hustled a sandwich or two when he was a teen in Times Square in the 1960s.

Peter Berlin: No, I never, never hustled because I knew I didn't have the credentials of a hustler. A hustler is selling his body and is doing what a client is telling him—and I don't want anybody telling me what to do. So, I wouldn't oblige, okay? People asked me, and I liked being mistaken for a hustler because that's what I looked like.

Jack Fritscher: Perhaps you were like Coco Chanel who was so modern, someone said, that even though she wasn't an out-and-out hooker or hustler, she'd settle for something in between being admired and being given gifts. Like you, she had two identities. One as a fashion designer. One as a singer in a cabaret popular with cavalry officers.

Peter Berlin: Oh! I don't know her story. That is interesting.

Jack Fritscher: Two designers. She had her little black dress. You had your Saran Wrap jeans. I think of you like her as a unique fashion designer who fit the times. Your movies came out [1973 and 1974] just after the movie *Cabaret* [1972]. As if Peter Berlin stepped out of a Weimar cabaret. Berlin. Nazis. And all that jazz.

> By now there are so many gender-variant live stage versions of *Cabaret*, I can see the role of the Emcee played by Joel Grey being played in a homosurrealist fashion by an actor playing Peter Berlin wearing Peter Berlin drag. I'd pay to see "Peter Berlin" coming on stage shouting over the opening song's powerful Kander vamp: "Meine Damen und Herren!" In truth, culturally and politically, creative director Armin's Peter Berlin is at least subtextually a triumphant anti-fascist creation and divinely decadent symbol because he emerged from the war as an avant-garde next-gen incarnation of the degenerate gay art the Nazis tried to destroy. He was his own art object.
>
> Standing in the shadow of his father killed by Nazi ideology, he grew up as part of his generation's postwar reaction to Nazis. His proud DNA is in his thin silhouette. His fashion runway was the yellow-brick road that ran from Berlin to Paris to Rome to New York to San Francisco where he put down roots on Polk Street, still often called today by its original name, Polkstrasse, because of the German immigrants who settled there in the nineteenth century.
>
> When Armin created Peter, he began performing beyond the narrow prescriptions of gender stereotypes. In the contours of global masculinity, Armin was all-male in body,

spirit, and personality, and yet, he was perfectly androgynous. In the form and fashion of homomasculinity, Peter was both metaphor and contradiction. On the Rainbow Spectrum, he wasn't hyper-masculine; he was homomasculine. He was perfect adjunct for the Cockettes crowd with whom he collaborated. He was too soft for the leather crowd which was why Peter was never featured in *Drummer* magazine—and why he had at first to pay Tom of Finland to draw his portraits which are now classic "Tom."

His independence in identity and style was his homo-surreal erotic power. His trans-Atlantic presentation of the platonic ideal of a sensuous European masculinity reads like "androgyny" which some queer progressives like as gender fluidity and some gay male conservatives hate as effeminate and decadent.

Everyone from fans to haters had an opinion about Peter Berlin. No one ever forgot their first sighting of him. When the immigrant Peter walked American streets during the Vietnam War doing his own thing, he upended conventions. He pushed boundaries. He was a challenge to the sliding order of gay masculinity on the Kinsey Scale. His aloof attitude and his *outré* clothing—a hybrid original of leather stylings for men not to be confused with drag for queens—were punk, years before punk rock. Mapplethorpe, attuned to the early 70s rise of punk through Patti Smith, first shot the punkness of Peter on Polaroid in 1974.

When Vivienne Westwood began designing punk fashions in the early 1970s, she who dressed the Sex Pistols in 1975 was influenced by gay leather and bondage culture and by Peter's disobedient style in his new films that thrust him into the international spotlight. Think of Peter's Technicolor designer selfie standing like a ballet dancer on a garbage can, *punk*, while wearing see-through gray tights from calves to tits, *punker*, and a stylishly reconfigured set of red suspenders holding up the tights and harnessing his chest, shoulders, and biceps in hints of bondage while wearing a red pillbox hat over a blond wig, *punkest*.

In March 2015, Lauren Murrow in *San Francisco Magazine* included Peter as the lead image in her photo-feature article "San Francisco: The Pioneers (The Pin-Ups, Porn Stars, and Provocateurs of San Francisco's Sexual Heyday)." The mature Peter in a photo by Cody Pickens appeared alongside Cockettes Fayette Hauser, Scrumbly Koldewyn, Sweet Pam, and Rumi Missabu, as well as beside Linda Martinez, David Steinberg, Joani Blank, Annie Sprinkle, and myself. It was the first time Peter and I were linked in the straight press after exhibiting our photos together for the SF Camerawork Exhibit: *An Autobiography of the San Francisco Bay Area, Part 2: The Future Lasts Forever*, 2010.

Peter Berlin: You have a good sort of overall view I don't have because I'm too close to myself. I became known as a person you might run into in the middle of the night in a bar or the street or a train station. Sometimes I meet people who remember me from that time, and they say, "Oh my God, you were a vision!" It was a thrill to have that effect on people. I always intended to be obvious because I tried to be an example, a role model, a blueprint, a template for guys to imitate. I always thought, my God, the best thing that could happen is that somebody looks at me and tries to imitate me. I encountered two or three who tried, but the imitations were always not as good as I did it.

Jack Fritscher: Right.

Peter Berlin: Now, you know.

Regarding "Peter Berlin impersonators," Dom Johnson reported on Vaginal Davis' blog: "November 27, 2009: I also met…writer Bruce Benderson [a marvelous friend, insightful scholar, and longtime champion of Peter Berlin]… What a riot he is! It was the most peculiar night, as he had a British Peter Berlin lookalike staying with him, who is living as 'Berlin circa 1975,' and doing a project where he gets photographed in Berlinish poses by superstar photographers. He even got the aging original Peter Berlin to photograph him as his youthful self, which is pretty perverse…. Slava [Mogutin] was photographing the new [not the original] PB (with a Dutch bowl haircut, in slutty white string pantyhose, cowboy boots, and a little silk neckerchief)."

Jack Fritscher: I know you're authentic.

Peter Berlin: I did the best with the body I was born with because my frame when I look at my body compared to a black guy—when I go to the internet, I say, "Oh my God, if I could have looked like that, sure and confident." I never was sure of myself even as I gave an impression of sureness and confidence. I was actually much more frail and insecure.

Jack Fritscher: How tall is Peter Berlin, and how much did he weigh?

Peter Berlin: Peter is five-foot-ten. I'm sort of five-ten, right? I was always on the thin side, 150 pounds. So I went to the YMCA to work out. My workout ran twenty minutes, lifting weights, but I never took it serious. I never liked the idea of a workout. I never liked the word *work*. I went to the gym because I could cruise and have sex there. I went there for the experience.

Jack Fritscher: As we all did at YMCAs everywhere.

Peter Berlin: I never got into the pleasure of lifting weights and feeling good the way runners get a runner high. Did you ever have a runner's high?

Jack Fritscher: Oh, yeah. I spent years on treadmills and working out at the Y and Gold's and the Pump Room.

Peter Berlin: If I run, I get a pain in my left or right side. So, I never had that runner's pleasure. I worked out not to get big but to get a little definition.

Jack Fritscher: But you did develop killer abs.

Peter Berlin: I never had killer abs. [Laughs] I never had killer anything.

Jack Fritscher: You have killer abs in *Nights in Black Leather*. Nobody slouches and presents his washboard torso for worship like Peter Berlin.

Peter Berlin: But when I compare myself with the best, with what I see in the black guys! My God, I never was really happy with myself. But I said, "Okay, it's not good enough" because for all the work I put in, I didn't have enough drive to put real work into anything. Not like Mapplethorpe. He had drive. He did a lot of real work. Besides his sexual life, he was a worker.

Jack Fritscher: You certainly are in shape in your films. In what I think of as your signature move on screen, you thrust out your pelvis and your very tight torso, and you twist it from the waist, and pivot your shoulders thirty to forty degrees away from the plane of your waist. It accents your sixpack abs. I've watched your films in theaters full of men. And that makes audiences swoon.

Peter Berlin: When I picked up my camera, I always had a plan. In every photo I took, I first watched myself move in a mirror. I had a big mirror, and I put in front of the mirror a camera looking back at me. So I could stand there and choose my poses exactly. I could maybe move a little bit my face and it would look awful. People think, "Oh, he's so photogenic." No. I'm everything else but photogenic.

Jack Fritscher: Sondheim wrote "My body's all right, but not in perspective and not in the light."

Peter Berlin: Yes. Yes. So it's tricky to be able to make a photograph.

Jack Fritscher: Each one a separate art object.

Peter Berlin: I have to look a very definite way to become Peter. I look and stare and study the image in the mirror, and the instant I see Peter Berlin in the mirror, I clicked and made it work.

Jack Fritscher: So you would direct yourself in the mirror. You'd shoot what the mirror was seeing. You did not shoot into the mirror. You shot yourself from the point of view of the mirror.

Peter Berlin: I shot at myself. I shot what the mirror saw.

Jack Fritscher: The mirror gave you the "proof" of what you were doing?

Peter Berlin: The mirror made me see how I looked. I directed the shoot. When you hire a photographer to shoot you, he tells you, "Okay, move here, move there, do this, and do that." Right? If I had to rely on another photographer, I never would have been Peter Berlin.

Jack Fritscher: How did you feel when Robert Mapplethorpe shot you in 1977? How did you two handle that. Two stars with one camera?

Peter Berlin: That portrait he shot on the boardwalk? On Fire Island? That I could have done myself with a tripod.

Jack Fritscher: Snap.

Peter Berlin: Robert was after me so he could shoot a picture. He was after me, my look, my pants, right? He shot several more photos of me [in 1976]. In one, I was sitting in the same spot he'd shot Patti Smith, where I was sitting in his studio against a white wall, and I look terrible. You can tell it's me, but I don't look like Peter Berlin at all. I never liked to be photographed by other people. I only did it because Robert asked me, and I said okay. I was stupid in a way, you know. I should have exploited my connection with Robert. He sent me that picture of me sitting in his studio and I hung it in my first apartment on Broadway, and somehow a fight broke out with some guy and the picture fell down, and was all messed up, right? And I didn't think twice about it. Yeah. I was stupid, right?

"Robert Mapplethorpe. 'Peter Berlin, N.Y.C.,' 1976. Gelatin silver print, Image: 13.9 x 13.94 in. (35.3 x 35.4 cm.). Signed, dated, numbered on recto in ink; Signed, titled, dated, numbered on verso with artist's [Mapplethorpe's] copyright credit stamp. Edition 3/10. Estimate: $6,000 to $8,000. Artnet Auctions. April 25, 2023."

In a perfect match on both sides of the camera, the thirty-year-old Mapplethorpe's exquisite technique embraces the energy emanating from thirty-three-year-old Armin's exquisite beauty. This quintessential image is important to both Robert's and Peter's work because Robert shot a portrait of Armin, not of Peter Berlin. Armin told me: "I don't look like Peter Berlin at all." This unmasked posture portrait of Armin sitting nude on the floor of Robert's studio matches Robert's series of unmasked posture portraits of Patti Smith crouched nude almost in the same spot, also in 1976, hugging the radiators below the windows of the Bond Street room.

Jack Fritscher: Did you ever meet Patti Smith?

Peter Berlin: I met her once, but I wasn't interested in her and she wasn't interested in me. So I never saw her perform. In fact, I never go to see anyone perform. I don't want to meet them that way. I want to meet the person they are.

Jack Fritscher: Robert really admired you and the art of your self-portraits because he shot so many self-portraits in leather and drag, and with that whip coming out of his butt.

Peter Berlin: I know. I must tell you because like you I knew Robert before he was famous. I was very surprised to see how he developed. I always said, "Oh, you know, Robert, yeah, he's a very nice, sweet, pleasant guy." He approached me the way many people approached me. He was impressed by the whole Peter Berlin thing.

Jack Fritscher: He liked you because you were a celebrity and he collected celebrities.

Peter Berlin: Robert was a starfucker. May I tell you, Robert clicked on me. He was so impressed when I'd be out walking with him wherever, you know, Provincetown, New York, Polk Street, and people would recognize me because my films were playing in theaters. And he'd say, "My God, I'd like that." So, I told him, "Robert, put your fucking face on a book so people can recognize you. That's all you have to do to be recognized. You have to be seen on TV or on film or in a magazine."

Jack Fritscher: Perhaps you emboldened Robert to continue doing his own self-portraits. He also studied himself in the mirror.

Peter Berlin: Yeah. The influence I probably had on him. The other influence on him was my friend, Jochen, who Robert had a fling with. Jochen was painting flowers—many, many calla lilies, calla lilies, calla lilies. Robert saw those. I have hundreds of potted plants in my apartment. I've shot hundreds of pictures of flowers, enough to make a good book. You know that one flag picture Robert shot?

Jack Fritscher: Yes, the tattered flag with the sun behind it.

Peter Berlin: We were living on Fire Island, and I looked up at that flagpole, and I said, "Robert, look, that looks nice, right?" And he said, "Oh, yes." So I know exactly the moment when he took the camera and made that picture.

Jack Fritscher: A moment in time.

Peter Berlin: I got a good, good feeling from that. Soon after, here in San Francisco, I met Marcus Leatherdale who met me as Peter Berlin. I hung out with him. He knew I knew Robert and he asked me, "Can you introduce me to Robert?" And they became good friends.

Jack Fritscher: Until they didn't. So, you had influence on Robert?

Peter Berlin: Yeah.

Jack Fritscher: You and Jochen.

Peter Berlin: Yes. My God! What a good time we had mixing it up back then. I remember the first time I went to Studio 54 and stood in line. The doorman came up to me and said, "Peter Berlin doesn't have to stand in line." I felt terrible because I was ushered in past all the people hoping to get in. One night when Andy Warhol came into 54 with his entourage, he saw me. I was shy. We greeted each other sort of with a nod, you know, that kind of thing. I never approached Warhol because I never approach people in my life. I'm not proud of that. [Later, Peter had supper with Warhol whom he permitted to shoot him.] I probably could have made a lot of nice friendships. But I was never interested in that.

I only got into Andy's Factory with my Dutch friend Koos Van Den Akker, the New York fashion designer. He's dead now. Everybody's dead. He had a string of stores in Manhattan and sold to Bloomingdale's and Saks Fifth Avenue. He was known for his collage dresses. A very funny guy. He had a house on Fire Island. That's why I spent so much time on the island. So I was living there when Robert and Sam Wagstaff rented Koos' house. So I always was with them on their weekends. They would all leave on Monday because they had to go to work. I stayed alone all week. Because of Jochen, I didn't have to work.

Jack Fritscher: So you and Koos and Robert and Sam were staying in the same house?

Peter Berlin: Yeah, yeah. That beautiful house. It had big windows. I was there living like a millionaire with no money in the pocket.

Jack Fritscher: Were you there when Wakefield Poole shot *Boys in the Sand?*

Peter Berlin: No. These things, I avoided. Porno didn't interest me. I was always an outsider. All that big porno stuff with groups of guys was not my cup of tea. I only did my little film because I wanted to be in a porno. I wish I would have been more honest in my film-making. That's why years later I don't like my films, you know. It's sort of all fake and stupid.

Jack Fritscher: I don't think they're fake and stupid at all. I think they're statements, documents of a time gone with the wind, about people who love to have sex.

Peter Berlin: There's a lot stuff in them I feel okay about. I've always wanted to make another feature film, but, um, you see, this is what, what I was not given in my life. I have no partner. You have a partner who helps you.

Jack Fritscher: Right.

Peter Berlin: Robert had a partner.

Jack Fritscher: Sam Wagstaff.

Peter Berlin: All the big stars they had partners.

Jack Fritscher: Marlene Dietrich had Josef von Sternberg.

Peter Berlin: You see, I have a lot of talent, but there are certain things that I just can't do and won't do. Right?

Jack Fritscher: That separation of tasks was one of the amazing things I felt about your films. I thought, Peter always shoots himself in stills, but he doesn't shoot himself in movies.

Peter Berlin: So true. The first film I tried was *Nights in Black Leather* [a spin on the Moody Blues' 1967 "Nights in White Satin"] with a very interesting friend [Richard Abel] who spoke better German than me. He was American and had a big beautiful reflex camera. He went to film school to make his master's in filmmaking. He showed me a ten-minute black-and-white student film that was nicely done. I told him, "You can show that film to your mother and to your sister, but let's do something more. Let's make a porno." He liked the idea. So, there I was in front of the camera and I told him, "Here, now, do this and do that." And when I saw the footage, I realized, no, he didn't do what I told him, right? So, I was directing and starring. The only thing he did without me was the editing which was all his doing. And the sound.

For that reason, I decided to make another film, *That Boy*, with another friend [Ignatio Rutkowski—with second camera by Phillip Martin] who had a Bolex H16 reflex camera. It was the same situation where I was telling him, oh, you know, motivating him, saying,

"The weather is nice today. Let's go shoot something." I was spontaneous. Not one word was written down. We made it up on the spot.

Jack Fritscher: So, no shooting script. Did your write down the
voice-over you added later?

Peter Berlin: It was all made up. Spontaneous. Like the idea with
the blind guy in *That Boy.* That came about when I told that guy,
"Now walk from there to here towards the camera." And he walked.
I said, "Oh, my God, look at the way he walks across the street." I
suddenly thought I should make him blind. It came to me as we shot.
I made the best of what I had with the friends I asked to be in it [like
Cockette Pristine Condition aka Keith Blanton].

Jack Fritscher: Actually, the blindness of a voyeur attracted to the
vision of Peter Berlin is a perfectly homosurreal contradiction. A
great provocative idea.

Peter Berlin: I just asked friends, "Oh, you want to be, uh, a star?"
And they obliged.

Jack Fritscher: In *Nights in Black Leather*, the voice-over is you
speaking. And in *That Boy*, the voice-over is the photographer.

Peter Berlin: Right.

Jack Fritscher: So no one "wrote" those scripts?

Peter Berlin: As I say about *That Boy*, it was spontaneous, just spur
of the moment. Just like I sewed my clothes without a pattern. I
certainly didn't write anything down. I was supposedly reading from
my journal which I was holding on screen.

Jack Fritscher: You are a performance artist. You were doing improv
theater. For my erotic films, I'm a writer dictating a story to get an
actor to improvise while I run a camera.

Peter Berlin: I had tons of other things to do with the film. I was
editing hours of film and asked myself what do I do with all that
footage? What do I do with all this crap? I had all the various pieces

of the film clipped up hanging on my wall. Not even the editing was premeditated. So I did the best I could splicing things together to tell a story. I worked hard, yeah? That was the only time in my life where I actually worked very hard because I'd look at all the cuts and splices I'd made that I hung side-by-side on the wall to sort out.

Jack Fritscher: You didn't use a storyboard.

Peter Berlin: I had to study the frames. Where was this? Where does this go? I tell you, I was sweating and, and I said, "Oh, God!"

> In Berlin in the 1960s, Armin trained as a photo technician to learn the basic tricks of the trade and started working as a photographer for German television shooting stars like Alfred Hitchcock, Catherine Deneuve, and Klaus Kinski.

Jack Fritscher: So you didn't edit both your films?

Peter Berlin: No, no, no. I had nothing to do with *Nights in Black Leather*.

Jack Fritscher: You were the actor.

Peter Berlin: I had nothing to do with the editing or the sound. None of that. On *That Boy*, however, I was the only one.

Jack Fritscher: You were the *auteur* director of *That Boy*.

Peter Berlin: I had never edited a film in my life. But I see myself as an editor because I always was very much strangely thinking what is so great about making a photo? You click, right? And a photo: what's the big deal? And then one day, I said, "It's not the clicking. It's the editing." That means you don't look here; you look there. You zoom in and do something. I grew up believing photography was not considered art. This is a whole other subject when I talk about art. I don't even like to mention that word. What is art? Of course, there is fine art, but then there is the art business, and this is where I think I will lose people who do not agree with my take on these things.

Mapplethorpe loved the business of art. But the art business is the reason I basically stopped having anything to do with it in my life because I felt there's something in it I find very distasteful and fake. Basically, when art became a matter of business where suddenly, you know, it became all about galleries. "Oh, no, no. Don't do it in this gallery. Do it in the other gallery." All that networking. It's like Robert's picture. I can't remember the name. You mentioned it in your article [*The Guardian*, London: "'He Was a Sexual Outlaw': My Love Affair with Robert Mapplethorpe," 9 March 2016, honoring the date Robert died in 1989.] You know. That ugly picture of that suit thing and the dick hanging out.

Jack Fritscher: "Man in Polyester Suit."

Peter Berlin: I love black men. I saw it and said *Nah*. It is completely showing the insanity of the art world. It has nothing to do with anything but money-making. For them, art is not the object of the photography. It's the art of selling it.

Jack Fritscher: Sotheby's recently sold that "Polyester" picture for half a million dollars.

> Artsy.net currently offers a Peter Berlin original for sale at the typical price for a signed Peter Berlin original: "'Peter Berlin,' Studio Self Portrait Nude, Erect, ca. 1970s, Gelatin silver print, vintage, 13 × 8 1/2 in | 33 × 21.6 cm, Hand-signed by artist in ink lower right: 'Peter Berlin.' Frame included. US $5,500."

Peter Berlin: I always gave away my stuff, you know? And when Mr. Sam Wagstaff [Mapplethorpe's wealthy lover] was in San Francisco, Robert told him you have to meet Peter Berlin. So Wagstaff came to my place and said he'd like some of my work. I gathered some of my prints together. Unlike Robert, I did all my prints, right? In my dark room. Wagstaff was sort of choosing, I don't know, two or three of my black-and-white prints, double exposures I made from color negatives of Peter Berlin in blue jeans. I had printed them blue. He chose one and asked. "What do I owe you?" I said, "Here." I gave it to him.

Jack Fritscher: Oh, Armin.

Peter Berlin: And he took it. I've thought about this millionaire attitude, right? [Laughs] I was thinking, my God! What a disappointment I am to the art world, just for being Peter Berlin, and living my life the way I did. That's just not done in the art world.

Jack Fritscher: You didn't want your art reduced to money.

Peter Berlin: I had many possibilities to meet rich people. I know you knew Edward DeCelle

> My longtime friend, art dealer Edward DeCelle (1944-2002), was a gallery owner, curator, and fine-art collector in Washington, D. C., and in San Francisco where he built his international reputation curating his daring 1978 exhibit *Censored: Robert Mapplethorpe* at his 80 Langton Street gallery, South of Market. He was an artist in New York and Europe before moving to San Francisco in 1972 where he ran the Lawson-DeCelle Gallery from 1972-1983 in the SOMA leather district which helped make him a formative force in the gay leather renaissance of art in 1970s San Francisco. He was also on the Board of Directors of New Langton Arts which followed at the landmark 80 Langton Street address. In my two-hour interview taped on October 30, 1990, DeCelle talks of Robert Mapplethorpe and the kind of commercial gallery life Peter Berlin faced in San Francisco.

Peter Berlin: Edward approached me and said, "Oh, Peter, I have to introduce you to the high society here in San Francisco." So I met these rich women and I went here and I went there. You've been to those parties. Champagne and stuff. But, you know, if an artist doesn't show interest in those ladies, they lose interest in you. I didn't find that scene very amusing.

Jack Fritscher: Robert loved shooting rich San Francisco women. I remember in 1979 when DeCelle introduced him to Katherine Cebrian.

> San Francisco *grande dame* Countess Katherine Cebrian whom Mapplethorpe shot in 1980 was so aristocratic she

out-queened queens when she said, "I don't even butter my bread. I consider that cooking."

Peter Berlin: I wish I would have been more interested, but I didn't need their money because back then was the only time in my life when I made some money. [Laughs] From my mail-order business selling my films in VHS and Beta and sets of photographs.

Jack Fritscher: Outside of bar owners, you were one of the first gay small businessmen after Stonewall, creating your own mail-order business. Your mailing list helped web gay popular culture.

Peter Berlin: But I myself never was a business. I never ran myself as a business.

Jack Fritscher: Mapplethorpe's mentor [the New Orleans painter and photographer] George Dureau, told me Robert ran himself like a department store.

Peter Berlin: My only thought was Peter Berlin had some pictures to sell. To start out, I made five sets of each color photograph that I developed at Walgreens or Safeway. I offered the sets for ten or fifteen dollars, and when people bought the five sets, I said, "Okay, make ten sets." Then I made fifteen sets. When somebody liked me, they bought everything I offered.

Jack Fritscher: That's how you built Peter Berlin's image in gay pop culture.

Peter Berlin: Yeah. The truth is I got really bored with all the work to choose and print and package the pictures and send them out. I was not professional. I never did anything really professional. I just didn't feel it. I didn't. I didn't. When I'd send out an envelope of pictures, I didn't feel it. It was sort of in a stupid envelope. So to be personal, I put a little note in it. Sometimes I made $1,000 a day because I sold these videotapes for a lot of money. That was how I lost interest in Armin running Peter Berlin's business. All I wanted was to get laid. All my clothes I made myself so I didn't have to pay someone else. I was always doing everything on a shoestring. And for those reasons, I'm amazed that my name is sort of there in the annals of gay history.

> Peter's pop-culture street styles encouraged French fashion designer Jean Paul Gaultier who followed street trends, and created, among other genderfuck bits, the skirt with suspenders that Madonna wore in *Desperately Seeking Susan*. When Gaultier reached out to discuss collaborating directly with Peter, Peter did not return his calls.

Jack Fritscher: Could you explain how you handled your photo prints as an artist? How you took prints that were blurry or discolored and worked each one over with brushes. That's what makes you a homosurreal artist. You shot reality from a unique angle, printed it, and then enhanced it by hand.

Peter Berlin: I never wanted to throw anything away. Sometimes I'd shoot a roll of film that turned out underexposed or overexposed. So I'd take my commercial prints from Walgreens, 5x7 or 3x5 inches, and sit and look at them, study them, and figure how to enhance them warts and all with watercolor or some oil color, whatever I had.

Jack Fritscher: As an artist layering basic frames, you upscaled your vision of Peter Berlin years before Photoshop. Think of what you could do now using artificial intelligence tools to interpret your images into enhanced images created through AI by your own hand. You could take all your zeroes and ones from 1972 and create Peter Berlin as a young hologram avatar who can live forever. Lots of men would like to watch a deep fake of you.

Peter Berlin: Yeah, the future. Let me tell you how in the 1970s this colorizing process happened. I was sitting in Jochen's big beautiful loft in New York on 100 Grand Street doing nothing while he was painting his flowers.

Jack Fritscher: Cool. This could be a pivotal scene in the Peter Berlin Hollywood movie.

Peter Berlin: It struck me that since he had oil paints and acrylics everywhere, and I had all these gray pictures, why not touch them up? I experimented and put a lot of time into it. We had music and much laughter. Jochen liked what I was doing. He had a very rich friend, the heir to one of the biggest companies selling fragrances and perfumes.

Jack Fritscher: Lauder? Lancôme?

Peter Berlin: I don't recall his name. I'll think of it in a second. He was a "Von Something" like I am. He was always coming to Jochen's. They were friends. I had no idea he was rich. He saw me painting my photographs and he said he liked them. I said, okay, and sold him one for fifty bucks. And he bought maybe four or five more. Von Amerling! His name is Von Amerling. And he just died a couple years ago. I forgot about him after Jochen died because Jochen was my connection to him. Jochen got sick in 1988 and when he died my world went from Technicolor to black and white. When my book [*Peter Berlin: Icon, Artist, Photosexual*] came out [in 2019], that stupid book, I thought of him again. You know what? I should really now actually give my opinion about that stupid book.

Jack Fritscher: Yes, tell me about it.

Peter Berlin: My manager Eric [Smith] and I really tried to work with the publisher, but we were mistreated because the book has none of my input—even though I was very careful not to offend the publisher by demanding this and that, you know. We were treated badly, Eric and me. We were excluded. Not the way one should have been treated. The book has none of my input. None of it. Just my photographs. Right? They did the rest and it's a terrible book.

> At the launch for *Photosexual* at the Tom of Finland house in Los Angeles, Peter, *immer lustig*, always jolly, and very Dali, covered his elder face with a large cut-out photo of his younger face mounted like a masquerade mask on a wooden stick which he held up in front of his head when fans asked for selfies with him.

Peter Berlin: Even so, when the book came out in New York, I tried to look up Von Amerling, and sure enough, I found I still had his phone number. So I called him and said I'd like to give him my book. Unfortunately, I made a mistake in the date and time of our meeting, and missed him and never did meet him again. I gave the book to the concierge. When we had spoken on the phone, I asked him if he still had the photos he bought. He said, "You know, I don't know." He had no idea where the photographs were which was not good news. The photos were really beautifully done, very intricate, very one of a kind. If he had them, I would have liked to have photographed them to make digital copies.

On the internet, entrepreneurs sell unauthorized individual pages sliced out of *Photosexual* at ten dollars each.

Jack Fritscher: Are you glad your book is not in print anymore?

Peter Berlin: I think it's not in print and I don't think they have sold anything. We didn't even have a book signing here in San Francisco.

Jack Fritscher: You did get reviewed in the *New York Times*.

Peter Berlin: Sometimes people say I like your book, and when I say I don't, and the reasons, then they suddenly agree with me. Such a missed opportunity in content and layout.

Jack Fritscher: Just as your working your photographs with paints makes you a homosurreal artist, I think your mode of dress as Peter Berlin is very homosurrealistic. I know that you once met Salvador Dali [Spanish surrealist painter, 1904-1989; Warhol called him an important influence on Pop Art].

Peter Berlin: I lived for awhile in Paris, and Dali was living in that hotel [Le Meurice] in Paris. Somehow, I don't remember, I was invited to a party there. I knocked on the door and Dali opened it wearing a paper mask. We just said hello. There were a lot of people at the party, and a naked guy standing in the corner on a pedestal. Every Sunday he had these gatherings of different people. Was I invited because I was Peter Berlin? I have no clue. He and I never spoke after we said hello. So I ended up sitting there for three hours talking to his wife [and frequent model], Gala, in German. I wish I would remember what we talked about. I had a good talk sitting there with her.

Jack Fritscher: What a woman. What a moment.

Peter Berlin: Yeah, yeah.

Jack Fritscher: Dali no doubt appreciated Peter's style. The early Surrealists often ran around Paris wearing costumes they'd made for themselves. Did that have any influence on the young Armin going out into the streets of Berlin costumed as Peter Berlin?

Cell phone rings

Peter Berlin: One, one, one second. Hang on, Jack. Hello, I'm doing an interview. Today at six? Okay.

Jack Fritscher: We can stop today if you need to.

Peter Berlin: No, no. A neighbor wants to come over. I always have my apartment door open and he always brings me some sweets. He reminded me at six o'clock there's a tenant meeting because the management wants to turn our building garage into apartments.

Jack Fritscher: Housing is more important than cars in a city.

Peter Berlin: Right, but this means a lot of big construction in our building. I live in a beautfiul rent-controlled one-bedroom apartment with a beautiful view of City Hall and downtown. If I'd ever move out, they'd knock out the walls and make it a two-bedroom. Is that brilliant? My $3000-dollar place will rent for $5000. That's why they would like to have me move out. [Laughs] I have good rent because I'm here already since 1989. Anyway, what were we talking about?

Jack Fritscher: I was asking if Dali and the Surrealists influenced Peter Berlin to dress up. Mapplethorpe certainly dressed thematically with leather and occult jewelry. When people compare you to others like Dali or Warhol or Mapplethorpe or Tom of Finland, are they jumping to conclusions to make it easy to fit you into art history?

Peter Berlin: I think so. Yes. My image is about my life. I never worked to become anything. I just wanted to get people off. I don't see that personal force or drive in me that I see in Warhol or in Mapplethorpe. I'm all about discovering all the entities of myself that I can be in becoming Peter Berlin. I'm sort of famous, right? Most older gay people have heard my name and they know my image, and that image is from head to toe. There is also my dick. The dick is sort of always there, but it's not this overwhelming dick for dick's sake. Dressing my dick is a fashion statement, right? In most art, there are very few dicks to be seen. The only parallel to me that I see is in the drawings by Tom of Finland. He's the only artist, even if not an influence.

Jack Fritscher: So you feel bonded with him more than any other artist?

Peter Berlin: Not with him personally. With his drawings. I could appreciate his drawings, right? I looked at his work and said, "Yes, this is it. He's got it." I never felt I would appeal to Tom as a subject he'd personally choose. So when he had his showing here at [Oscar Streaker Robert Opel's] Fey-Way Gallery in 1978, I went and I timidly approached him and asked him if he would draw me. It wasn't like Tom approached me and asked, "Can I draw you?" He didn't approach me at all. No. I approached him and we agreed on some drawings at $300 a piece. I told him. "I don't want to be naked. I want to be in jeans." And he said, "Yeah, I like that too." [Laughs] I'm glad I did that to get these drawings.

Jack Fritscher: As *Drummer* editor, I was one of the hosts at that opening. I wonder if Tom noticed that you have a Tom of Finland body? Tom, who was also very shy like you, told me on that same visit to San Francisco when I hosted a *Drummer* magazine supper for him and his lover Veli that he preferred men in uniforms and leather over nude men. He said he was turned on by the uniforms on both sides during the war.

Peter Berlin: Not one shred of Nazi uniforms ever turned me on. My uniform and boot fetish has nothing to do with Nazis. One of my dreams, like making a film of my life, would be the American government asking me to design a new uniform for the army. [Laughs] Tight pants and boots. A very Peter Berlin look.

Jack Fritscher: [Laughs] In the 1960s, the horrible President Nixon designed uniforms for the White House security police, but everyone laughed and said the uniforms looked like costumes in a Banana Republic musical comedy.

Peter Berlin: How funny.

Jack Fritscher: In *That Boy*, there's a sequence that shows a guy wearing a Nazi arm patch which was not an uncommon insignia among Hells Angels and leather fetish players in the 1960s and 1970s. In that scene, you tell him that you voted socialist. Very amusing.

Peter Berlin: You know, I don't remember that because I keep my distance from people and I don't watch my films.

> The postwar 1970s was Nazi-obsessive as American men continued to re-fight the war in their psyches. Nazis were everywhere in American popular culture. Men's spank-bank fascination with the enemy did not mean they were Nazi sympathizers. People deal with post-traumatic stress as best they can. Immensely popular straight men's adventure magazines like *Saga* and *Argosy* (that inspired gay men's adventure magazines like *Drummer*) featured cover paintings of scantily uniformed Nazi women topping shirtless muscular American soldiers tied up on lurid dominatrix covers and in soft-core S&M stories. Nazis were everywhere in pop culture.
>
> In addition to Richard Goldstein's 1975 essay attacking leather culture as fascism in the *Village Voice*, Susan Sontag reacted with her 1975 essay, "Fascinating Fascism," in *The*

New York Review of Books to analyze the 1970s obsession with Nazi uniforms, sex, and the power of "SS" S&M. Nazis were in homes on television in series like *Wonder Woman* and *Hogan's Heroes* as well as in mainstream John Wayne war movies and in *Cabaret, The Night Porter, Seven Beauties, Salo,* and *Ilsa: She-Wolf of the SS.*

Gay filmmaker Kenneth Anger (February 3, 1927-May 11, 2023) featured Nazi regalia prominently in his iconic leather-biker movie, *Scorpio Rising.* In San Francisco, the influential Catholic leather priest Jim Kane was collecting Nazi insignia pins and jewelry as gifts for friends, the pointillist artist Rex was drawing his pictures next to a video monitor playing Nazi rallies with Nazi marching music, and the most popular footage screened in leather bars was the "Springtime for Hitler" musical number from *The Producers.* Nazi fantasies did not make a man a Nazi. At *Drummer,* I who grew up loathing Nazis had to fight the publisher who loved to print pictures of Nazis in Hollywood movies. I begged him to stop inserting ads for the National Socialist League whose tag line was a spin on the title of the Hitler Youth song in *Cabaret,* "Tomorrow Belongs to Me."

Jack Fritscher: So, considering the gay *Zeitgeist* back then, I must ask. Because you're German, has anyone tried to get you to play a Nazi scene? Did anyone try to turn your nationality into a sex fetish?

Peter Berlin: No. I never was in a situation like that. I would never allow a situation like that.

Jack Fritscher: I know you never would, but did anybody ever ask you to?

Peter Berlin: No, no, no. Nobody asked me. I'm always careful not to get used. I wouldn't allow that situation to occur. If anything, Peter Berlin is a very un-Nazi image. Nazis would have killed me as a decadent artist. I'm careful who I meet. Sometimes I'm introduced to interesting people, but I don't know who they are. So I wouldn't know what they were into or wanted to get into with me in their fantasies. You go to a party and don't know who's who or what they want. Famous people should all wear name tags.

Jack Fritscher: Right.

Peter Berlin: I regret not developing friendships with people I met or with fans who bought my movies. Like Sam Steward had his *Stud File*, I have a cardboard box of my mail-order clients with names, addresses, and what they bought. When Gerard Koskovich [the San Francisco-Paris archivist and one of the founders of the San Francisco Gay and Lesbian Historical Society] inventoried my papers and art collection two years ago, he was delighted he found that box. As I said, I sent some of them notes. Some of them were probably interesting people, but I've always kept my distance. So, I'm not really collected, but there is the Clamp Gallery in New York which is selling my work. I had an exhibition there once. I don't remember these things. Eric always has to remind me of my own history. "Oh, yeah, Peter," he says, "you have shown here and there." You know the Clamp Gallery?

Jack Fritscher: Yes, I do. I read the interview they did with you.

Peter Berlin: Thank you.

Jack Fritscher: Another question I have about iconography, about your stylizing Peter Berlin. In the 1960s when long hair meant everything, where did your Dutch Boy haircut come from?

Peter Berlin: I don't know. Is there a Dutch Boy thing? Is the Dutch Boy actually Dutch? What is it?

Jack Fritscher: The guy with the Dutch Boy haircut. That's how guys used to describe your look. A lot of us grew up watching our fathers buy Dutch Boy Paint while we played with Dutch Boy coloring books for boys and girls. It comes from the popular advertising campaign selling Dutch Boy Paint. The blond boy in the ad wears a blue flat cap shaped like your leather cap, and has a Dutch Boy haircut.

Peter Berlin: Some long hair with bangs or what?

Jack Fritscher: Like a pageboy hair style. Cut in a bob, straight bangs, side and back hair chopped off right below the chin line all the way around the neck almost like a helmet.

Peter Berlin: Oh, oh, oh, you see, I didn't even know that. All I know is that Dutch Boy painting.

Jack Fritscher: Right. The drawing of the Dutch Boy brand is based on that famous painting. ["The Dutch Boy" by American Lawrence Carmichael Earle, 1845–1921.] It comes out of the story of Hans Brinker and the Little Dutch Boy who saved Holland from flooding by putting his finger in the dike.

> American author Mary Mapes Dodge wrote the original Dutch Boy story in *Hans Brinker and the Silver Skates* in 1865.

Peter Berlin: Oh, oh. That all went over my head [Laughs].

Jack Fritscher: [Laughs] Of course. The Dutch Boy story is part of American pop culture, not European. So Americans trying to figure you out in the Pop Art scene of the 1960s and 70s looked at your hippie hair and connected you to him in the Pop Art of advertising. He is as iconic as a Warhol painting. People love the Dutch boy.

Peter Berlin: I hear you. [Laughs] I never had that explained to me.

Jack Fritscher: The Dutch Boy Paint Company should hire you and put some of your color-coordinated pictures of Peter Berlin on the paint cans. Not that you want to end up on a paint can.

Peter Berlin: My not knowing proves how I live so outside the box. I know nothing about business, but I am surprised that nobody ever approached me to make a Peter Berlin doll. It would sell, right?

Jack Fritscher: Yes. There are Tom of Finland dolls and Village People dolls and Divine's "Simply Divine" cut-out paper dolls. Even today a Peter Berlin doll would be snatched up as a collectible.

Peter Berlin: But I'm not interested in making money, or meeting people. Facebook is now where people contact me. Eric put me there. If he hadn't, I wouldn't be there. He posts and answers things to support the Peter Berlin image. I get links from the Tom of Finland store always selling something new. Tom of Finland cologne. Tom of Finland soap. They must make some money. But someone has to produce the goods.

Jack Fritscher: Right. Tom of Finland himself never did it. His guardians Durk Dehner and Steve Sharp work hard at marketing to keep the art and archive of Tom and many other artists alive. Durk says they sell all those things so everybody can have a little Tom in their lives.

Peter Berlin: Durk is a good friend. Maybe I should ask him. There was a guy who contacted me through Facebook. He said, "Oh, Peter, can I use your…" and I said, "George, you want to make, I don't know, magnets for the refrigerator and some of this and that?" And then he made all kinds of stuff. I let him do it until Eric said, "You know, Peter, you should tell him to stop it." But I said no. I always in my life gave things away.

Jack Fritscher: You've been very generous. I'm sure you've pleased many grateful people.

Peter Berlin: I'm just not a businessman.

Jack Fritscher: You're an artist.

Peter Berlin: I don't know. What makes an artist? Unfortunately, Eric had a stroke a year or two ago. So life's a little difficult.

Jack Fritscher: Did you ever meet the artist Rex whose studio was at the Magazine Store on Larkin Street?

Peter Berlin: I probably was introduced.

Jack Fritscher: He's very reclusive too.

Peter Berlin: I know his drawings from the magazines back in those days with *Drummer* and *In Touch*.

Jack Fritscher: I bring him up because like us, he's now eighty himself. He is living disabled in a wheelchair in subsidized housing in Amsterdam where he moved, an immigrant, ten years ago because he couldn't stand the politics and the way he was treated as an artist in the United States.

Peter Berlin: Ahhh.

Jack Fritscher: Rex left some of his belongings and some of his drawings behind in San Francisco with Trent and Bob at the Magazine store where he worked for years.

> Trent Dunphy and Bob Mainardi, The Magazine, the gay pop-culture archive store, 920 Larkin Street, closed after fifty years in 2022 and is now the headquarters of the Bob Mizer Foundation, publisher of the revived *Physique Pictorial*.

Peter Berlin: I often used to stop in and say hello to Trent and Bob when I'm walking the dog.

Jack Fritscher: So Rex needing income has been trying to resurrect himself as a business in Holland. Then last year, I heard a couple guys from San Francisco, one a "millionaire," I think, have connected with him and rescued him, producing Rex drawings on T-shirts and in X-rated books. Rex now has a restored income which is helping him survive. I thought you might like to know how a person our age has managed to find guys younger who can produce him.

Peter Berlin: Yes, but, unfortunately, I never could survive on income from Peter Berlin. Like I said, that's because of me. I'm more concerned about other things, everything in life.

Jack Fritscher: Right, it's about the art, not the selling of art. Speaking of your life, may I go back to your roots and ask you about your famous uncle, Baron George Hoyningen-Huene.

Baron George Hoyningen-Huene (1900-1968), born in Russia into Peter's large clan, was a fashion photographer famous for his beautifully lit glamour portraits of Hollywood stars. He fled the Russian Revolution with his two sisters, Helen de Huene and and Betty aka Mme. Yteb, who were fashion designers. His lover was fashion photographer Horst P. Horst. He was chief photographer at *Vogue* in Paris and *Harper's Bazaar* in New York. In Hollywood, his name is reverenced as a peer of George Hurrell and Cecil Beaton. He worked closely with gay director George Cukor as a visual and color consultant for the 1954 Judy Garland movie *A Star Is Born*, and the 1960 Marilyn Monroe film *Let's Make Love*.

Peter Berlin: It's often written that he is my uncle. He's not an uncle. We have the same name, but our whole clan of Hoyningen-Huenes is very big. So he is maybe a cousin or something.

Jack Fritscher: One source claims he's your paternal grandfather.

Peter Berlin: I only regret that I never contacted him when he was in Europe.

Jack Fritscher: Why not?.

Peter Berlin: I knew of him. I knew his name and his influence. I knew of Horst when Horst was still living in New York. I wish I could have met George, but I was too young and very shy, and then he was dead. I saw something on YouTube, a documentary about him that said what a beautiful human being he was. Frankly, I don't think I would have liked him very much because he looked sort of what I would call sort of gay, you know. But who knows? Like I say, I never contacted him. Maybe I should have, but I never contacted anybody. Unfortunately, I don't reach out.

Jack Fritscher: Well, you were, let me figure, twenty-six in Germany when he died at sixty-eight in Los Angeles [in 1968]. I thought you might have had an interest in him because he photographed Marilyn Monroe, and you have identified with Marilyn Monroe's self-creation.

Peter Berlin: Yes. Yes. It's true. I think so much about Marilyn. She herself, Norma Jean, created Marilyn. She was not created by somebody else. I wish I would have met her, but I'd want to have met her as a person not as a star. I myself never want to meet people as the star. I want to meet them like you talk with me now as Armin. I never found that star thing interesting. I prefer the person behind it, and Marilyn would be the first one I'd like to meet from all the great names. She is on that level where there is no other level higher. Once, when you reach that plateau!

Jack Fritscher: [Laughs]

Peter Berlin: Like Robert Mapplethorpe reached a plateau of his own self invention. I don't want to come up with a number, but there are probably many, many, many, many, many other photographers as good and maybe better than Robert.

Jack Fritscher: Many of them think so.

Peter Berlin: So he made it, not, my God, that his art is so outrageous. No. It was ambition. Business. If you want to be on that plateau, you have to climb it; but I never climb. I feel fine with that. When you mentioned that Rex can't stand the politics in America, it reminded me of that singer Ozzy Osbourne who says, yeah, he wants to leave America.

Jack Fritscher: Him? He said if Trump tells you to do something, do the opposite.

Peter Berlin: He said he didn't want to die in America.

Jack Fritscher: He's British.

Peter Berlin: There's something bad happening here politically in America, and I am more concerned about that than the Peter Berlin thing. Peter left the building a long time ago. You've refocused me on Peter Berlin because Eric asked you to do this. I'm glad he did, but I wouldn't have presumed on our friendship to ask you because I don't want to put people in a position where they have to maybe say *no*.

Jack Fritscher: This is enjoyable for me. I always like our times together. Don't worry about that. [Laughs] I've always enjoyed our friendship. I just wish that as editor I could have convinced the publisher to promote you in *Drummer*.

Peter Berlin: I remember always you being so very nice, but because I don't keep contact with anyone, after awhile I lose contact. You live your life. I live mine.

Jack Fritscher: Mostly we've talked on the phone. Last summer, we had a two-hour phone conversation that I remember very well.

Peter Berlin: But you see, I have not even a clue that we talked. This is how bad my memory is. The only thing I remember is the time you and I did the questions and answers on stage with the audience at the Castro Theater [after the premiere screening of Fenton Bailey and Randy Barbato's HBO documentary, *Mapplethorpe: Look at the Pictures*, 2016]. I remember because there are pictures of you and me all over the internet and in the press.

Jack Fritscher: I love those [Getty Images] pictures. [Laughs] How you cuddled into me on stage and held my hand.

Peter Berlin: Memories come in my mind and then they disappear. In a way, I'm living without a memory. And there's something appealing to it, you know?

Jack Fritscher: Some things are better forgotten. "Some dance to remember. Some dance to forget."

Peter Berlin: On the other hand, while we talk, I'm reminded of all kinds of things. We are each of us like a comet with a big, big tail trailing behind.

Jack Fritscher: As the song says, we are stardust.

Peter Berlin: The older a comet gets, its tail diminishes and the tail is the whole history of our experiences. It's in our DNA and our memory. You, like most people, have a good memory, but I forget a lot of stuff. So, to tell the truth, for Armin the old Peter Berlin experience was yesterday, and it's evaporating.

Jack Fritscher: It's not just you evaporating. Even Polk Street, the street where you lived, is evaporating. The San Francisco we knew, like the Castro and Folsom world we knew half a century ago, is evaporating into the fog. The 1960s and 1970s were a different country. What did "Armin slash Peter Berlin" think in 1969 when you saw Joe Buck walking down the streets of Manhattan in *Midnight Cowboy*? You shot yourself in the 1970s as an urban cowboy wearing what looks like a boy's cowboy hat on your head like a crown.

Peter Berlin: I don't know. I didn't pay attention to movies then. I only remember two guys walking and one is in a cowboy hat. I don't remember anything else, but I assume I didn't like it much.

Jack Fritscher: One of the reasons I ask is that the film won the Oscar for Best Picture in 1969 at the same time as Stonewall while you were finalizing the creation of Peter Berlin. The first half of your *Nights in Black Leather* is as much a wonderful documentary of Polk Street in San Francisco as *Midnight Cowboy* is of cruising the streets of New York. In a sense, Peter Berlin was a midnight cowboy walking down Polk Street.

Peter Berlin: If only I could make a film of my life.

Jack Fritscher: You created your first movies just after Warhol shot Joe Dallesandro as the sexy lone-wolf hustler avatar in his films [*Flesh*, 1968, *Trash*, 1970, and *Heat*, 1972].

Peter Berlin: I don't remember Warhol's movies.

Jack Fritscher: Ha! Lots of guys who were there in the 60s don't remember the 60s.

Peter Berlin: One of the few films I remember is *A Streetcar Named Desire* because I saw it many times. I liked *My Dinner With Andre*.

Jack Fritscher: Which is two old men talking. Like now.

Peter Berlin: [Laughs] But when I see one film one time, it goes away. As for the *Tom of Finland* film, it's a good movie, but for me the scenes were too long. When the script made a point, I said, "Okay, I got it, I got it." I'd want a movie of my life to move faster. My own talent is limited. Looking back, it never has really been able to flourish and bloom.

Jack Fritscher: Even so, you've had an immense influence on several generations. Wait till the Millennials and Gen Z discover you.

Peter Berlin: My photos are remembered because their subject was honesty. As I told you, directing yourself creates a different picture than a photographer directing a model.

Jack Fritscher: What you call your honesty, I call your authenticity.

Peter Berlin: You should have seen me shooting myself in the mirror. So amusing. When I shot my double exposures [his famous signature doubles work, smacking of "twincest," which Peter Dubé who limns Peter Berlin so well in *Queer Surrealism: Desire as Praxis* called "the dialectic of look"], I had to remember with my bad memory whether I was supposed to stand on the right side this shot or the left. Little things. Sometimes I'd suddenly end up twice on the left side.

Jack Fritscher: [Laughs] What a comedy scene to put into your movie! Peter shoots himself.

Peter Berlin: Right. One thing I have acquired in America is a sense of humor. Humor is the main thing that gets me out of bed. I have a good friend in Holland. We've never met, but we talk on the phone. He is my age. He was in the diplomatic sphere in Holland so he's had to work with the Queen, and yet, here he is on the phone. He said once, "I like to listen to your voice because you always bring me to laugh and laugh."

Jack Fritscher: You make me laugh.

Peter Berlin: That was the secret best thing with Jochen. We laughed constantly. Constant humor and constant good life, and my God, what a good life I've had. Poor Jochen. But the life I live now is a complete 180 degrees different. If you put a reality-TV camera in my apartment to livestream my life, or videotape it, theaters full of people would laugh at how Armin became Peter and Peter became Armin. Like with the Peter Berlin documentary Jim [Tushinski] made. A woman in Canada saw it and wrote me a letter saying she found it touching the way I talked about my lover James as a person. After twenty years, James died like everybody dies on me. So my daily life now is walking the neighbor's dog every afternoon for six years, sitting on a bench, feeding the pigeons. That's a scene for the opening and closing of my movie. I had to cut the dog's walk short today because I had to be here for you.

Jack Fritscher: Poor dog.

Peter Berlin: And, oh, that reminds me. Oh, I have to get him. Yeah. Uh, do you, do you think you have enough, or do you maybe call again or what?

Jack Fritscher: You've been most generous and forthcoming. I think we almost have enough, but if you'll indulge me, I have a couple more questions just to finish our train of thought.

Peter Berlin: Okay.

Jack Fritscher: I think that as influencer, you inspired Michael Zen's film *Falconhead* [plotted around an antique mirror that sucks each sucessive owner into a mirror-fuck sex fantasy].

Peter Berlin: Did I?

Jack Fritscher: I know you were an influence, a person under consideration, for casting in the iconic leather movie, *Born to Raise Hell*, in 1975 because director Roger Earl told me when I interviewed him [in 1997] that he wanted either Colt model Ledermeister [Paul Garrior] or Peter Berlin to star in what is now that leather classic.

Peter Berlin: That's interesting. I didn't know. I'm learning so much today.

Jack Fritscher: It would have been perfect dream casting if Derek Jarman had directed you as Saint Sebastian in his first film *Sebastiane* [1976].

Peter Berlin: But I, uh, don't take direction. I know there was a lot of interest in the persona of Peter Berlin in the 70s and 80s and 90s; but I was always sort of, "there not there." That I'm not forgotten is a miracle because I didn't do anything to further it.

Jack Fritscher: There's that old Latin saying, "Vita Brevis. Ars Longa." "Life Is Short. Art Is Long." I think it is your art that calls attention to you. I don't want to take any more of your time because that poor dog is probably dying to pee, but thank you. Thank you so much, Peter, for your time and the pleasure of your company.

Peter Berlin: It's too bad that there's always mileage between people. I, uh, would like to, you know, to be closer to you.

Jack Fritscher: If only we could be in the same room again. I'm still in quarantine because of Covid. So I'm not going anywhere soon.

Peter Berlin: Are you at some time in the future going out?

Jack Fritscher: Until Covid ends, I'll not go out again.

Peter Berlin: I no longer travel. I'm living completely sort of like you quarantined only that I don't do it because of Covid. Do you talk to friends?

Jack Fritscher: I used to, but I'm like you. The close ones are all dead now.

Peter Berlin: But some are left, not dead?

Jack Fritscher: Not really. No, because of AIDS and age, there's nobody left. Everybody from *Drummer* is dead. All my "Black Leather Swan" friends from Folsom Street are dead. My straight friends from school are dead. In fact, many of the university students I taught starting sixty years ago are dead so I no longer hear from them. Although one survivor did email me last week.

Peter Berlin: Think of all the friends we've lost. Can you imagine the life we'd all be living now as old men if all our friends had lived?

Jack Fritscher: I think of that often. Would we all retire to Palm Springs? I try to keep them alive in my head and in my fingers when I write about them.

Peter Berlin: A whole different ball game. I think about it so much because I'm so basically by myself. Even with Reggie asleep in the bedroom. Not having a partner now is a very big problem in my life. It'd be a completely different life if those people we knew were alive. I can have sex with myself, but to share it is a whole different level.

Jack Fritscher: Armin, I figure those of us who survived AIDS have to live for those people who died and couldn't live. If you and I can tell their stories, say their names, that keeps them alive a little bit longer.

Peter Berlin: When you die and I die, then what is left in your case? The books, right?

Jack Fritscher: Right now in this moment, you and I have my words and your images that may survive us. We're both floating in a life-boat from the *Titanic*.

Peter Berlin: Oh, yeah. It's a similarity.

Jack Fritscher: A metaphor for the Titanic 70s party that cruised on unware of the iceberg of HIV that lay dead ahead.

Peter Berlin: I have so many stories. There are some episodes in my life like when I was nearly killed when some, some queen who was a mad queen, you know, uh, threw a sort of a, a, a beer bottle, a full beer bottle at my head in Rome, and it hit my forehead hard.

Jack Fritscher: That must have poured the bitters into *La Dolce Vita*.

Peter Berlin: Also in Rome, my interlude with [fashion designer] Valentino in the 60s is a vignette.

Jack Fritscher: Hey, another lovely scene in the script of the Peter Berlin movie.

Peter Berlin: It's a very beautiful little story. The Colosseum in those days was open at night, and it was a gay hunting ground.

Jack Fritscher: I know. I've been there at night. But after the 1960s.

Peter Berlin: Can you imagine? Inside that beautiful setting, people were cruising in the catacombs. And in front of the Colosseum, there was parking where the hustlers were. So I was in the parking lot being Peter Berlin and this beautiful guy comes to look, and we sort of start cruising, and he started talking, and I said, "Oh, you know what? I like silent cruising. I don't like talking." He said, "I have a friend who would like to meet you." I said okay."

Jack Fritscher: This is so Fellini.

Peter Berlin: So we walked out and there's this big black limousine parked, and then he opened the door and there was Valentino sitting there and, he said, "Hello," and I said, "I'm not into threesomes." But they gave me their phone number and invited me for tea. So I took Jochen with me. I said, "Jochen, I don't want to go by myself." So picture this very chichi apartment of this designer with his very beautiful, very elegant demeanor.

Jack Fritscher: This kind of scene is why Gore Vidal and Tennessee Williams and Truman Capote lived in Rome at that time.

Peter Berlin: So we had tea, and the music was playing. It was sort of a slow song I don't remember, but Valentino got up and bowed in front of me. He bowed! I was sitting and he asked me for a dance.

Jack Fritscher: Ah.

Peter Berlin: And I get up and we sort of embraced, sort of slow dancing, and I looked over Valentino's shoulder at Jochen, and I sort of rolled my eyes. Peter who was Armin who was Peter was slow-dancing with Valentino. Don't you think it's a beautiful scene?

Jack Fritscher: Yes, it is.

Peter Berlin: There I am, Armin, dancing as Peter Berlin with Valentino and then his friend, his partner, a very beautiful guy joined the two of us in the dance. He is still living with him. Now they're both very gray-haired. Both look fantastic because they have had a lot of work done. Anyway, that is the kind of a beautiful picture that I can see in the Peter Berlin film.

Jack Fritscher: [Laughs] I can see that too.

Peter Berlin: Yes. Don't you, when I talk, don't you see it immediately as a movie?

Jack Fritscher: Well, I was just going to say what you've given me here today and the way you've talked about these various scenes and the way you've thought about them and the way you hooked them together, there's a through-line here that's a kind of draft for the beginning of a film script.

Peter Berlin: Whenever I talk to people and they say they read books, I ask why don't you write a book? And then I tell them if you write a book in this day and age, you should write it as a screenplay.

Jack Fritscher: Exactly.

Peter Berlin: Because that is what people want. They sit in front of the TV and they look at Netflix, and then on the computer at my stuff. So if you write a screenplay, people are more ready to invest in that because it's kind of "in."

Jack Fritscher: Calling all angels.

Peter Berlin: But it's so good to talk to you.

Jack Fritscher: Yes. If you're not too exhausted tonight, take a look at *My Policeman.*

Peter Berlin: Okay. Today, what is it? Monday? Oh, Monday at six o'clock I have to go to that stupid tenant meeting.

Jack Fritscher: Right. I better let you go.

Peter Berlin: No rush. First, I have to get the dog and then I go to the meeting. So I have to record Rachel Maddow on TV. Or I can just watch the repeat at nine o'clock. So say hello to your friend Mark. Your husband. It's good to talk to you.

Jack Fritscher: Thank you, Peter, for your time and all your information. You've been grand.

Peter Berlin: Thank you for you.

Jack Fritscher: As a journalist and friend, I thank you. May I say I love you.

Peter Berlin: Thank you.

Jack Fritscher: Til soon. Bye.

Peter Berlin: One never knows when it's the last goodbye. *Auf Wiedersehen.*

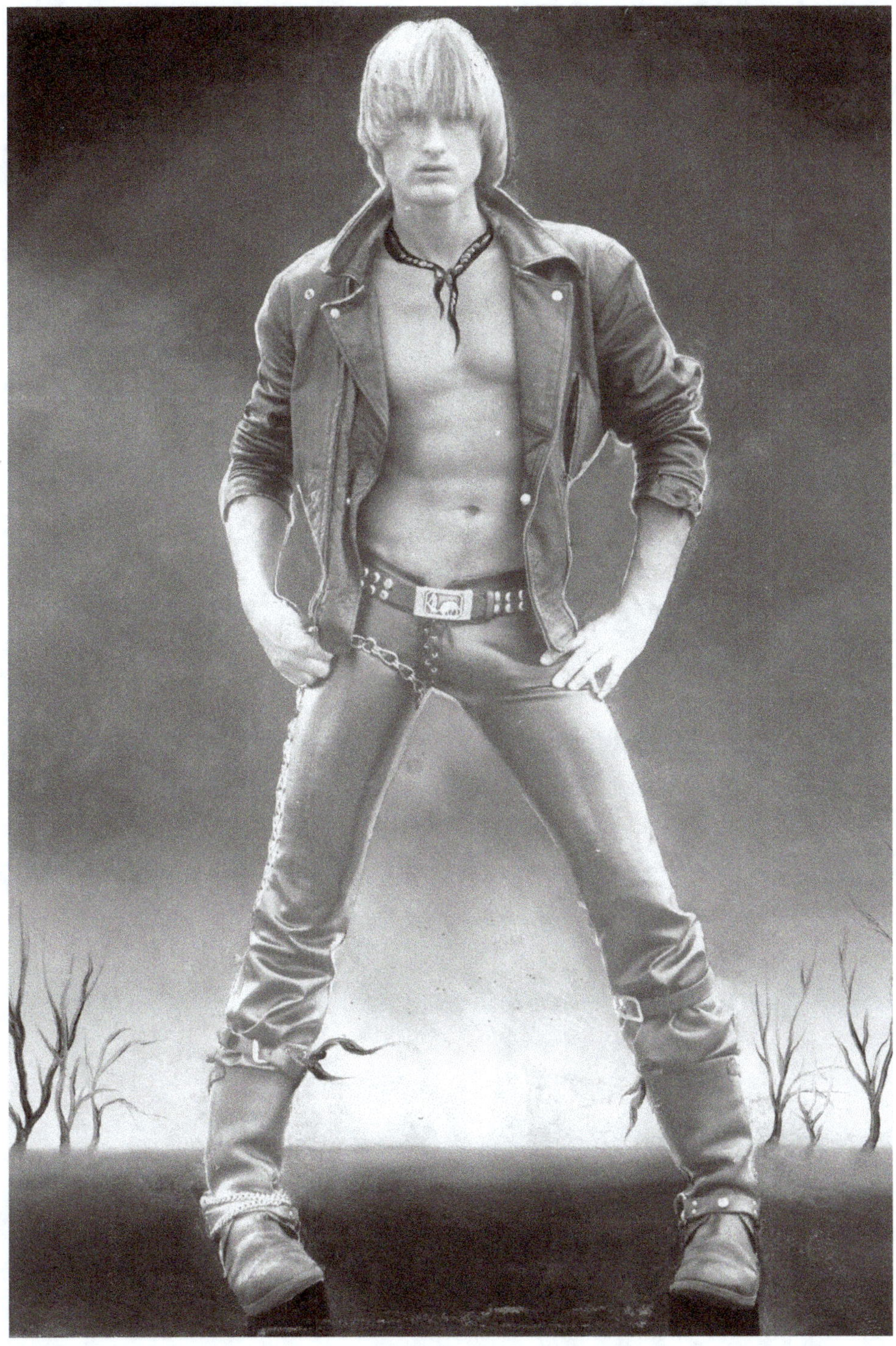

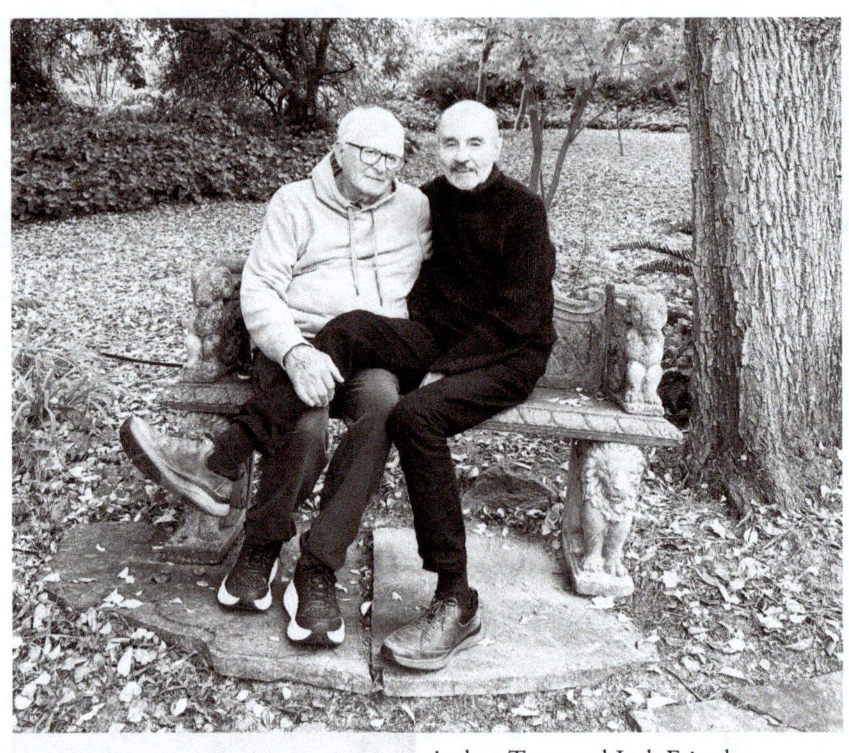

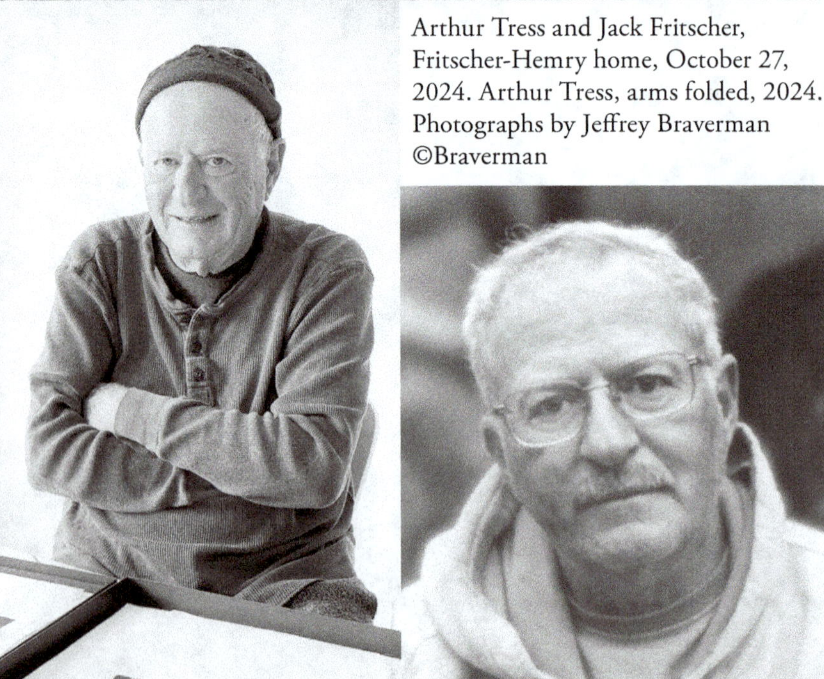

Arthur Tress and Jack Fritscher, Fritscher-Hemry home, October 27, 2024. Arthur Tress, arms folded, 2024. Photographs by Jeffrey Braverman ©Braverman

ARTHUR TRESS
Tressian Homosurrealism

"My gay life shapes my art."

**A Living Master of Photography
At Millennium's End
in Conversation with Jack Fritscher
April 20, 1999**

Arthur Tress: Hello?

Jack Fritscher: Hello, Arthur. It's Jack. How are you?

Arthur Tress: OK. Is this connection clear for you?

Jack Fritscher: Fine. How are you feeling? Your morning's gone well?

Arthur Tress: Yes. I took a nice walk on the ranch out here [Cambria, California]. We have about two miles of ocean front. You'll have to come down some time.

Jack Fritscher: Thank you. I've never been to Cambria. How long have you lived there?

Arthur Tress: About five years [1992]. I kept my apartment in New York for the first two years and then I gave it up to be here full time. Did you get that stuff I mailed?

Years later, in 2015, Tress moved to San Francisco to a home inherited from his sister, attorney Madeleine Tress.

Jack Fritscher: Yes I did. The clippings. The photos from your thousands of photos. Thank you very much. It was very interesting and

I've spent the last few days brushing up on "Arthur Tress." So today I should pretty much be up to speed on some of the mass amount that's been written about you. Also, for some time, I've been working on a series of eyewitness books of oral history under the series title *Profiles in Gay Courage.*

Arthur Tress: I see.

Jack Fritscher: It's interviews with photographers like George Dureau, Crawford Barton, Joel-Peter Witkin, Miles Everitt, and Peter Berlin as well as curators like Edward DeCelle and critics like Edward Lucie-Smith. It may take years to assemble. I'm grateful to be able to include you speaking your unfiltered thoughts as the year, decade, century, and millennium grind to an end in nine months. I'm taping by the way so I can't misquote you. Is that okay?

Arthur Tress: Yes.

Jack Fritscher: The first thing in my intent is to create text for a page or so of information about your forthcoming book [*Male of the Species Four Decades of Photography of Arthur Tress*, 1999, introduction by Edward Lucie-Smith], but the larger historical purpose is to record you speaking at this *fin de siècle* on your origin story, on your perspective on life, where you've come from, what you've tried to do, your reaction to the way the art world treats artists, and so on. So let me first ask your birth date. I figure it must be 1939 or 1940?

Arthur Tress: November 24, 1940.

Jack Fritscher: We're the same vintage. You're seventeen months younger. Where were you born?

Arthur Tress: In Brooklyn, near the Brooklyn Museum and the Botanical Gardens. As I child, I used to explore the Museum and the Gardens.

Jack Fritscher: Do you think those buildings, art and nature, had an effect on your work?

Arthur Tress: Yes, certainly. The Brooklyn Museum was like an old attic. It was kind of run down. It was filled with all of these Egyptian mummies, and it has an amazing ethnographic collection which is now more properly displayed, but in those years, it was just sitting in old cases. As a young child, I could just walk up the street and hang out there. Also nearby was the Brooklyn Public Library where I would spend a lot of time in the children's library which was a WPA project and so the children's library was huge and I would spend a lot of time looking at the illustrated books, art books, and things like that. And in the Botanical Gardens there was a Japanese Garden which was closed because of World War II, but I could sneak under the fence and I used to hang out there with some of my friends. It had waterfalls, but the waterfalls were turned off. I remember that we would play war games there, like hanging dolls and things on clothes wire, and we would play Hitler games and things.

Jack Fritscher: As kids during the war, we all played those kinds of war games, throwing rocks like hand grenades and yelling about Hitler and Tojo and "Bombs over Tokyo!" You were in kindergarten and I was in grade school when the war ended.

Arthur Tress: I just gave a lecture in Tucson and opened it up with a photograph of Cartier-Bresson [who corresponded with Tress] of bombed-out buildings in Hamburg which he took in 1946, and I was kind of wondering why I picked this picture out of all the Cartier-Bresson pictures.

I used to play a game with my sister. Even though I was a young child, three or four years old, the war did affect me. I remember playing Hitler prisoner games with my sister who would slap me as she "interrogated" me.

His photo, "My Sister and Father," New York, 1978. When the honorable lesbian attorney Madeleine Tress (1932-2009) died, Arthur discovered 900 of his negatives from 1964 stored in her San Francisco home. He published 64 of them in his book *Arthur Tress: San Francisco* 1964 (2012).

Arthur Tress: But the reason I mentioned the World War ruins is that later in the 1950s the Museum of Modern Art, the Whitney Museum, where I would hang out a lot, would have these paintings of these romantic surrealists like Pavel Tchelitchew [gay] and Eugene Berman [gay], and Paul Cadmus [gay] and they all used that imagery of ruined cities, bombed-out cities, and that affected a lot of my later work when I was doing the series about dreams. So I think that coming into childhood during that war period, even though we were far from the war, affected a certain kind of imagery that I was to produce in all those "bombed-out" buildings later on.

Jack Fritscher: How interesting. I was about to ask you about the special generation of us war babies. Any child who came to consciousness during World War II is a different kind of person than anybody who came before or after because the war was everywhere on radio and in newsreels at the movies, and we kids heard it and saw it and it terrified us even as we freaked over the images of the war: bombed cities, refugees, small children being tortured in the newsreels between double features of a musical and a western.

> "Boy in TV Set," Boston, 1972. At a time during the Vietnam War when sociologists claimed that violence on TV caused children to become aggressive and anxious, Tress said he created his powerful picture of a boy—sitting cramped inside the box of a broken television set with his big toy gun pointing out like a sniper from the missing TV screen—to make the point that media deliver violence from around the world to children who must somehow find their own defense.

Arthur Tress: Oh yeah, I've always had a fascination with photographs of concentration camp victims. Of course, being Jewish, I have a consciousness of that. My father's brother was a rabbi and he saved a lot of European Jews bringing them to Cuba and to Mexico. He's very famous for doing that.

Jack Fritscher: What was his name?

Arthur Tress: Michael Tress. Someone [Yonason Rosenblum] even wrote a book about him.

They Called Him Mike: Reb Elemelech Tress: His Era, Hatzalah, and the Building of an American Orthodoxy, Artscroll History Series, 1995.

Arthur Tress: He founded an important Jewish refugee kind of association [Zeirei Agudath Israel]. I bought a book by a German-Jewish artist who, well, I better not get into that because I don't have his name, but that imagery of the kind of persecuted person alienated in this kind of bombed-out landscape was something that was part of my childhood, of my family. And then in my high-school years, I started seeing this war representation on the walls of the Whitney and the Museum of Modern Art done by gay artists who were the popular artists of the time. This was before the abstract expressionists came in. So you had Cadmus's famous painting of the sailors ["The Fleet's In" (1934)], and some of his other works. Also Tchelitchew's paintings of children in the trees where their faces are hidden. This mixed in with stage design from the New York City Ballet and movie design like the film *An American in Paris* where you had these very de Chirico kind of landscapes. These all shaped my early idea of art, but I think I was unconsciously relating to those paintings because I was gay, that sense of alienated molding that you had in high school, being a gay person in the 1950s.

Jack Fritscher: You and I came out in the worst decade to be gay in America in the twentieth century. You calculated that you became aware you were gay around the age of ten.

Arthur Tress: Yes. I played homosexual games with other boys, but I could sense they were growing out of that. We might jack off together, measure each other's penises. They seemed to grow out of that, but I [Laughs]…

Jack Fritscher: …you made a life out of it, art out of it. When did you take your first photos?

Arthur Tress: Like all kids back then, I was given a camera when I was eleven or twelve. So I photographed my school trip to Washington, [D.C.], and things like that, but I really became a serious photographer when I was sixteen to eighteen and did amazingly mature photographs, many of which are just as interesting as the work I'm doing now. I was basically self taught. There was a little darkroom in the Brighton Beach Community Cultural Center and I learned to use that.

Jack Fritscher: Was your "eye" there in those first photos? Has it changed much since?

Arthur Tress: Actually, I go back and look at some of those early photographs. I had a little Rolleicord camera [a medium-format twin-lens reflex camera manufactured from 1933-1976]. And I would go out after high-school hours and roam around the abandoned summer housing, bungalows, and ruined amusement parks at Coney Island near my high school [Abraham Lincoln High School] and my home.

Jack Fritscher: So after school, you were outside instinctively cruising abandoned sites of the kind gay men instinctively cruise, and you were capturing images of your loneliness and estrangement as well as the fascination of the war imagery?

Arthur Tress: Yes. I would photograph kids in leather jackets who had pigeons on their roofs. I just recently did a photograph at the house of a model who had just finished college here in San Luis Obispo. I went with my friend Kevin and wanted to photograph these two college kids together. They had a microscope.

Jack Fritscher: I know the picture.

Arthur Tress: And the microscope reminded me that was the way I would try to seduce boys in high school. I would get them to give me a sperm sample and we would look at the sperm through a kind of toy microscope.

Jack Fritscher: You were already looking at life, framing life, focusing on life, through a lens.

> In his photo, "Elmer Looking at the Brooklyn Bridge," 1977, Tress shoots his camera past an obscured profile of Elmer's head as Elmer peers down from a great height on the out-of-focus faraway bridge through a big magnifying glass in whose eye-like circle the span is in focus.

Arthur Tress: Yes. [Laughs] The sperm looked like tadpoles squiggling around.

Jack Fritscher: What boy doesn't look at his sperm to see if he can see it moving, or see babies in it. I know I did.

Arthur Tress: [Laughs] I was very good at subterfuge. I just looked at *XY Magazine* and they have a sports issue with all these photographs of gay teenage athletes—runners, swimmers—it shows their names and schools. They are all talking about coming out in high school. They are practically campus heroes. They get elected prince of the year. It is so different from my experience. Some of them had anti-gay trouble, but…

Jack Fritscher: The world has changed. Guys now make sex "work" for them.

Arthur Tress: It's really wonderful. It brought tears to my eyes to read that. They are going to have their own set of difficulties, of course.

Jack Fritscher: Everybody does, but at least being gay may no longer be the prime issue. This change may create a different kind of gay boy and gay adult, may even change the face of gay art, because of that inclusion in society. Gay art is often based upon alienation and resistance and the existential otherness of being other. I recently dug out some photographs I shot when I was fourteen. What amazes me is that the angles I use as an adult were already present. It sounds like you find the same thing. Certainly, you, as a Jewish boy during and after World War II, experienced disintegrating worlds when you visited the shuttered Japanese garden ruined by war—and the summer houses in ruins. That kind of set the stage for your gorgeous work of gay men cruising the surreal ruins of the Christopher Street Piers where you caught us all like the endangered folk culture you shot in Appalachia.

> In 1968, ethnographer Tress had his first one-person exhibition *Appalachia: People and Places* at both the Smithsonian Institute and the Sierra Gallery in New York City. *Appalachia: People and Places* was one in his inter-related series including *Open Space in the Inner City*; *Shadow*; and *Theater of the Mind*.
>
> The Christopher Street Piers jutted west out over the Hudson River at West 10th and West Streets in New York. Tress also shot closer to his home preferring the piers at 72nd street near the abandoned Railroad YMCA with its 200 rooms where he took models for more privacy.
>
> In the way that sex in Samoa and New Guinea fascinated anthropologist Margaret Mead, and the Dust Bowl fascinated photographer Dorothea Lange, the piers, in that first decade after Stonewall, were an irresistible magnet of human behavior for photographers wanting to turn the free photo-ops of raw promiscuous lovely sex into art like the pier peer-group of Arthur Tress, Frank Hallam, Leonard Fink, Peter Hujar, as well as David Wojnarowicz whom Tress introduced to the piers on a night-time tour in 1978.

Jack Fritscher: Yet, in the context of the queer space of those abandoned piers, the decade before AIDS, you filmed a flourishing, vibrant, haunted life of sex that's now gone with the wind. First you shot empty ruins, then people in the ruins. As you grew up, did you change your angles, your way of holding the camera?

Arthur Tress: Actually, my photography has always been fairly straight forward. I tell my students, "Make the picture. Don't censor yourself about what's a good picture and what's not." I'm sorry that you don't have my *Stemmele Monograph* [Peter Weiermair, editor, University of Michigan, 1995]. The first four pictures in the book are pictures I took at Coney Island when I was sixteen and seventeen. It's mostly that I set up little still lifes. The photographs also have kind of a dark melancholy about them, a very surreal feeling, and that's what's been pervasive in my best work until now.

It's kind of interesting that surrealism really started in 1910 with de Chirico [Giorgio de Chirico, Italian, 1888-1978]. He was a gay man and later the gay scene became more evident in his paintings, but he always had these great long vistas with a great chimney or a factory chimney looming at the end of the arcade or a bunch of bananas. There were always these obvious phallic symbols. It was quite amazing. Within a short period of time from 1910 to 1915, he created these great "metaphysical paintings" which he called them—and then false realism grew out of that, although the French made it very heterosexual later on. Everyone has just taken his themes. The people who collected him were mostly gay.

Jack Fritscher: The passionate few create classics.

Arthur Tress: Yes. I've had encounters with one of them named Monroe Wheeler, at the Museum of Modern Art. [Monroe Wheeler, 1899-1988, partner of novelist Glenway Wescott, 1901-1987] Most of the curators and administrators who were running the Museum were gay in the 1950s. So there was always a very gay sensibility in that world.

Jack Fritscher: I find your sense of figure in the landscape to be, in filmic terms, very akin to the loneliness of Antonioni, the gay men lying on the beaches with the whales or seals in the background. You capture a certain kind of 1960s international filmmaker "look" like Fellini in the last scene on the beach with a sea monster in *La Dolce Vita* [1960]. Your photo of two boys—one on a rock, the other standing over him.

Arthur Tress: Yes. Both are wearing scuba-diving face masks ["Spear Fishing," Florida, 1976].

Jack Fritscher: It's a gladiatorial image out of the Colosseum where the phallic "trident" is pressed down against the bare chest of the vanquished boy by the victor. The sea water below them looks like it could be from Roman Polanski's *Knife in the Water* [1962]. These images, the frames you design, oftentimes look like stills from a larger Arthur Tress movie I'd pay to see. You are a filmmaker.

Arthur Tress: I think a very formative period was my college years when I ran the film program at Bard and chose the films for our Saturday night screenings.

Jack Fritscher: I was doing the same teaching university in Michigan.

Arthur Tress: It doesn't say so on my biography, but after Bard College [Bachelor of Fine Arts, 1962], I immediately went to film school in Paris for a couple of months and have made some films.

Jack Fritscher: It shows.

Arthur Tress: Yes. Probably an even earlier effect on my photography were the black-and-white films of [photographer Irving Penn's brother] Arthur Penn [*The Miracle Worker*, 1962; *Mickey One*, 1965] and Elia Kazan [*A Streetcar Named Desire*, 1951; *On the Waterfront*, 1954; and *America, America*, 1963].

Jack Fritscher: When you mentioned "pigeons on the roof," I thought of *On the Waterfront* immediately.

Arthur Tress: Definitely, because those were the films that we saw as teenagers, like *Rebel Without a Cause* that had homoerotic overtones because of Sal Mineo.

Jack Fritscher: And because of James Dean's own homomasculine image in the 1950s, as always, the worst American decade for being gay—when you and I were teens—and both straight men and gay men were butching up their own masculine and homomasculine images as gender declarations. I notice in one of your later photographs you picture a man leaning against a wall on which hangs a poster of James Dean in *Rebel*.

Arthur Tress: Oh, that's the director of the film.

Jack Fritscher: Nicholas Ray.

Arthur Tress: Yes, he was living as a kind of alcoholic in the East Village in a tenement apartment. I read recently, it might not be true, that he was having an affair with Sal Mineo.

> The bisexual Ray reportedly had sex with teens Natalie Wood and Sal Mineo and some sort of "relationship" no one wants to "recognize" with James Dean. My own feature article on the seductive eros of the closeted James Dean was published in 1961.

Jack Fritscher: The way you pose Nick Ray up against James Dean's photo is such a succinct juxtaposition of existential decay. He is very much identified with the creation of the iconic 1955 James Dean image. He even looks a bit like James Dean in ruins, as James Dean might have looked had he lived a long dissolute life like Oscar Wilde's Dorian Gray.

Arthur Tress: Time makes ruins. The camera helps organize the chaos.

Jack Fritscher: And clocks. You often include clocks in your work ["Electrocution Fantasy," 1977; "Blue Collar Fantasy," 1979; "Elmer Inside Clock," E.H., 1978], but the "clock of the body" is something that you use so well in showing a trajectory from very young people to very tender older men like your father. May I say your pictures have added resonance now because of the incredible speed trip of aging that occurs with AIDS. Your historical photos have become mourning *tableaux* of lives now lost.

Arthur Tress: Actually, I did my *Hospital* series [in an abandoned hospital on New York City's Welfare Island aka Roosevelt Island] in the mid-1980s. Around 1983, I stopped shooting models for ten years while AIDS happened. I only began shooting models again in 1993 after I moved to California.

Jack Fritscher: As the epidemic was growing worse. I wonder if your boyhood microscope experiences, counting sperm, might have been the beginning of your inclusion of technology in your photos.

Arthur Tress: Oh, I hadn't thought of that. It might be there. [Laughs] That's interesting, yes, that could be there.

Jack Fritscher: An artist intends certain things in his work, but once the art object exists, it exists independently from the artist in the eye of the beholder. How do you feel about people interpreting your art?

Arthur Tress: I find that my best photographs are metaphorical or allegorical and the more interpretations and feelings that people can bring to them, the better. I'm always very pleased with that. That's why my photos are purposely ambiguous.

> Examining a Tress picture some time ago, my husband of forty-five years asked me if I was one of the two men in Arthur's capsized telephone-booth photo, "Secret Conversation," New York (1980), part of his *Facing Up* series. He who knows my face said, "Is that you? That's you." In the 1970s, we all looked alike, leading parallel lives, sporting porn staches and clone crewcuts; but as best as I can recall from those hazy golden days of sex, I wasn't in that photo, even though the man sitting shirtless in the corner reading a book looks exactly like my look then when I first published Tress's pictures. To my eye, it even "feels" like me, like something that happened in a forgotten dream which makes it perfectly Tressian. It's not me, but do we all see ourselves emerging in the gay mirrors of his photos? The uncanny resemblance in this 1980 picture can be vetted against the portraits Mapplethorpe shot of me and him together in 1978.

Jack Fritscher: And that ambiguity is one of the beauties of your work because it allows the person to see what you are doing, and what your model is doing, and then—thesis, antithesis, and synthesis—take it to heart and enlarge upon it personally.

Arthur Tress: Yes, I do usually get specific feelings, inspirations, from the model and the location. I do try to include from their input some little psychological [narrative] "clues" when I can.

Jack Fritscher: I think that, like Robert Mapplethorpe, you transcend literal S&M and its conventions and make its rituals something transcendent, something metaphorical. Could you explain how you went from playing Nazi war games to seeing S&M emerge in New York at the piers and in the bars?

Arthur Tress: Actually, I never really participated in sex or S&M on the piers. I'd go there during the day because there was light to shoot. It could be a little dangerous cruising through the ruins at night.

Jack Fritscher: When you could fall through holes in the floor and drown in the Hudson River.

Arthur Tress: Even so, day and night, lots of guys, sailors, for instance, would be cruising and having sex, but everyone wasn't involved with S&M.

Jack Fritscher: I'm thinking of your many photos of leathermen. Instead of outright S&M, perhaps your photos capture the kink of sex, of domination and submission and bondage.

Arthur Tress: I'm very interested in images of things being tied and bound and meshed and the feelings that you get from that.

Jack Fritscher: What feelings are you going for?

Arthur Tress: Well, it's a combination of a kind of oppression with an escape to liberation in the background. There is one photograph where I tied up a model wearing Calvin Klein underwear—and *that* I did enjoy doing. I'd never done that before. It was recent. So I probably am a closeted S&M person.

> In Tress's "I Dreamed I Was Fit to Be Tied in My Calvins," 1995, a nude male figure lying on a disheveled mattress stretches out full length tangled in a bondage of a long winding cloth (like the linen cloth with which Egyptians

wrapped their dead), and almost a dozen pair of white Calvin Klein underwear—a gay fetish like jockstraps and condoms—slipped up his legs, hobbling him, with one pair masking over his face with his eyeglasses on the outside of the underwear. The title spins the popular 1960s ad campaign for Maidenform Bra meant to support women liberating themselves with the ever-changing tag line: "I dreamed I…(went back to school, won the election, etc.) ….in my Maidenform Bra."

Jack Fritscher: Perhaps you are. And more out than closeted. Personally, you may not be involved with S&M, or approve of this label, but your fans, especially *Drummer* magazine readers, find you to be an iconographer of S&M.

Arthur Tress: Yes, on a subconscious level, I guess I am. I did write a little essay called "Blue Collar Fantasy" for an image [*The Book Dealer*] from my first book. It's a man dressed in a suit standing and reading a ledger book spread out over a nude man [in a hard hat lying on his back] on the desk in a kind of Michelangelo pose.

I used to take my portfolio [his ledger] around to art directors [in suits] so they could see my work. You realize the power situation [of the business world of art] and just realize the S&M undercurrent of everyday life. That to me is very interesting where you're getting all kinds of plays on power and exploitation.

Jack Fritscher: Of course, but is that what S&M is? Isn't S&M *sensuality* and *mutuality* also? And *sex* and *magic*? Maybe there is an essential nexus between your photography, your high-school experiences, and S&M. In many ways, male S&M is the acting out of coping rituals that through magical thinking transform the bullying in high school into fun in the dungeon. I read you once said, "A photographer could be considered a kind of magician, a being possessed by very special powers that enable him to control mysterious forces and emerge outside himself."

Arthur Tress: Oh, I see.

Jack Fritscher: You seem to find something heroic in suffering, in masochism. In terms of Western culture mythology, you could be illustrating the *Martyrology: The Holy Roman Book of the Martyrs*. You have a very, maybe Tarot-like, maybe Christian, picture of a man hanging upside down in a cruciform position on a ladder near another man almost in shadow who is holding a pointed spear in his fist. It looks like he's getting ready to pierce the side of the inverted crucified man like the Roman soldier with a spear stabbing a hunky Jesus crucified on Golgatha. I appreciate how some very iconic Western culture images of transcendent suffering infuse some of your work.

Arthur Tress: I find a sense of anger in my pictures. It might come from sexual frustration.

Jack Fritscher: But you don't strike me as angry. Are you sexually frustrated? Or do you mean frustrated by our puritan culture?

Arthur Tress: Well, I think for many years, I was frustrated by my experiences in high school. Now I'm older, the situation has improved. So when I'm working with a model, I think I am sometimes acting out a kind of erotic hostility that goes back to my teen years in high school. I think one of my erotic fantasies was I could have sex with my straight fellow students if they were sleeping or drunk or in some helpless state.

Jack Fritscher: You have a lot of "sleeping beauties" in your psychological surrealism where you play the handsome prince and kiss them with your camera to make them come alive.

Arthur Tress: So on one level I'm still acting out that teen fantasy as a sexually frustrated person. I don't see these images of passive victims as negative images.

Jack Fritscher: Because you regard them like the high-school hero asleep or drunk and you get a chance to rub his dick.

Arthur Tress: Yes, well, that was the covert sexuality that was allowed to me in that period and I've been exploring that for many years.

Jack Fritscher: You have said that you thought S&M passions dramatized the darker side of the human condition, but perhaps this passivity of the sleeping beloved is almost like Michelangelo's dead Christ being held reclined in lap of his mother in the *Pieta.*

Arthur Tress: Yes, or Michelangelo's *Prisoners*, the standing sculptures where the figures are emerging from the marble.

Jack Fritscher: You have also said that you thought photography's function was to reveal the concealed even if it was repugnant to society. What do you think you are revealing in these photographs, overall, if you just had to capsulize your career in terms of the specific concealed thing that you are revealing?

Arthur Tress: I would say, when I'm really getting down to it, I try to release all the inhibitions around a subject. My own and society's.

Jack Fritscher: So you're trying to release inhibitions so that people can see inside themselves or inside the human condition?

Arthur Tress: Yes, but recently I've been thinking about a title for my new book. I was sitting around with friends and they came up with the title *Constrained Silence.*

Jack Fritscher: Sort of *Bound and Gagged* [the gay S&M picture magazine published by Bob Wingate's Outbound Press, New York, 1987-2005].

Arthur Tress: Which sort of fits all the pictures. But I'm feeling a little different from that at the moment. There's another metaphor for my own personal sexuality, and that's as an artist you are taking chaos and giving it form. What I used to like to do in backrooms at bars was go up to men and reach into their button flys and get them hard, and I thought that was like the greatest thing and then I'd walk away.

Jack Fritscher: That was you.

Arthur Tress: That was me. I came up with this idea for a title because we're using my photograph of the guy in the hot tub with his head emerging from the hot tub bubbles. ["The Deliquescence of Elliott," 1995]

Jack Fritscher: With his eyeglasses and his two hands breaking the surface of the water, it's a beautiful picture. His eyeglasses are steamed. He's up to his neck in water, virtually blind, sightless, on the cover of a book meant for the eyes.

Arthur Tress: Yes, I hope we use that in the book. I thought of a phrase called *Breaking the Surface* as a title. Do you like that?

Jack Fritscher: Yes, I do.

Arthur Tress: So I'm thinking that this wonderful virile idea of penetration, of going into something, breaking a membrane, but also rising up out of the water in a "wonder" sort of phallic way.

Jack Fritscher: You certainly feature a lot of water in your pictures on beaches, in bathtubs and hot tubs, in shower rooms. And you are not shy about male frontal nudity which is courageous in a culture whose ultimate taboo is penis.

Arthur Tress: It is interesting how accepted the female nude is. It's never seen as erotic in the all-world setting, but the male nude…

Jack Fritscher: A male photographer and a female photographer can each shoot the same nude male at the same moment, but one photo will inevitably be labeled as gay and the other celebrated as brave and more acceptable.

Arthur Tress: I've had a forty-year shooting career. I spent four years from 1977 to 1981 doing my first group of male nudes. I spent another four years doing my male nudes here on the Central Coast. So 20-25 percent of my photographic career has been dealing with very specific gay male imagery. And, you're right, it's true that my nudes are usually glossed over a little bit in the retrospective catalogs and essays about my work. But if you consider my overall work, I think it is important to know about my nudes and my sexuality. We often know very little about artists' sexuality. What did Picasso do in bed? What did Suzanne ever do? [Picasso's 1904 "Portrait of Suzanne Bloch"] Of course, you know all that about your friend Mapplethorpe.

Jack Fritscher: Yes, we all know quite a bit about Robert Mapplethorpe. Been there. Done that. Loved it.

Arthur Tress: [Laughs] His official biographies don't seem to mention what he was doing sexually with Sam Wagstaff, but they all like to mention how Robert and Sam collected American silver.

Jack Fritscher: Edward Lucie-Smith [British critic, born 1930] told me that Robert's flowers have importance and cachet hanging in somebody's dining room precisely because in the bedroom they have a fisting photograph. Perhaps your nudes also give *frisson* to your surreal catalog? Robert started out in the 1960s pasting up collages of other photographers' nude work cut out of gay physique magazines he bought in adult bookstores on 42nd Street. He learned a lot that way.

Arthur Tress: I wasn't doing that kind of collage work with male imagery. ["Father of the Bride," collage, New York, 1983] I got to my homoerotic imagery through a different track than Robert. I started with my early high-school pictures of Coney Island, with a kind of alienated gay loneliness which is my work from the 1950s. You will get to see this when I send you my book. I'm lucky. I still have my teenage negatives in good shape and I'm printing them up. I have several of them as vintage prints. Soon after college, I traveled for several years in Asia, Japan, and the work became a little bit more documentary, photographing different primitive tribes, people in Appalachia. I loved having that opportunity to travel. I had really no sex during those years.

Jack Fritscher: Was there any moment of revelation for you staying with some tribe, some family, some culture?

Arthur Tress: Actually, I've written an essay about it which I can send you. What I learned from my experiences with different cultures is the metaphorical connectedness of everything in their societies, the way they were connected to nature, to each other, and the little huts and sculptures and their ceremonies. It all seems to be of one piece. Most ceremonies deal with cycles, the life cycle of youth to old age. You know, birth ceremonies, initiation ceremonies, death and funeral ceremonies, which is the way I usually like to structure my books. Even that little book you have goes from youth to old age. In the use of ritual and ceremony in these cultures, the people are constantly moving between different levels: from earth to heaven, from earth to hell, to the underground. There is tremendous cycling of movement to paradise or to hell. Then you have natural God and demonic God. So you see in a lot of my photographs that they are always striving to get into these alternate states. Among these people in their initiations of boys into men, I saw these wonderful elemental gestures of birth ceremonies in tribal initiations when men are dragged naked through each other's legs and covered with feathers and blood and quite often semen.

Jack Fritscher: No disrespect to the tribes or you, but in pop culture how wonderfully *Mondo Cane*! All those ceremonies, all those rituals, reaching for the low, reaching for the high, every one of those primal things you mention seem akin to gay culture which is also very *Mondo Cane*. In fact, *Drummer*, the magazine of leather rituals of initiation which I edited for years, is very *Mondo Cane*.

> *Mondo Cane* (1962) became a global box-office hit and a camp classic with its ethnographic travelogue scenes documenting taboo cultural practices around the world designed to shock movie-goers in scenes of tribal rituals of sex and death staged or creatively directed like reality televison shows to enhance the shock appeal. Its beloved Oscar-nominated love theme "More" won a Grammy. In the revolutionary 1960s, the transgressive High-Concept of "Mondo" Style encouraged the media "outing" of taboo subcultures like homosexuality and S&M, and stimulated the eye-opening

and mind-blowing images of Warhol, Mapplethorpe, Arbus, and Tress.

Jack Fritscher: Your work affords a lens of analogy that helps explain why gay culture is looked upon as something primordial and separate beyond the pale of our straight American culture holding its nose about homosexuality. For all your photos are, they are also often psychic windows into the gay soul revealing what is concealed in gay hearts, minds, libidos, and closets.

Arthur Tress: I was involved with several primitive tribes, Eskimos, Lapps, tribes in India, mountain tribes, people in Tibet, and they all worship the horned god. It was a kind of shamanistic northern Arctic culture. Every culture that I would visit would have great piles of bull horns with which they would decorate their homes, or the shape of their houses would be horn-like. ["Boy with Magic Horns," New York, 1970] I was with one tribal group in India where once a year the young men of the tribe would wrestle with the bulls. They would let the bulls run in the streets, sort of like Spain. If they manage to grab the scarf off the horns, they get to marry the chief's daughter, or something like that. These are very ancient rituals. I tried to join in, but the fascination of being gored in the ass by a bull, the idea of penetration, was actually very frightening.

Jack Fritscher: You literally ran with the bulls?

Arthur Tress: Yes. For about ten seconds. It's very frightening, but at the same time very exhilarating. The bull horns also relate to the shape of the horned moon. When I did my book *Shadow,* there is a lot of bull and flight imagery. In fact, in that book I wear the mask of a bull and go into a bull's ring. Do you have my book *Talisman?*

Jack Fritscher: No. You have so many wonderful books that this interview can perhaps introduce to new fans who don't know where to begin with an artist as prolific as you. I mean in 1964, you shot a thousand photos of "pre-historic life" in San Francisco—before the Summer of Love [1967] and the rise of the gay Castro Street *arrondissement* [1970]—shooting the Republican Convention

[1964], the Beatles concert [1966], civil rights demonstrations—and that's just a fraction of your global career.

Arthur Tress: I don't usually mention my books to interviewers, but I'm talking about them to you because you're interested in my gay life which reflects on and shapes my art. That time I ran with the bulls was pre-AIDS. I was looking to get fucked, but to find a bullish guy to do that, well, you know how that story goes. So I turned to the arts around the worship of that animal. I found that kind of image in Picasso's "Minotaur" in which a very voluptuous woman is sleeping all in white.

Jack Fritscher: Like your high-school jocks.

Arthur Tress: Yes. And there is this great beast with a bull's head lifting the veil from her body. It's very much the metaphor for the artistic experience.

I use the camera in a very aggressive way. I do. I don't know Mapplethorpe's process, but when I start to photograph, I'm very impolite as far as complimenting, "Oh, you look great!" I don't do that. I yell at them. I do that for ten rolls, and I think by the tenth roll, they're all looking very tired and anguished because they've been hanging upside down for an hour.

Jack Fritscher: Suffering for art. And willing.

Arthur Tress: My new theme is around an installation I'm doing with the working title *Well of Sacrifice.* It's based on Mayan and Aztec sacrifice rituals. If you look at those Mesoamerican statues, they all have their mouths slightly open as if they're inhaling. To me that is the ecstatic moment of the heart being ripped out, and you see that on a lot of the faces of my models. I say to a model, "Open your mouth." My picture of the boy with the boat pressing into him? His is the sacrificial victim's expression which looks the same as when you have an orgasm.

Jack Fritscher: This explanation will help anybody looking at your many books. I've a note I wrote here that "Many of your bodies look as if they were dumped in the woods by a weird serial killer."

Arthur Tress: I know. We may use one of Thom Gunn's poems that he wrote about [gay serial killer] Jeffrey Dahmer.

> International British poet, MacArthur Fellow, and leatherman Thom Gunn (1929-2004) left London permanently for San Francisco in 1954 to teach at Stanford University. In his award-winning poems, he voiced the gay sensibility of motorcycle bikers, sadomasochistic leathermen, rough-trade hustlers, serial killers, skateboarders (akin to Tress's book *Skate Park*, 2010), drug visionaries, and people with AIDS. His phantasmagorical books, all of which could be aptly illustrated by Tress, include *My Sad Captains* (1961), *Jack Straw's Castle* (1976), *Boss Cupid* (2000), and his AIDS masterpiece *The Man with Night Sweats* (1992). Having known Thom since 1969, I eulogized him in my essay (2019), "Thom Gunn: On the 90th Anniversary of His Birth, a Memoir of the 'Leather Poet Laureate' of Folsom Street and His Pop-Culture Life in San Francisco."

Jack Fritscher: You stage and improvise so well within our weird popular culture. Thom Gunn is a good friend and I like your photo of him ["Thom Gunn," San Francisco, 1995] sitting in his kitchen surrounded by a collage of photographs on two walls holding what looks like a comic cookie jar of the face of the Man in the Moon with his ceramic tongue licking Thom's left nipple. It's almost a Hamlet-Yorick homage.

Arthur Tress: Yes, that's Thom's collage [of hundreds of pictures of men].

Jack Fritscher: Which prominently includes Warhol Superstar Joe Dallesandro. You also capture Thom's signature black panther tattoo on his right forearm [inked by Lyle Tuttle].

Arthur Tress: You know, the other side of penetration is consumption. When I'm dealing with the male nude, I'm dealing with models.

Jack Fritscher: Did you have sex with Thom Gunn?

Arthur Tress: No.

Jack Fritscher: Thom and I first did the deed back in 1969 and have traveled together and been friends ever since.

Arthur Tress: I've seen the [1978] picture of you with Robert Mapplethorpe in your book. You were very cute.

Jack Fritscher: [Laughs] Everyone is cute when they're young. I always thought Robert was cute. That's why I tried to include cute unstaged candid pictures of him in my book, and not his dramatized self portraits. Do you ever put yourself into your portraits?

Arthur Tress: Actually, if you're interested in my relationships to the model, we can get into this. I was going to write an essay on this—but I probably won't—about how I usually meet my models and so on. Different photographers have different techniques for getting models. I'm a little shy about it. I just can't go up to strangers the way Duane Michals does.

> Duane Michals, born 1932, age thirteen at war's end, widowed 2017, lenses his subjects in their environments and not in a studio. In the 1960s, he innovated shooting his still pictures like storyboard frames for a narrative movie or for a graphic novel as in his 1970 book *Sequences*. In 2019, Tim Sotor, a photographer friend of Michals who intentionally became friends with Tress, published *ForTress (A Book about Arthur Tress by Tim Soter)*, a handsome insight into the personal Arthur Tress.

Arthur Tress: He really likes straight guys who I would be intimidated to ask because I would feel that they could sense that I was gay and might call me faggot or something, but Duane will just go up to a waiter or someone and take his chances. David Sprigle dares to photograph mostly the kind of straight young types that he finds around Venice Beach.

> David Sprigle edited *Male of the Species: Four Decades of Photography by Arthur Tress*, 1999. In 2001, Tress's *Beefcake Plus*

exhibit opened at the Orange County Center for Contemporary Art in Santa Ana.

Jack Fritscher: That's the gay ideal, isn't it? The outdoor jock. That's why [photographer] Jim French moved his Colt Studio [founded 1967] from cold Manhattan to the sunny beaches of Los Angeles. No matter what we say on the politically correct side, if you look at the gay classifieds, which are really the gay voice expressing the Id of its desires, they all want straight acting, straight appearing, straight males who won't call them a fag. Or will. If that's what they want.

Arthur Tress: It's funny, most gay people today are so kind of "bland American" that they look straight to me. Very rarely do you see an effeminate guy any more. I mean, they're not even clone-y types, but just average Joes, which I guess is the part of the ultimate resolution [of assimilation].

Part of the problem when I shoot gay men is that they're more image conscious, more attuned to what is trendy or fashionable, than the straight models. They arrive knowing what they want to look like whereas a straight model is more a *tabula rasa*. Gay guys always have to construct an image to survive, so they're always projecting an image. Sometimes it's just awful because they're just imitating posing for you right out of poses they saw in some magazine, but I use that too because that's part of the process.

Jack Fritscher: Everyone wants to grow up to be a Calvin Klein underwear model.

Arthur Tress: So to pick up a model I'd go to situations where I think I'll feel comfortable introducing myself as a photographer. I might go to a party and carry my photo book around with me as a way of getting to know men. I don't feel that I'm that attractive or interesting on my own; but if I pull out my book, I can get people's phone numbers. It's a little bit of my personality that I feel that without my book and my photographs I'm not important or interesting enough to seduce or attract other men. I think every artist might also have those kind of feelings. You use your art to create more art and get attention. Perhaps fifty percent of any artist's motivation, gay or straight, is to use their art to get attention and make themselves more attractive to other people. The two or three lovers I've had in my life are people who showed up at my lectures, or people I've met at my openings, because you get that kind of admiration that you can use as part of a seduction and building of a friendship. So I do that. Is this interesting to you?

Jack Fritscher: Yes, please. It's the something new I'm seeking for your origin story.

Arthur Tress: So at events I will get their phone numbers. It does no good to give them your card because they will never call you back. In a week or so, I might call them and ask, "Are you interested in modeling for me?" I ask them what they do because sometimes that can be an interesting source for photographs. Like with the fellow who was a butcher—I shot that early image in a butcher's shop. Or I'll go to see what their apartments are like, if they have any interesting objects. Quite often, when I go to their apartment, I can find an interesting prop, like that stuffed sheep ["Man with Sheep," San Francisco, 1974] or the microscope or something like the cookie jar for the Thom Gunn photograph. Thom and his roommate [longtime husband Mike Kitay] had a lot of interesting objects.

Or I may find an interesting location here on the Central Coast where there are not many abandoned factories or empty buildings, although I have found some. I have some models who are very good like this boy Kevin or Bob Rice who's an older guy. Sometimes a model can be photographed many times, and some can only be shot once. With my early models, if they're available, I use them again and again. What makes a good model is that they're usually kind of athletic and they don't just stand there. They'll come up with ideas on their own. They'll climb around things. Sometimes when I photograph a man who's never modeled before, one of the reasons he might be doing it is that he wants to have someone photograph him jacking off. I probably won't have any jack-off photographs in my book because they're a little one dimensional.

Jack Fritscher: Not if you're using a 3D camera.

Arthur Tress: But I do love to see them take off their clothes. Sometimes I volunteer to help them get hard, but it's all for the purpose of playing together with them in this very creative, erotic experience.

Jack Fritscher: It's the art of seduction you've been doing with microscopes and cameras since you were a boy.

Arthur Tress: Yeah, but it usually doesn't make for very good photographs if it ends in sex.

Jack Fritscher: In other words, the sex has to go into the camera not into a Kleenex.

Arthur Tress: Yes. But sometimes if I've photographed a model for ten rolls of film, he's been climbing a tree, and I've been hanging from a branch. It's a little like the shooting sequence in *Blow-Up* [1966]. David Hemmings on the floor with the models. A bonding.

Jack Fritscher: We're back to Antonioni.

Arthur Tress: Yeah, and Hemmings didn't have sex afterwards with the models because he had a kind of creative camera sex with them while he was photographing them. Quite often, a shoot becomes a total experience in itself. For instance, when Kevin was climbing the tree, sex might enter only as an afterthought, but I never tried to impose myself on the models.

Jack Fritscher: People ask me all the time how can I keep shooting an erotic video with hot men sweating in front of my camera. They say they'd jump the model. You and I try to put the model's personality and sexuality, and any sexual tension between us into the camera so it shows up in prints and on screen.

Arthur Tress: Yes. That happens. I'm happy when anybody will model for me for free and will sign a model release. So I'm happy to use eager gay models who know the score. I think I might even feel a little guilty about using straight models because I put their photographs into a gay context. However, when I shoot a straight model, like teenage runners, it usually makes a better-selling picture. ["Teenage Runners," New York, 1976] I don't know whether I should do that or not, but frankly I don't feel too guilty about that. I show prospective models my photographs and books so they know what they're getting into. I find there is a new generation that is generally bisexual. In fact, I think my last lover, Vince, is back living with a girl. Some young guys will start an affair with you to see what they can get, but others like you as a person and, being gay or bisexual, they are not so bound by the straight social conventions. They have a little bit more freedom.

Jack Fritscher: In your works, I spy themes of flight and fall. An Icarus equation. You suspend gravity. You stage people upside down, caught high up in tree branches, astronauts who fall to the shore, to the earth ["My Feet in the Air," New York, N.Y. 1969]. I think of your remarkable photo of the boy sitting in the bath tub with the sailing ship. That could be the ironic cover of a twenty-first-century edition of *Billy Budd*.

Arthur Tress: Oh yes, that's the title of the photograph. "Saint Billy's Thesis."

Jack Fritscher: That homage comes through so clearly. In the book I have the photo has no title.

Arthur Tress: That's exactly what the title is meant to be.

Jack Fritscher: I know that we've discussed this personally, but your photograph "Squirt [Just Call Me Squirt, 1997]" is a fresh new archetype acting up in an age of AIDS, a very hot and spermy shot of soda pop and body fluids that points in a happy direction. I also love the picture of the man in the truck cab filled with flowers. "Squirt" is one of the happiest pictures you've done. "Squirt" is certainly a joyous side of Arthur Tress. It's a comic, vivid, and hopeful photograph.

Arthur Tress: I think we called that "Big Squirt and Little Squirt," but we're a little worried about putting it into the book because of the company owning the Squirt soft drink brand [Keurig Dr Pepper].

Jack Fritscher: But what an appealing ad. The slight blur of the nude athlete's body behind the plastic "Little Squirt" statue offers some "modesty." You may recall that Mapplethorpe appeared with [gay photographer] Norman Parkinson in a full-page ad in *Vanity Fair* [May 1987] advertising Rose's Lime Juice for Schweppes.

Arthur Tress: That "blur" has a story. Back then, I had this young lover, Vince, for three years, who's also a very good photographer and like many of his generation, he's in this kind of Nan Goldin school of photography.

> Influenced by Antonioni's *Blow-Up* and photographer Larry Clark's approach to bonding with subjects living marginal lives, Goldin (born 1953) focuses on the queer LGBTQ underculture.

Arthur Tress: Vince's photographs are much more loose and less structured than mine. He uses a 35mm camera and did all these kind of odd compositions. So while living together, he'd look at my work and I'd look at his work. He got me to loosen up a little bit in terms of incorporating accidental movement into my photographs. So there is also some purposeful blurring in some images.

Jack Fritscher: Which adds a ghostly touch. I think of your photo of a man being wheeled out of an intensive care unit on a gurney [part of his *Hospital* series] and you've caught him twisting his head in a blur from left to right.

Arthur Tress: Actually, that's a picture I did for AIDS when there were only 2,700 cases.

Jack Fritscher: And that blur is there like a gay spirit soul exhaling and circling a stricken body like a grieving lover.

Arthur Tress: Yes. I've learned to relax more and be loose as in that "Squirt" picture because of living here in California in a house on the ocean where I have these very expansive open views while at the same time I'm dealing with some of these California models. This is a very different world from New York.

Jack Fritscher: Thom Gunn said the same thing of how his poetry loosened up after he moved from London to San Francisco.

Arthur Tress: Unlike Vince's 35 mm, I do think its very difficult to catch movement with the Hasselblad that's kind of clunky. When you press the button, the movement is already gone.

Jack Fritscher: How long have you used the Hasselblad?

Arthur Tress: Forty years.

Jack Fritscher: Our generation's analog childhood has evolved to digital adulthood. Might you be changing to the new digital cameras?

Arthur Tress: No. I'm so comfortable with my camera.

Jack Fritscher: In the way that George Dureau shoots men who are amputees, you have men whose limbs you obstruct in certain ways or bend in certain ways that kind of reference broken classic ancient statues. You and he both fancy disabled men hobbling on crutches.

> After I published four photographs by Arthur Tress in *Drummer* 30, June 1979, photographs by George Dureau appeared in two issues of *Drummer*: issue 93, April 1986, and issue 129, June 1989. In March 1991, my husband, Mark Hemry, and I traveled to New Orleans to shoot a documentary video interview with painter-photographer Dureau who was famous for his exquisite photographs of black men, ex-cons, and physically challenged men missing arms or legs. In 1996, three years before interviewing Arthur, when George and Mark and I were in Paris, our video documentary *Dureau Verite: Life, Camera, Canvas!* as well as our video short *Dureau in Studio* were inducted into the permanent collection of the Maison Européenne de la Photographie, Ville de Paris.

Arthur Tress: My poses are a bit like that. But whereas Dureau or Diane Arbus or Joel-Peter Witkin start with freaks and freaky things, I like to take normal people and make them look rather freaky and disabled, hovering on death. I kind of deform them on purpose. I think it's more challenging to start with normality and make it deformed—or start with deformity and make it beautiful.

Tress's contemporary, Joel-Peter Witkin, a World War II baby born a twin in 1939, began his career as a combat photographer documenting the Vietnam War. Born like the Jewish Tress in Brooklyn, Witkin, the devout Catholic son of a Ukrainian Jewish father and an Italian Catholic mother, often shot on location on Coney Island: "Puerto Rican Boy," Coney Island, ca. 1956; "Christ," Coney Island, 1967. In their similar themes, Witkin's straight gaze is a perfect match for Tress's gay gaze.

In Witkin's 1982 photo, "Le Baiser (The Kiss)," he pictured two same-sex male heads kissing lips to lips in profile, but the heads that look like identical twins are actually one head cut in two for autopsy with the halves arranged face to face by the artist whose twin brother is the painter Jerome Witkin (born 1939). The photo created such an uproar that the negative was destroyed in 1983. Tress's own photo of heads, "Platonic Friendship: The Last Symposium," 1995, is two decapitated stone statue heads facing each other. The internationally collected Witkin is a recipient of the Commandeur de'Ordre des Arts et des Lettres de France. His books, like *Gods of Earth and Heaven* (1989), survey his work around the mythology of transsexuals, cadavers, and animals. When I interviewed Witkin in 1992, he told me: "Robert Mapplethorpe went out, as I do, into life's darknesses. It takes courage not to be totally seduced by the dark. It takes courage to come back in, unconfounded by the darkness. Without the dark side of the soul, there is no saint." In 2019, Soudabeh Shaygan published the case study, *Mythoanalysis of American Contemporary Staged Photographers Works: Arthur Tress, Joel-Peter Witkin, and Gregory Crewdson.*]

Jack Fritscher: You work so well with the textures of flesh and also the textures around flesh. For instance, your athletic bodies often appear caught in the incongruity of ruins of factories and piers and the detritus of the industrial age. Man in ruins. That's as romantic as it is existential. In our high-tech age, you picture men almost back in the heart of the industrial age and the collapse of the industrial age. I so admire how you shoot so successfully on location. Mapplethorpe stayed safe in his studio with exceptions like shooting outdoors at the abandoned bunkers on the Marin Headlands which are like a mini-version of the New York piers. Like an avant-garde filmmaker, you march out with your models into the midst of nails and screws and the falling down structures of our civilization.

Arthur Tress: Because of that, I got arrested for the first time. For lewd behavior. It cost me $1,000. I had to get a lawyer for the model. But it's a great picture.

Jack Fritscher: Where were you shooting?

Arthur Tress: I thought I was shooting in a fairly isolated place at Cal Poly [California Polytechnic State University, San Luis Obispo]. They have this area called Cal Poly Canyon that's like a big nature preserve with a jogging path through it. That's where I did the wonderful photograph of the boy lying muddy and kind of broken in the ruts of the road with the distant horizon [*Road Kill* series, 1974, a nude male lies in the deep ruts of a muddy curved trail]. We were doing fine until a girl jogger came along and reported us to the police. Actually, I saw her in the distance and I would have normally ended the shoot because I don't want to have problems, but what we were doing to get the picture was so good, I knew that we would never get it again so I kept him there.

Jack Fritscher: That adds an edge of risk to your work that one doesn't get in the studio.

Arthur Tress: Jack, I have to send you this video that deals with some of this stuff. These people made a half hour video about me around 1985. It's called *Arthur Tress*. I talk about the male nudes for about five minutes in it, but it's also when I was doing the *Hospital* series when I did fifty installations in the hospital. They were sculptures I made expressly to photograph them.

For five years in the 1980s on Roosevelt Island in an abandoned hospital with 500 rooms that Tress turned into his own pop-up studio and his own museum, he created "junk" sculptures out of antique medical equipment and spray-painted them to re-animate them to photograph them. As a folklorist, Tress says that descending into ruins he becomes like a shaman medicine man in an ancient tomb. For this project, he hand-made *in situ* hundreds of brilliantly colorful psychedelic mixed-media installations, very toy-like, very Willie Wonka candy-color palette, very Alice in Wonderland, very Disney *Fantasia*, very abstract to set-decorate hundreds of photos that preserve the "still life" installations that lasted only a few days and no one ever saw because of vandals and rain. It was his first serious work with color and some of the visual textures of the pictures suggest a pairing with the drip paintings of Jackson Pollock.

Arthur Tress: I like the decay and loneliness of industrial ruins. Like I'm cheating death with these little bursts of life. I talk about how I enjoyed it being a dangerous building and how I got very turned on by the danger and the fun of the danger, so I'll send you this. Of course, now with Photoshop you can "place" a model anywhere.

Jack Fritscher: We discussed image manipulation at the exhibit in San Francisco where you were giving a talk, and I asked you during the Q&A if, because you make your installations and collages by hand, will technology be altering the way you work, and you said you didn't really think so.

Arthur and I first met in May 1994 at *The Male Nude Exhibit, Vintage and Contemporary Photographs by Paul Cadmus, Arthur Tress, Peter Stackpole, Biron, and Others*, Scott Nichols Gallery, 49 Geary Street, San Francisco. Arthur was also represented in San Francisco by my friend Edward DeCelle at the Lawson Decelle Gallery (1972-1983), 80 Langton Street, in the bohemian SOMA leather district, South of Market.

Arthur Tress: No, because I can get the effects I want with very simple means.

Jack Fritscher: You do most of your bespoke effects [as in the *Hospital* series] hands-on before you shoot, not after.

Arthur Tress: Yes. I try to shoot my subject matter the way it exists. My friend, Richard Lorenz, went through my travel pictures and my Appalachia pictures, and he found hundreds of pictures of attractive, interesting men.

> In 1994, Richard Lorenz published *Fantastic Voyage: The Photographs of Arthur Tress.*

Arthur Tress: So on an unconscious gay level [his gay gaze], I was photographing all these coal miners, sons, and workers, young guys in Mexico, whatever, catching their innate sex appeal. So Richard also put together a second little book called *Male of the Species* which he showed to some publishers, but it never really clicked.

So now I've my early documentary photography that became *Open Space in the Inner City* [his 1968 four-volume series] which pictured empty places where children could make their own parks and playgrounds in the city. I was photographing them and abandoned cemeteries and factories—these places where kids could make their own vest-pocket parks.

> In 1970, the New York State Council on the Arts made *Open Space in the Inner City,* first exhibited at the Smithsonian and the Sierra Gallery in 1968, into a fifty-plate boxed portfolio in an edition of 1000 that was given free to schools and libraries.

Jack Fritscher: Are the photographs erotic in themselves or is eros in the mind of the beholder? People find sex in the underwear photos in the *Sears Catalog.* A fetish exploited by Calvin Klein.

Arthur Tress: You're right. It depends upon the predilections of the viewer. For years, people have been photographing children as in Steichen's *The Family of Man* [1955]. So my documentary photographs of children living in the ruins of the city became my project *The Dream Collector* [1972] for which I audio-taped children talking about their real dreams and nightmares, and then photographed them acting out some of those dreams like the boy metamorphosing into a tree while lying on his belly alone on a wet walkway with tangles of roots coming out of his sleeves ["Boy with Root Hands," New York, 1971].

Jack Fritscher: Your "Arthurian Grimoire" of role-playing fantasy.

Arthur Tress: It was children being crushed by cars or tractors, children flying, children being chased by monsters, children being suffocated by giant trash cans. The children seem very much like victims, all lying back, but it was a whole new take on childhood and really upset people in the 1970s, more than my male nudes ever did.

Jack Fritscher: Is our pace all right with you? We've been chatting for an hour. I don't want to tire you. We'll finish soon.

Arthur Tress: I'm okay. I have a new glass of water.

Jack Fritscher: Please go ahead with the children again in 1970, and *The Family of Man.*

Arthur Tress: So I picture the children flying against the sky ["Flying Dream," Queens, New York, 1971]. A Heaven-Hell kind of thing, dream-like states-of-being which verge on the ecstatic and the sexual as well as the Jewish racial memory of the pogrom, of the war. Many of them I photographed at Coney Island or in the slums of the Bronx. I never thought of them as erotic imagery. The pictures were making a social comment, partly on the archetypes of dreams, but also maybe on the state of children in the city. The pictures exist on both levels.

I've written a little bit about this, how childhood experiences never quite end. Since childhood, I've always felt, emotionally, when I would go to the baths or to the piers, that I was not the physical type. I didn't have that aura of sexuality or penis size or physique that turns other men on at the piers or bathhouses. I was a bit of a wallflower. I would say to myself, my God, this is just like high school again.

Jack Fritscher: Gay life is one eternal high school.

Arthur Tress: In my work, I think there is a certain amount of the angry nerd getting his revenge on the cool guys who back in the 1950s and 1960s were not thinking about relationships. It was not on the table for discussion. Back then, I really wanted to have a boy friend, or at least have sex, whatever, but it rarely happened. So I think there is a little bit of angry revenge in those pictures, you know, like the Nerd's Revenge. Sissy Spacek getting revenge at her high-school prom in *Carrie* [1976].

Jack Fritscher: The prom queen's got a gun…and it's a camera.

Arthur Tress: The element of revenge in that movie is an element in my photographs which gives them an edge. I know it. But don't want to admit it. Part of my motivation in shooting those pictures was a male thing. I wanted to show I was "one of the boys."

Jack Fritscher: That's one of the main goals of masculine-identified gay guys. Of homomasculinity. Driven from gyms in high school, we join gay gyms to prove we're one of the boys. A photographer is a kind of voyeur.

> Gay voyeurism is a factor of the closet where you can't be seen and all you can do is look. Boys who want to play must watch boys who won't let them play. Like spies, we pick up our cameras like guns and we shoot them, objectify them for the divine revenge of masturbating to their captured images.

Arthur Tress: Yes. And I did gain acceptance from some men and in the art world although not from Mapplethorpe [1946-1989] or from Wagstaff [1921-1987]. They would never acknowledge my existence.

Jack Fritscher: Don't take those two Manhattan islanders personally. As much as I liked Sam and loved Robert, and as nice as they both were to me, they did rub some people the wrong way. You were competition.

Arthur Tress: I like to think that Wagstaff knew I was as good or as tough as his little Mapplethorpe boy. But he never bought one of my photographs or anything. That caused me to have a certain feeling of alienation even while I had a desire to be part of that Mapplethorpe group, to get that cachet, to be one of those boys, to be able to say: "I can do all this just as good or better than you, Mapplethorpe."

Even if we're talking shooting S&M. I've seen some of Mapplethorpe's unpublished S&M pictures. There is a Chinese man who has a collection of his work that included a lot of his un-published male nudes, fist fucking with a lot of blood, penises all pinched and tied up and nailed down. I never did that. I was rarely that literal. My pictures actually have a more metaphorical poetic quality. They are, perhaps, a little bit more interesting. So there was that Mapplethorpe competition I worked around [as in the very lit-eral picture with the title pun, "Vice Grip," 1980, a close shot of the torso of a naked man squashing his hard penis in a giant metal vise grip].

I was, however, accepted by gay magazines. That started one summer when I had very little money and my friend Perry Brass [born 1947, author of *The Manly Pursuit of Desire and Love*, and founder of Gay Men's Health Project Clinic, New York, 1972] who used to write for *Mandate* magazine took me down to the publisher [George Mavety] and he said, "Do some more," and I was able to sell them for $50 each.

Jack Fritscher: As a note of comparative value of the going rate in the 1970s, that was the same amount we offered Tom of Finland for one of his drawings to appear on the cover of *Drummer*.

Arthur Tress: My rent was only $200 in those days. In the 1980s, many more gay magazines appeared. So if I could sell four or five pictures a month.

Jack Fritscher: A great cross-marketing scheme for you and for the magazines. At *Drummer* [with 42,000 copies published monthly], we launched hundreds of photographers, artists, and writers. What were some of the first pictures you sold to the gay press?

Arthur Tress: There were two male nudes: the "Hermaphrodite" ["Hermaphrodite behind Venus and Mercury," East Hampton, 1973, from Tress's *Theater of the Mind* Series] and "Man with Sheep" [San Francisco, 1974] which kind of grew out of my *Dream Collector* series, etc., etc.

Jack Fritscher: Which magazines did you sell to?

Arthur Tress: *Honcho, Drummer, Christopher Street, Mandate.*

> Arthur Tress: a partial magazine bibliography: *Honcho*: April, 1978; June 1978; January 1979; July, 1980; April 1981; April, 1983; *Drummer*: June 1979; *Christopher Street*: April 1979; *Mandate*: January 1978; July 1980; August 1980; January 1981; May 1981; January 1983; May 1994; June 1984. Arthur was also listed on the *Mandate* masthead as a 'Contributing Photographer" with a dozen other erotic photographers. *Drummer* did not pay Tress because his gallery sent his photos in trade, as did Mapplethorpe, to cash in on the international publicity of our big monthly press run.

Arthur Tress: And a couple of other magazines that have changed their names or gone under. Just a couple of years ago, I sold a portfolio to *Honcho* [June 1996].

Jack Fritscher: To Doug McClemont? He's a pal and a great editor.

Arthur Tress: Yes, but it's still the same [straight] owner in the office, George Mavety, a little guy with a big cigar.

Jack Fritscher: George is a nice guy whose Mavety Media Group publishes dozens of magazines. I've written many articles and stories, straight and gay, for him since the late 1970s.

Arthur Tress: So I was becoming part of that [magazine] culture which I had never really been aware of.

Jack Fritscher: Gay magazine publishing, you mean? It was slow to develop. It was my playing field. When the Supreme Court ruled [1962] frontal nudity could be sent legally through the U.S. mail, it opened the door for gay photo magazines like *Tomorrow's Man* and *Blueboy* and *Drummer* to be sold by mail-order subscription across the country.

Arthur Tress: Yes. Then I had some portfolios about "Loving Couples" in *Christopher Street* magazine [*Christopher Street*, volume 3, number 9, April 1979].

Jack Fritscher: Because you mentioned in your pictures there is often S&M behind the hidden psychological agenda in our daily lives, I thought you'd be perfect for *Drummer*. So on March 17, 1979, I wrote to your New York gallery [Robert Samuel in which Mapplethorpe was a secret and driving silent partner] for prints and permission, and published four of the eight photos Sam Hardison sent [March 29]. To your great acclaim, I must say.

> The four photographs in *Drummer* 30 were: "Boot Fantasy," New York, 1979, a naked man kneeling in ruins with his submissive head bowed into a bucket and a dominant leather boot on his horizontal back; "Blue Collar Fantasy," New York, 1970, a Black man turning the wheel of an industrial machine which adds race presentation to its source influence, Lewis Hine's "Power House Mechanic Working on a Steam Pump," 1919, that also influenced Herb Ritts' "Fred with Tires," Hollywood, 1984; "Sebastiane," a brutalized and smudged naked man tied up, hands over head like Derek Jarman's signature movie poster for his 1976 film *Sebastiane*, standing in a divine swoon among the burned out ruins on the New York piers; and "Electrocution Fantasy," New York, 1977, a naked man, gagged and blindfolded, tied into a chair in front of a ruined industrial electrical panel wired to a clock counting down to execution, knees spread revealing the vulnerable penis.

Jack Fritscher: Subscribers liked discovering the sex vibe in your work. They tore out your photos and hung them like sexy pin-ups on the wall. Your pictures have a certain sexual *frisson* not found in Mapplethorpe's pictures. Your work seems reflective of the actual leather lifestyle of ritual and kink. Some critics say your pictures parody gay masculinity with camp. I think your photos document the homomasculinity lived by a majority of gay men, especially leathermen.

Drummer was a homomasculine gender-identity magazine of magical thinking. The imaginative fiction in Tress's photos matched the imaginative fiction we published. His magical realism matched the magical thinking of the readers' masturbation fantasies. His gothic dramatic stagings matched their role-playing as well as their gothic fantasy narratives of power and submission in homomasculine culture. My goal was to promote him as I did Mapplethorpe.

I published "Men Under Stress, Meditations on Arthur Tress: Male Apocalypse Now" in *Drummer* 30, June 1979, our fourth-anniversary issue for which I shot the ambiguous cover which looked like an arm-wrestling photo that the readers understood as a coded fisting photo. I opened the introduction to my "Four Meditation Poems" on Tress with two short editorial paragraphs meant to sell the pictures:

"Manhattan. One Arthur Tress photograph is worth a thousand words; but meditations on Tress, like "Meditations on the Way of the Cross" expose access to the secret world of masculinity at once dominant and submissive, aesthetic and sexual, urban and urbane.

"Tress's recent exhibition at New York's Robert Samuel Gallery was hung as an insight into the night-time fantasy of 'Male Apocalypse Now.' Tress is a man of distinction, a real big splendor, good to look at when so inclined. Eight hundred dollars: the complete *Tress Portfolio*. Robert Samuel Gallery, 795 Broadway, New York, NY 10003."

Arthur Tress: Those gay magazines with thousands of readers helped my work be seen. Have I said enough? Is this interesting? I don't know. Keep asking me some questions.

Jack Fritscher: Thank you. You are very interesting. How did you manage to shoot your Ramble photographs back then, out in public, when gay men out cruising did not like cameras?

> From its opening in 1859, the woodsy Ramble in Central Park with its bushes and winding paths has been a gay cruising ground, fun by day, dangerous by night. The term "The Ramble(s)" became gay code for public sex by ramblin' men. The park's designer, Frederick Law Olmsted, chose the title-word *ramble* as in *rambling* because it means *wandering…* or *cruising.*

Arthur Tress: I'm glad you brought that up. That's an interesting series. That was 1964-1965. I lived at 72nd and Riverside. That had two interesting aspects. One was that at that location, the Railroad YMCA and the piers were right there. I didn't take too many pictures on the downtown piers, because we had piers and docks at 72nd street. There was a pier where males would nude sunbathe. I would go there and find models and then take them into the abandoned Railroad YMCA where I would also have props like abandoned vacuum cleaners. I had 200 rooms all with river views.

Jack Fritscher: That's like having your own private backlot at MGM.

Arthur Tress: Yes, it was a fabulous location…like shooting the *Rambles* series [in the 1960s] within the Ramble.

> This early *alfresco* work is published in *Arthur Tress: Rambles, Dreams, and Shadows*, edited by James A. Ganz, Getty Publications, J. Paul Getty Museum, Los Angeles, 2023.

Jack Fritscher: Like David Hemmings photographing in a park in *Blow-Up.*

Antonioni's *Blow-Up* features stills of the cinematic murder in London's Maryon park shot by Don McCullin (b. 1935, a straight British war-baby photojournalist who began by shooting bombed-out ruins), and production stills by Arthur Evans (1908-1994). Released in 1966 when Tress was twenty-six, it is a cult film based on Swinging Sixties photographer David Bailey, husband of Catherine Deneuve. *Blow-Up* became an immediate classic prized among inaternational photographers for the aesthetic psychology behind its then innovative concept that the artificial-intelligence eye of the camera sees more than the human eye.

Arthur Tress: At that time before Stonewall, people didn't want to have their pictures taken so much, but I would go up to guys and photograph them. I didn't send you too many of the images from that. People then were very almost paranoid and certainly very furtive.

Jack Fritscher: But that adds a candid *paparazzi* insight into the way we lived in the closet before Stonewall. You began as a street photographer [with his "Gay Activists at First Gay Pride Parade," Christopher Street, New York, 1970]. You capture the open faces we had to keep masked before gay liberation. Your anthropological dive into and out of the Ramble turned risk into revelation. Your pictures made us visible.

Arthur Tress: Yes. But for those there are no model releases. Even so, some of them could be published. I published one in the *Stemmle Monograph* which I'll send you. I titled it "Boy in Central Park" [1965] because I couldn't *then* call it "Boy in the Rambles" or "Men Cruising." [It is now titled "Boy in the Rambles."] I had to code the title. I had to let people draw their own conclusions. A picture may be worth a thousand words, but sometimes it's really what you title a photograph that makes all the difference. Anyway, I think I was, even at that early date [four years before the Stonewall Rebellion in 1969], trying to deal with gay imagery, homosexual imagery.

Jack Fritscher: You were a pioneer, a gay ethnographer living and working inside the scene, documenting the gay sexual underground a decade before Stonewall, before Mapplethorpe, before Peter Hujar and Marcus Leatherdale.

Arthur Tress: A little bit. It was funny how I handled that scene. The portraits were documentary, and almost more than documentary. I remember from those days that I felt the Ramble was kind of a labyrinth of the gay mind. The Ramble was a perfect metaphor. I'll try to send you some more of the photos. I had them all pulled out, but they recently got re-filed. I remember I shot twenty rolls of film, 200 or 300 photos. If I had a time machine, I'd go back and do more because no one else shot it.

Jack Fritscher: Were there any other writers, artists, thinkers, photographers who crossed your path?

Arthur Tress: Throughout the 60s, 70s and 80s, I've always shown my work to Duane [Michals] who has been very encouraging. He's about the only photograph/artist mentor I've had. I liked Eugene Smith's work and met with him, but I didn't show him the gay material. I showed him the documentary material.

> Straight photojournalist William Eugene Smith (1918-1978) developed the documentary photo-essay style in *LIFE* magazine.

Jack Fritscher: How long have you known Edward [Ted] Lucie-Smith?

Arthur Tress: I guess he last wrote me about two or three years ago. I met him years ago in London when Marco Livingston [art historian, born 1952] did my book and show called *Talisman* [1986], and then I stayed with Emmanuel Cooper [1938-2012, potter, painter, and author: *Fully Exposed: The Male Nude in Photography*] at his house while I was in London and he invited Lucie-Smith over and the three of us had dinner. But I don't remember too much else.

Jack Fritscher: Ted is a wonderful man and a great friend. Like you, he is prolific and much published.

Arthur Tress: Yes. Actually, I like his new photographs. Have you seen his own photographs?

Jack Fritscher: Oh, yes. He's given Mark and me a lovely stack as house gifts. In fact, on one of his long-stays, we took him on a photographic safari to San Francisco so that he could shoot in the streets packed with thousands of leathermen at the Folsom Street Fair. We kind of protected him, assured him it was okay to shoot, convinced him that Folsom Fair was a model-fest filled with guys eager to be shot. We met up with Thom Gunn and Ted shot Thom and me together. He had a good time and got a lot of good images. He wasn't particularly interested in shooting guys' faces, but more in closeups of body parts which reflects his interest in matching nudes with classical statuary. [Lucie-Smith's photo book of statuesque men and statues is *Flesh and Stone*, 2000.]

Arthur Tress: I think he's calling his new series *Men Who Have Just Had an Orgasm*. His models are interesting kind of rough types that he gets up to his apartment and photographs by lamp light, giving the photo a very harsh contrast with a blur blurring the expression. A lot of people have done that before, but it is kind of exceptional and unexpected coming from him.

Jack Fritscher: I've met some of his rough men. They appeal to him the way rough guys appealed to E. M. Forster, Tennessee Williams, Francis Bacon, and the rest of us bougies out slumming. I think of Ted as a born aristocrat, but he came to the UK as an immigrant from a well-off family in Jamaica. He says he's a bit of mixed race. So he's traveled across classes and continents in his own life. He's a great fan of the street hustlers shot by [Los Angeles photographer] David Hurles whose work with hustlers is his current inspiration. It's rather brave of Ted at his age [70], having been a critic for so long, to emerge as a photographer because it opens him up for all kinds of potshots from other critics and from photographers he's reviewed. He's a wonderful man and a genius.

Arthur Tress: He's selling the prints. I think that's his new career.

Jack Fritscher: It's certainly another act in his long life [as critic, poet, and novelist]. There is one photograph of yours that I must ask you about directly and that's a surreal image of a foot in a refrigerator with a filth-covered boy who looks like he's sitting on a kitchen floor in Kosovo. [The war *du jour* in Kosovo 1998-1999] You talked about Joel-Peter Witkin starting out with body parts. Body parts are strewn through your images: feet, hands, heads.

> "Hand on Train," Staten Island, New York, 1972, a hand emerging between the cushions of a train seat. "Hand," c. 1976, a hand with fingers splayed emerging out from the crack of naked buttocks like a reverse of Mapplethorpe's fisting photo. "Ancient Singer," 1981, a nightmare shot of disembodied head emerging from the ruins of a tattered upholstered chair sitting out in a snowy bramble.

Arthur Tress: That boy is Kevin. He's in a lot of my recent photographs mostly because he's a very good model. I pay him $40 each shoot. He's also an artist. He made a plaster cast of his foot and his hands. So we took the casts out to this old junkyard and covered them with mud and I think I put a little mud on him too.

Jack Fritscher: *Nostalgie de la boue.* It's a beautiful picture.

Arthur Tress: Do you think so? I wasn't even going to consider it for the book.

Jack Fritscher: Oh, no. Absolutely you must. As a card-carrying war baby you must! With Kosovo under siege now, it sums up this terrible warring end of the endless wars of the 20th century perfectly.

Arthur Tress: I would appreciate it if you Xerox me back ten or twelve selections of your favorite photographs. I showed that photo to the publisher [David Sprigle, Fotofactory Press, Santa Monica, CA], but he doesn't want to put any unpleasant pictures in this book.

Male of the Species Four Decades of Photography of Arthur Tress, 1999, based on the exhibit Tress was planning at the time (April 1999) of this interview: *Male of the Species*, David Aden Gallery, Venice Beach, California, December 3-19, 1999.

Arthur Tress: So I'm really knocked out and a bit conflicted. Insofar as I'm fairly insecure about the strength of some of my stronger images, I tend to go along with his safer choices. You know his books. He does those uniform male-bonding books. They tend to be non-controversial. They're very nice books but…

Jack Fritscher: His books are glamorous, fun, idealized versions, champagne versions, of a young, clean, and hot gay world of hunks on a never-ending shore leave. He likes the aspirational beauty of homosexual bodies in uniform. Many of your pictures, for all the spoofing of sex you do, seem to contradict that kind of frivolity and surge with an urgent underside that adds a bit of existential terror that intensifies the beauty of homosexuality.

Arthur Tress: Yes. We need to put some of those pictures in the book.

Jack Fritscher: Right. To reveal the strength of gay humanity in your work so that your images of men are not discounted as gay fantasy porn.

Arthur Tress: Yes. Actually, the Kevin picture looks too much like the photographs David Sprigle likes to take. As an artist, sometimes I know when a picture is good, but a lot of times I just do it and see what happens.

Jack Fritscher: What inspired you to do that foot in the refrigerator shot? It's so surrealistically "planned."

Arthur Tress: Yet spontaneous. Maybe you can't see it in the Xerox, but there's a real live lizard that came out and sat on the refrigerator which makes it even more strange. It sat there through the whole shoot.

Jack Fritscher: [Laughs] A gift of the gods to you.

Arthur Tress: If you could let me know ten or twelve of your favorites, I'll feel more reinforced.

Jack Fritscher: OK. There's one other photo I would like to mention and ask you about. There's a blond man [John Boyer], nude, standing on a block or box in front of a phallic chimney and he's twisting a piece of iron around like a rope.

Arthur Tress: It's iron cable.

Jack Fritscher: He's like a gay martyr in the Pantheon of Suffering Gay Saints. He's seems akin to Saint Valentine and Saint Sebastian.

> During the same gay-lib moment Tress was shooting these pictures, British artist Derek Jarman thrilled the gay world with his startling S&M film *Sebastiane* in 1976, reviewed in *Drummer* 22, May 1978. What collaborative visions of genius might have been conjured if Jarman had hired Tress to shoot the film stills for the boxoffice hit. In 1991, in this gay-pop culture masochistic genre, Joel-Peter Witkin—to shoot his photograph "Queer Saint"—arranged a sculpture of a real human head, skeleton, and penis, and pierced the composed corpse's chest with arrows to elaborate upon the martyrdom of Saint Sebastian. In 1996, Tress shot "Spinal Tap," a nude male standing back to camera holding at the back of his neck the top of a human skeleton spinal column that hangs down his back to his hips.

Arthur Tress: Yes, We're going to use that picture as a start of a fold-out display of four consecutive images as there are several more similar images of him twisting that wire cable. The shots are very interesting when you see in a sequence how he twists the coil around.

Jack Fritscher: That he twists the cable into a kind of heart shape is a great subliminal.

Arthur Tress: That's my friend John Boyer. He's a very good model I've used several times. He knew this abandoned mansion in the hills above Santa Barbara. When we got there, it was very foggy and cold; but I kept him up there for an hour.

Jack Fritscher: It's a wonderful photograph. You have many very fine "coffee-table" art books in print. Have you considered an affordable calendar to reach guys who can't afford a book or a print?

Arthur Tress: David Sprigle does do calendars. Hmmm. I should suggest that we do a calendar. He does those sexy kind of *Playgirl* calendars.

Jack Fritscher: Your signature kind of "beefcake" might have great appeal to young and old collectors on a budget. The images of your "average" attainable men compared to his unavailable gym gods might appeal to young men just coming out searching for relatable images on which to build their own identity.

Arthur Tress: Interesting. We don't expect to make much money off the book.

Jack Fritscher: Just a couple more questions. May I ask you about your *Condom Series*? What was your intent?

Arthur Tress: I'm trying to think how that began. Usually a series begins with an idea for one photograph. As happened, I had several little salesmen statues and I put a condom over one of them, and it kind of began to look interesting. So I began playing, buying lots of condoms, and putting them over the salesmen. The condom became a very interesting metaphor because it is like imprisonment and constraint.

Jack Fritscher: Again a theme of bondage—and the erotic fetish around condoms.

Arthur Tress: The breaking of the condom, losing its protection, has so much to do with our fear of death and AIDS. Condoms are a kind of lifesaver, but as I was putting them on these objects, the condoms were breaking all the time. Condoms promise safety, but are also a risky kind of thing—and controversial among people who react against using them.

Jack Fritscher: You were wrapping objects in condoms at a time Christo turned wrapping objects into an art form in popular culture.

> "Monument to a Tattered Hero," a color iris print in Tress's *Condom Series* published in Sprigle's book *Uniforms*, Foto-Factory Anthology III, 1998. His "Plastic Wrapped Man" photo shows a model wrapped in a plastic bag like a penis in a condom.
>
> Christo Vladimirov Javacheff (1935–2020) and Jeanne-Claude Denat de Guillebon (1935–2009) wrapped the Reichstag, L'Arc de Triomphe, and open land running to the ocean just north of San Francisco near my home with their *Running Fence* (1976)—panels from which were used to set-decorate the wildly decadent San Francisco disco party, *Stars* (1978), held on a re-purposed abandoned pier under the Bay Bridge. No one then had a clue that the white fabric panels were a ghostly foreshadowing of the panels of the AIDS quilt, some of which would be made from Christo's panels.

Arthur Tress: I've also put condoms over little fighting cavemen with the title "Weapons Ban." It's a kind of pacifying our raw instincts for good or for bad. The condoms became very interesting as a metaphorical series that deals with masculinity and it's also rather funny. I have a collection of some Egyptian mummy statues and, of course, they are "wrapped." The French have word for a condom: *Le préservatif.* Wrapping is life preserving. So the condom deals with all these interesting issues, and yet I was trying to work with them in a humorous way.

Jack Fritscher: I like your gothic humor. You have a photo of a model dressed as Father Time standing in the woods holding a scythe with the world of Mother Nature behind him. He looks very human, but he also seems to be the Grim Reaper staring at us gay men growing older even as our friends are dying prematurely of AIDS. You have a photo of a collage of photographs of Rock Hudson with a man in a suit and a condom in front of his face.

> Closeted gay movie star Rock Hudson died of AIDS in 1985. He was one of the greatest actors in the world because he made the "performance of heterosexuality" believable.

Arthur Tress: My publishers are afraid to use that photograph too. That we'll be sued by the Rock Hudson estate. What is your take on that?

Jack Fritscher: In this pop-culture age, artists sample other artists. Warhol does it. The question is what is Fair Use?

> Warhol based his Marilyn silkscreen, "Shot Sage Blue Marilyn," 1964, on a still from her movie *Niagara* (1953). It was a studio publicity shot so it was probably Fair Use. He based his "Orange Prince" (1984) painting on a photo of Prince, the singing star, shot by Lynn Goldsmith. For that use, in 2023, the Warhol Foundation was found guilty of a violation of copyright law.

Arthur Tress: I also have a photo of two older men holding a Judy Garland photograph. David is afraid of the Judy Garland estate. The man in the photo worked for Judy Garland and that's a signed photograph from Judy Garland to him. So I think we should use it.

Jack Fritscher: I think one of the criteria is: would it stop anybody from buying the original?

Arthur Tress: It's not like I'm using it as an ad for TV.

Jack Fritscher: It's not a commercial icon in the sense of the Squirt bottle.

Arthur Tress: Right.

Jack Fritscher: As a man now grown older, I respond to your longtime coverage of older men. In fact, when I edited *Drummer*, I introduced older men, like porn actor Richard Locke, into our pages as Daddies. Actually, it was inside the issue I made with the Mapplethorpe cover [featuring his portrait of a seasoned leatherman biker, *Drummer* 24, September 1978]. Our readers liked *Drummer* daring to break the age ceiling in gay publishing. Very few gay men remain twenty-four with a twenty-eight-inch waist forever. Daddies are now a fetish of their own.

Arthur Tress: Yes, and I think when you're younger, when I was younger, in the gay world, I was looking for a kind of father figure to replace my father.

> Tress, ever the Telemachus, shot a remarkable homage to older men picturing in his *Theater of the Mind* series his father sitting like King Lear on a throne-like chair bundled up in winter clothes in a deserted snowy woods in his "Last Portrait of My Father," New York, 1978. The picture with its setting and season so similar to Ingmar Bergman's Swedish films *Wild Strawberries* and *The Seventh Seal* (1957) pairs with his "Death Fantasy" aka "Young Boy and Hooded Figure," New York, 1971. It's a magical realism photo from *The Dream Collector* series picturing a child standing trapped on a creepy deserted path in a barren winter landscape with his very white face peering out from under the very black cloak of Death with Death's cold white hands holding the child's body and soul in place against his legs.

Arthur Tress: I was never successful at replacing my father. Is anyone? As I've become older, my relationships are mostly with the young people who are attracted to me, younger guys like Vince. So I've become a more fatherly mentor type. But that's a very complex relationship, especially when mixed with sexuality.

Jack Fritscher: Essentially, your work ranges from young men to older men. Your mythology goes from Apollo to Zeus. That is wonderful to see because during AIDS so many gay men have died young with no chance to grow old alongside us. AIDS has robbed us of the pleasure of their company.

Arthur Tress: And here we are.

Jack Fritscher: One last question about sampling art and gay men dying young. I think I see James Dean, or a James Dean look-alike, in one of your condom photographs. He's wearing glasses with the open necks of sperm-filled condoms attached around both lenses and hanging down below his cheeks. His mouth looks prissy with lipstick. You may have altered the mouth as an androgynous comment, but the hair looks like Dean.

Arthur Tress: That's just a painting I found at a flea market.

Jack Fritscher: So you worked with it. Made it subversive. You surrounded the painting with the keys of a typewriter keyboard, and draped the face's eyeglasses with condoms.

> In the 1970s, condoms were sex toys used for fetish play during sex. They were especially popular at piss parties and in breath-control scenes. Some fetish men haunted Lovers Lanes where straight men tossed used condoms from parked car windows out into the bushes. The artist Rex for his April 8-19, 1978 exhibit, *Rex Originals* at Fey-Way Gallery in San Francisco, sent out handmade invitations on card stock printed with one of his condom drawings to which he attached a fresh unrolled condom. The September 1978 special issue of *Drummer* titled *Son of Drummer* published my photo series of "condoms as fetish" in the photo feature "Rude Rubbers."

Arthur Tress: Yeah. That's meant to be another "high-school" image. That photograph is called "Encrypted Message" [Cambria, 1996].

Jack Fritscher: Yes. Is it like graffiti in the boy's toilet? The [eight scrambled] typewriter keys you pasted in collage on his forehead spell out "Love D-ck." Did you not have a key for the letter "i"?

Arthur Tress: You look at the picture and you think it says, "I Love Dick."

Jack Fritscher: I couldn't break the code of what the rest of the keys spelled.

Arthur Tress: They don't mean anything. [Laughs] I just didn't have enough keys. I have shot some older men for *Bear* magazine [specializing in hairy Daddies]. I also have an interesting photograph of an older man on a bed with a younger boy sitting up, and it says, "I love daddy." I think that's an interesting photograph because of the amazing love that this man has for his boy—Larry or Randy or somebody—but despite all the boy's many problems, drugs, drinking, running off with girls, the older man exhibits patience because he's deeply in love with the guy. It's just amazing. At the very end of the new book, we're going to use the photograph of the men standing at the urinal.

Jack Fritscher: I love that picture. How we live. So real.

Arthur Tress: I shot it at the New York Public Library.

Jack Fritscher: Did you stage that?

Arthur Tress: No.

Jack Fritscher: You found them standing there waiting at the urinal?

Arthur Tress: Yes.

Jack Fritscher: No wonder it feels so real.

Arthur Tress: I went into the toilet intending to shoot this older man, Elmer, who I hired once again to be my model, and these other two men were already standing there cruising. Elmer's in the middle. I just directed him to go and stand there between the two who played along. So the picture is partially staged.

Jack Fritscher: That cruising scene now long gone, killed by security cameras.

Arthur Tress: We may use it as the last image of the book, but again, perhaps not. It may be too dark containing a message about the sadness of the human condition that we all end up lonely and gray and looking for love.

Jack Fritscher: Standing in a toilet stall looking for connection? Now *that's* surreal. We're all veterans of the gay-lib wars standing at a urinal waiting like Godot for the next trick to arrive. Finishing up with age, could you please tell me the story of how you shot your father in the chair in the park and then shot yourself in the same chair in Palm Springs.

Arthur Tress: I hope the Fax I sent you was clear enough.

> In 1999, at the time of this interview, people were just beginning to sign up for email addresses.

Jack Fritscher: Yes, it was. I understand the picture, but I'd like you to talk about the picture so we can collect here in one place how you shot your father.

Arthur Tress: I lived at 2 Riverside Drive and my father lived at 46 Riverside Drive. I always liked that neighborhood and wanted to be near my father. He remarried in his 60s. When he was in his 70s, his health began to fail. That chair was in my apartment. That was the chair I sat in all the time. It was my desk chair. I took it out to Riverside Drive Park and called my father during this snow storm and asked my father to sit in it in the snow. It's kind of James Joycean.

Jack Fritscher: Joycean. Freudian. Jungian. Bergmanian.

Arthur Tress: The snow is falling on him. People feel it's one of my strongest images.

Jack Fritscher: Its gathered *memento mori* intensity reminds me of Robert Frost's sublime "Stopping by Woods on a Snowy Evening."

Arthur Tress: It's in a couple of museums. That one frame contains all my feelings for my father and my concerns about his age and health. I had mixed feelings of sympathy and horror, morbidity and attraction and avoidance. When I left New York for California, I gave the chair to some friends in the East Village who themselves have recently moved out to Palm Springs and brought the chair with them. When I found that out about a month ago, I took the chair out to the desert and photographed myself in the same chair as though I was becoming my father. But being only fifty-eight, I decided I'm not really ready to sit in this chair like my father. So I shot myself sitting naked in the desert and it's freezing cold. Fifty degrees and the wind is blowing. I see what I'm putting my models through. But what I did in addition to sitting, I stood alongside the chair and tilted it over like I was angry at it and didn't want to sit in it. I think I'm rebelling in a way against sitting in that chair. I don't know how the pictures are going to come out.

Jack Fritscher: It's a great pairing of Tresses. Your father sitting in the snow. You refusing to sit in the chair in the desert. Both of you feeling the cold. Your own private *Le Morte d'Arthur*.

Arthur Tress: [Laughs] I began sitting in the chair and then thought, I'm getting out of it. I was hiding my belly.

Jack Fritscher: To sum up, you're doing Jung's dreams and Freud's acts in much of your work which is so very archetypal in dream material and so Freudian in dramatization. Arthur, I'm going quick through my notes here. You also channel [psychiatrist] Hermann Rorschach in the shadow "inkblots" ["Shadow Graphs," 1974] of hundreds of your photos like your 1970s series *Transformation* [and *Illumination* and *Magic Flight* and *Calls and Messages* and *The Ancestors*]. You also connect food and sex. I see pictures of naked men with pestles, and grain stuck to the outside of human bodies, and two men standing in a kitchen, with knives, themes of castration next to heavy-duty industrial equipment. When I first wrote about your work in *Drummer* [1978], I called it "Industrial Sex."

Arthur Tress: Oh yeah. That's kind of an interesting term for shooting people in abandoned factories, which I don't really do too much anymore because so many people are doing the male nude now, shooting them in urban ruins. Also there really are no abandoned factories around here [Cambria, California], but there are instead a lot of suburban houses, the suburban kitchen, these gay men with their knives, ovens, and garages filled with all their garden machinery. That's the new gay frontier. One of the guys I shot did have a tractor, a real one. Well, we've been doing this for two hours.

Jack Fritscher: Yes. What good stuff. New info at century's end. Thank you very much.

Arthur Tress: I'm going to send you this video, if you're interested.

Jack Fritscher: Oh yes. I'd love to see it. Perhaps you can tell I've read everything you sent me.

Arthur Tress: Yes. Yes, you have. That's great. Thank you.

Jack Fritscher: Thank you for taking the effort to send so much background material and also for the prints. I think the picture of the muscle man on the ladder is extremely wonderful ["Caution: Man at Work (Nude Construction Worker Clad Only in Boots Climbs Ladder)," 1995]. Now that's a calendar picture [as emblematic as Herb Ritts' "Fred with Tires," Hollywood, 1984].

Arthur Tress: Send me a list of ten or twelve that you like so you can write about them if you wish. I can send you some of the little more oddball ones that we've edited out of the book, even though I can, if I really want, insist on certain pictures.

Jack Fritscher: Arthur, thank you so much.

Arthur Tress: Thank you so much. Have a great day.

Jack Fritscher: That was Arthur Tress. April 20, 1999.

The handsome Crawford Barton, the prolific street photographer of Castro Street men in the Titanic 1970s, published his homomasculine book *Beautiful Men* during the American Bicentennial in 1976.

In 1994, in homage to Barton's iconography, Mark Thompson, editor *emeritus* of *The Advocate* published *Crawford Barton: Days of Hope: 1970s Gay San Francisco*, Gay Men's Press (GMP), London

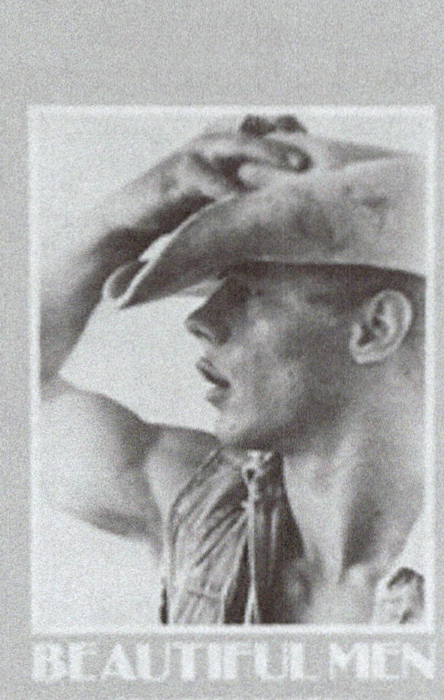

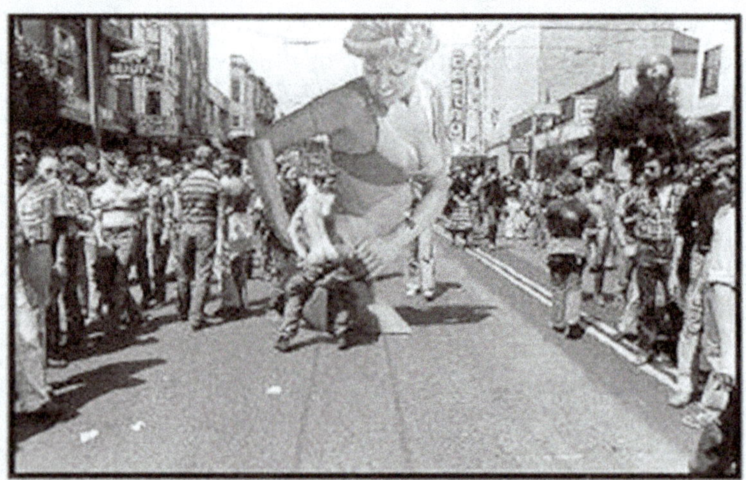

CRAWFORD BARTON
(June 2, 1943 - June 12, 1993)

San Francisco Photographer
of *Beautiful Men*

In Conversation with Jack Fritscher
October 2, 1990

"You can see anything
by looking out your front door in San Francisco."
—Crawford Barton

Crawford Barton: Is this the Fritscher dude?

Jack Fritscher: Is this the Barton dude?

Crawford Barton: How are you? I'm scorching over here sitting around in my underwear. What's happened to the weather in San Francisco?

Jack Fritscher: I'm nice and cool up here north of the Golden Gate Bridge. Are you having a good weekend?

Crawford Barton: I should have gone ahead and talked with you yesterday instead of going into the dark room. It was one of those days when I couldn't get anything to go right and I got really frustrated. I get funny right before the full moon sometimes. I really felt it yesterday and last night. Yesterday morning I thought everything was okay, but I had a lot of trouble getting out of the house. Because I haven't had my own dark room in years, I belong to the Harvey Milk facility. Everyone I met wanted to yakety-yak. Rink [as Rink Foto since 1960, documentary photographer of art, social, and political events] was there.

Jack Fritscher: I haven't talked to Rink in about a week. He's such a man about town. He's always full of news and dish when he calls on the phone. He sent some really interesting photos he shot of Robert and me together at the Lawson-DeCelle gallery that he hopes to sell to the publisher of the Mapplethorpe book I'm writing.

Crawford Barton: Are you going to tape this?

Jack Fritscher: Yes. If that's okay?

Crawford Barton: Yes. Do you send copies to the interviewee?

Jack Fritscher: I always do.

Crawford Barton: Do you want this to be totally spontaneous, and done now? If I think of something later, should I send you a note?

Jack Fritscher: We can talk again whenever and add what you wish. Be spontaneous. I have a few questions.

Crawford Barton: I have a sinus allergy condition and you'll have to put up with me clearing my throat and coughing.

Jack Fritscher: Everyone I've talked to in California this week has been on antihistamines. Would you like to begin? Or would you like me to ask you a leading question?

> The photo book, *Days of Hope: Crawford Barton Photos*, edited by Mark Thompson, was published posthumously in 1994 by Editions Aubrey Walter, London, and, as a portal to the past, constitutes a collector's gallery guide and reference survey of his work. Where possible in this interview, Barton's photos presenting gay men's bodies are listed by title and page number in *Days of Hope*: *DOH*. To clarify many of his photos which are untitled, descriptive "titles" have been added to aid the reader searching the internet. For instance, his 1977 *Castro Street Scene* series having few individual titles often appears as individual frames titled "Castro Street Scene" minus subtitle or specific description like "Castro Street Scene, Two Couples (a kiss on the steps)," 1977.

Barton captured the evolution of the gay male look from 1960s long-haired hippie to 1970s crewcut Castro clone. In his 1976 book *Beautiful Men*, his come-and-get-it homomasculine photo of a shirtless, hairy-chested, bearded, curly-headed hunk standing hands on hips beneath the Golden Gate Bridge, backed by a high-breaking wave, references gay icon Kim Novak standing below the Bridge in Alfred Hitchcock's *Vertigo.*

It has all the jazz and jizz of a gay Tourist Bureau poster celebrating the City. To the gay gaze and the queer eye, it shows how orgasmic it felt, explosive as a foamy climax, to make a big splash and dive into the freedom of the Gay Mecca of San Francisco in the 1970s when we were escaping laws that prevented us from giving consent to our own bodies. Its frothiness is in the manner of Mapplethorpe's phallic "Gun Blast," 1985, a virtual cum shot that sprays the blast like sperm shot from a pistol—as well as of Arthur Tress's carbonated camp in "Squirt (Just Call Me Squirt)," 1998. I seem to remember Barton's "Splash" model as a guy named "Joe" on Castro. A working title: "Joseph, Arms Akimbo, Golden Gate Bridge Splash," 1975.

Crawford Barton: I can begin. You're interested in the basic way Robert Mapplethorpe affected me?

Jack Fritscher: You, your career, your opinions about him. While your memories are fresh. Next week, he'll be gone seventeen months. The good, the bad, the indifferent.

"Crawford Barton was famous for documenting the blooming of the openly gay culture in San Francisco from the late 1960s into the 1980s. By the early 1970s, he was an established photographer of the 'golden age of gay awakening' in San Francisco. He said, 'I tried to serve as a chronicler, as a watcher of beautiful people, to feed back an image of a positive, likable lifestyle, to offer pleasure as well as pride.' He was as much a participant as a chronicler of this extraordinary time and place." —Elisa Rolle, "Crawford Barton and Larry Lara," *Days of Love: Celebrating LGBT History One Story at a Time*

Crawford Barton: As I told you the other day when we were visiting, I was jealous of Robert. I was envious. He sometimes made me angry. Basically, I thought I was better than he was. He was getting rich and famous and I wasn't. Is this okay?

Jack Fritscher: Yes, because you are saying what so many other gay photographers are saying.

Crawford Barton: I must clarify I haven't seen every picture he did, but some of the work I have seen is truly memorable. Some of the photos are terribly important around racism, rough sex, sexual liberation. He was lucky he found his rich patron [Sam Wagstaff]. For years, I've tried to find a representative or manager or a secretary or a gallery that would get behind me. With all the support he got, Robert went zooming along. That made me mad. I thought in fair play I deserved it too. I also didn't like him perpetuating dark and negative images about homosexuals.

Jack Fritscher: How so?

Crawford Barton: I was struggling here in San Francisco. I started my business as Arts Unlimited [1973-1978]. I felt like I was working my ass off as hard as he was in New York. I was shooting for publication [in *The Advocate*, the *Bay Area Reporter*, the San Francisco *Sentinel*, and the *Los Angeles Times*]. I was trying to create some beautiful, memorable, positive stuff about gay men, and here he is taking pictures of people drinking piss and mutilating their genitals. That is just too much—and I refuse to do that. I thought the leathersex pictures were kind of tacky and made to get attention. I will admit he was technically proficient; but, face it, anyone can take a bunch of tulips and make a pretty picture.

I don't think it takes a "perfect moment" to do that. I do think that *The Perfect Moment* [portraits, figure studies, flowers, leathersex] was a wonderful title for that show. I ended up going to see it three or four times [at the University Art Museum, University of

California, Berkeley, January 17 - March 18, 1990]. I was planning not to. I didn't want to give him the credit, but people kept calling me up, especially black friends, saying. "Would you please go to this show and explain it to me and help me?"

Jack Fritscher: Black friends wanted a white photographer to explain a white photographer's work about black men?

Crawford Barton: Well, they were curious with doubts, and they thought maybe if Crawford goes with us, we'll get some insight. I don't mean everybody that asked me to go was black, but a few were. Their curiosity roused mine so I went to the exhibit I was planning not to attend.

Jack Fritscher: How did you explain Robert to your black friends?

Crawford Barton: [Laughs] They ended up explaining it to me. I don't remember anything precisely other than that they were fascinated that he was so interested in blacks—and I think that is one of his strong points of appeal because some of the pictures were quite ordinary, technically very nice, and relatable.

You know the one with the man sitting on the stool in four different positions? ["Ajitto," 1981; see also "Phillip Prioleau, NYC (on pedestal, side facing)," 1979.] I just don't think that took any imagination at all. On the other hand, the one with the guy in the business suit with his cock out ["Man in Polyester Suit," 1980] is, I think, kind of neat. There's a couple more like the two guys with torsos and legs in the same position.

Jack Fritscher: Why did you think "Man in Polyester Suit" was "neat"?

Crawford Barton: I think it's a classic statement. It's perfect and provocative. At the Berkeley exhibit, I heard the stories [instant urban legends] of people looking at the photos in the museum. A friend said when he was there, there were two little old white-haired ladies and there was a giant black guard standing in uniform near the picture, and they would look at it and look at him, look at it and look at him, and kind of like shiver. That's interesting. A lot of things he shot, I did earlier, but I didn't do S&M. For instance, in the de Young in 1974, I had a picture of my lover pissing. ["Larry Lara, Buena Vista Park," San Francisco, page 13, *DOH*.] It caused quite a stir. People were dragging their children away from the wall. I enjoyed standing there and watching reactions.

In 1974, the M. H. de Young Memorial Museum in Golden Gate Park featured Barton's prints in an exhibit called *New Photography, San Francisco and the Bay Area*. His photo-book, *Beautiful Men*, with a cowboy-hat cover photo of his constant model Merritt Warrington that rivals Jim French's homomasculine esthetic at Colt Studio, was published in 1976 by Liberation Publications at *The Advocate* with a second edition in 1978. His pictures, published in the *Time-Life* series, *Photography 1976*, also illustrated the book *Look Back in Joy* (1990) by Malcom Boyd, the famous beatnik Episcopal priest and author of the 1960s bestseller *Are You Running With Me, Jesus?* Boyd was the longtime husband of *The Advocate* editor Mark Thompson, my longtime friend, who collected the photos and wrote the foreword to *Crawford Barton: Days of Hope: 70s Gay San Francisco* published posthumously in 1994 in London by Editions Aubrey Walter which also published photo books by Arthur Tress, George Dureau, Chris Nelson, Jack Fritscher, and others.

For two decades, gay faerie Mark Thompson, the author of *Gay Spirit: Myth and Meaning* was senior editor at *The Advocate*, and, along with influencer Boyd, a constant champion of Barton's work. Thompson hired Barton to help support him as a staff photographer, but Thompson and Boyd were minor-league patrons compared to Mapplethorpe's Sam Wagstaff with his old money and his New York and European connections. In the 1980s, Barton wrote his epic novel of the golden age of gay awakening, *Castro Street*, and a book of poetry, *One More Sweet Smile*. Both unpublished.

His photo, "Harvey Milk, 18th & Castro Street," San Francisco, 1973, page 37, *DOH*, is in the National Portrait Gallery, Smithsonian Institution, a gift from the Trustees of the Corcoran Gallery of Art and of Edward Brooks DeCelle. His street photo, "Harvey Milk Campaigning on Castro Street," Summer, 1973, is part of the permanent Crawford Barton archival collection at the San Francisco GLBT Historical Society.

Barton's most iconic queer pop-culture picture, "Castro Street Scene, Two Couples (a kiss on the steps)," 1977, depicts his staged scene of two juxtaposed couples. One couple is bourgeois with a straight man in a suit sitting on the steps with a woman in a light-colored dress, knees closed, clutching a big purse, both staring off in the direction of the nearby intersection of 18th and Castro, looking away from the gay couple—while in another frame the exact same straight couple look into each other's faces. The other seated couple engaging in a kiss, knees open, are Castro clones, gay and bearded and perfect in white T-shirts. Barton's quartet says everything about the working-class Irish couples with families who lived in the Castro, sold their homes to gay couples arriving with money, and came back to their old neighborhood to see how their Eureka Valley had become The Castro.

The photo was shot in black-and-white on the famous Rainbow Steps of the gay bookstore Paperback Traffic at 558 Castro Street. That afternoon at that location, Barton directed and shot several alternative frames, some with blue-jean legs behind the two couples, some without, as well as other frames of two different couples straight and gay with the gay one kissing. (Page 36, *DOH*.) Like the iconic *Gone with the Wind* poster of Rhett kissing Scarlett, this instantly recognizable "postcard" photo has taken on an emblematic life of its own as a poster for the Castro gayborhood before it became a war zone of AIDS. As a signature totem of nostalgia, "Two Couples" has appeared in several films: *Gay USA*, 1977; *The Butch Factor*, 2009; *We Were Here*, 2011. In 1994, I published it as a totem in *Mappletthorpe: Assault with a Deadly Camera*.

Jack Fritscher: So you think Robert's leather pictures exploit gay men? That his S&M pictures are a bad press release for homosexuality? Would you rather he show gays in suits and ties and loafers like *The Advocate* [under publisher David Goodstein] advises us to be in its pages so people accept us?

Crawford Barton: Healthy looking pictures of gays? Yes. Guys in loafers, T-shirts and jeans, And Castro clones, I guess. I'm basically a documentary photographer, and I do portraits too, but my work is positive and, well, California, not New York.

Jack Fritscher: In the early 1970s, Robert, like you, went outside to shoot healthy beautiful men lolling poolside in the Fire Island Pines. ["Scott Bromley," 1972; "Peter Berlin," 1977; "Tattered American Flag," 1977]

Crawford Barton: I always thought all his work had an unwholesome feeling. Even his still-lifes of flowers were shot indoors, never outside in a garden. I think he once said, "Oh, my flowers are New York flowers."

Jack Fritscher: His studio was his hothouse. He and Patti who did his reading for him were always comparing whatever they did to Baudelaire and Rimbeau. Like working for extra credit after school. They grafted his night-blooming New York flowers on to Baudelaire's *Flowers of Evil*.

Crawford Barton: He shot everything behind closed doors. After growing up in a closet in Georgia, I like to get out of the studio, out of the closet, and into the streets.

> Barton's street photography in which one picture can illustrate a thousand words also invites the kind of literary comparisons promoted by Patti Smith. His street fair and parade photography contains multitudes like Walt's *Leaves of Grass*. For instance, in "Two Shirtless Men Embracing," Gay Freedom Day, San Francisco, 1977, two men standing in a huge crowd embrace one another like Whitman's Calamus lovers in his tender poem, "What Think You I Take My Pen in

Hand to Record?": I "… record of two simple men I saw to-day, on the pier, in the midst of the crowd, parting the parting of dear friends; The one to remain hung on the other's neck, and passionately kiss'd him, While the one to depart, tightly prest the one to remain in his arms."

In his candid alfresco series *After the Parade, Lafayette Park*, he documents crowds of clothed and nude gay men cavorting and dancing in what Whitman celebrated as "He-festivals" in *Song of Myself* in which he applauded "He-festivals, with blackguard gibes, ironical license, bull-dances, drinking, laughter." Pages 42 to 45, *DOH*.

In his staged improv-performance photo of four Dionysian men, Barton again channels Whitman with his shirtless duo of Merritt Warrington (left) and Larry Lara (howling, center) standing with an unidentified third man (shirted, right) around a fourth man seated (rich, left) in his MG convertible double-parked in the middle of Castro Street where A-list Castronauts lived the high life with no visible means of support. The picture might be descriptively titled, "Castro Street Scene, Four Men and an MG Double-parked in Front of the Castro Theater." He pictures his lead actor, Larry Lara, the black hole of his mouth agape, teeth bared, shouting, yawping the yawp of Whitman's "Barbaric Yawp" of male autonomy, joy, and radical freedom on location in front of the towering blade sign of the Castro Theater. The exact line from the poem is "I sound my barbaric yawp over the roofs of the world." Barton's pictures could illustrate Whitman's poetry in *Leaves of Grass* the way Mapplethorpe's pictures illustrated Rimbaud's poetry in *Arthur Rimbaud and Robert Mapplethorpe, A Season in Hell*, New York: Limited Edition's Club, 1986. Edition: 1000.

Crawford Barton: Robert's still-lifes have such a claustrophobic feeling.

Jack Fritscher: Cut flowers are dying flowers, dead flowers.

Crawford Barton: The flowers, especially the ones in color, are so uniquely sharp and clear that there's nothing unusual about them. Mechanical. No interpretation. He wanted to focus on a tulip and take a perfectly rendered picture of it.

Jack Fritscher: More literal than metaphorical? It's not faint praise to say some look like beautiful commercial photographs he could have sold to Kodak to advertise its newest film stock.

Crawford Barton: I just feel like flowers are pretty. So it's easy to take a pretty picture. Flowers are the sex organs of plants. I think that's why he liked them.

Jack Fritscher: That's one reason he liked them. He could show sex and beauty in flowers where people didn't mind the combination. Pop culture is mass culture. It thrives on the public curiosity to see what's behind the green door. Everyone wants to see inside everything.

Crawford Barton: I think that's why *The Perfect Moment* was so popular. People could not resist...

Jack Fritscher: ...his Traveling Peep Show?

Crawford Barton: ...because they wanted to see something naughty that they could see nowhere else. They got off on being a little bit bad by going to a museum and not some carnival to see the freak show.

Jack Fritscher: So, after Stonewall, it was a way for straight people, gay friendly or not, to check out gay things they'd only starting to hear about.

Crawford Barton: I think he could have been more educational, less sensational. I haven't thought a lot about it, but he could have made his work less gruesome. I have a problem with S&M. I don't understand it. I don't understand why anyone would want to do it and I don't understand why someone would necessarily take pictures of it.

Jack Fritscher: Maybe because like Mount Everest, it's there and hasn't been shot before. When you see paintings of torture like the Passion of the Christ, Saint Sebastian, Saint Peter, or even "The Flaying of the Satyr Marsyus" [Robert's *X-Portfolio* picture, "Dominick and Elliot"], do they suggest that Robert is creating inside a religious esthetic of suffering endured by willing victims like Christ or Sebastian? Robert was first and last a Catholic.

Crawford Barton: I don't know about religious overtones because I'm not a religious person. I don't understand religion either. It's just violence.

Jack Fritscher: Yet, the people who are looking at his pictures and having the worst response to it are the most "religious."

Crawford Barton: That's true.

Jack Fritscher: Did he bait them to make news and sell pictures? He takes religious art and spins it around gay sex and his subversion drives them mad. Fundamentalists hate art because they are literal about the Bible and don't like the ambiguity of art.

> The Protestant Reformation, suspicious of art and metaphor, led to today's fundamentalist censorship of art. When Protestant reformers destroyed monasteries and stole Catholic church buildings, they white-washed the walls, paintings, sculpture and ornamentation to erase centuries of idolatrous "Roman" art because its metaphorical ambiguity was contrary to their literal reading of the Bible and the Second Commandment that forbids making graven images. Scholars estimate that in the 16th century, militant iconoclasts destroyed 97% of the Catholic art in England. The Puritans brought this critical gaze to Plymouth Rock and installed its anti-art fundamentalism in American consciousness and politics, especially in the South where Barton was raised.

Crawford Barton: I grew up learning all the problems about sexually unliberated church people. They can't stand seeing other people having some degree of total freedom. They draw the line at sex. The 1970s were the most sexually liberated period in U.S. history and maybe the world.

Jack Fritscher: Maybe the Cosmos. Rome. The Weimar Republic. The Meatpacking District. Castro Street.

Crawford Barton: So it's not surprising he did it when he did.

Jack Fritscher: He was a man of his times. He lived his life and shot what he knew. So how is he different from the hundreds of photographers who shot for all the gay magazines like *Blueboy*, *Honcho*, *Christopher Street*, and *Drummer*? What makes Robert's pictures fine art?

Crawford Barton: Aside from the fact that he's technically very good like Ansel Adams, he pushed and shoved to get into galleries and museums, and the people in *Drummer* did not. You could say he had the balls.

Jack Fritscher: He had career balls to get institutional endorsement.

Crawford Barton: He could stand there and say to people. "I'm an artist. I'm a serious artist."

Jack Fritscher: If they balked, he had a great sales pitch: "If you don't like this picture, maybe you're not as avant-garde as you think." If you repeat something often enough and get other people saying these things in your social circuit...

Crawford Barton: You get shows everywhere and sell your prints for lots of money. The only thing today is to "be" an artist and stick with that. Don't sell out. That doesn't mean what you produce is going to be a masterpiece and be remembered ten years later, but it means you're honest. Robert may have been honest, but he wasn't honest enough.

Jack Fritscher: Is there anything in Robert's work that you think will be remembered in the history of photography?

Crawford Barton: Most of it is technically good and pretty to look at. I think his attitude, his new thinking of photography as a fine art, which he learned from Wagstaff, is more important than his work. Robert was a liberating teacher in the art world.

Jack Fritscher: He and Sam kept repeating "Photography is a fine art" until the art world finally believed them and sent prices sky-rocketing. Do you think that Robert was at all political, or did he pursue his own career and get political by accident when the world turned on him?

The essential Robert Mapplethorpe, who became an icon of the Culture Wars, favored pure static form over the fray of politics, but around issues of race, sex, gender, and identities, one could consider that Robert's coverage of disenfranchised gay men, women, and blacks was start-to-finish a slow-burn political mission of visibility that grew in subversive intensity. The jurors at the Cincinnati obscenity trial decided his work was "artistic and politically important, no matter how disturbing the homoerotic images might be." After the manner of Dan Nicoletta's photo of Harvey Milk on a U.S. postage stamp in 2014, Robert's "Ken Moody and Robert Sherman," 1984, is a virtual U.S. postage stamp of race relations.

In 1981, Robert shot a devastating political portrait of Donald Trump's then attorney, Roy Cohn (1927-1986), the loathsome gay lawyer who was infamous for his part in Republican Senator Joseph McCarthy's House Un-American Committee that did so much damage to the country, to gay people, and to the arts in America in the 1950s. The eerie photo of Cohn's disembodied head floating in a black void and titled "Roy Cohn," now in the National Portrait Gallery at the Smithsonian, might have been better titled "Bring Me the Head of Roy Cohn."

In 1989, thirty-seven days before Robert died, he shot United States Surgeon General C. Everett Coop who led the national fight on AIDS during the presidency of George H. W. Bush after Republican President Ronald Reagan who could not even speak the word *AIDS*. *Time* magazine published Robert's portrait of Coop on the cover of its April 24, 1989 issue. It was Robert's last commissioned portrait. On May 27, 1988, ten months before he died, Robert founded the Robert Mapplethorpe Foundation to promote photography as fine art and to support HIV/AIDS medical research.

Crawford Barton: I didn't know him that well. I feel like saying he got political by accident.

Jack Fritscher: The big controversy about him didn't begin until a hundred days after he died. He got no joy from it. He never knew how famous he'd become.

Crawford Barton: I never really sat down and had a long conversation with him about his opinions.

Jack Fritscher: When you look at his photographs, do you see political content? Declarations of sexual independence?

Crawford Barton: Unlike others, I always thought of sexual freedom as non-political. I think it's everyone's right. Maybe he set out to explore his sexual fantasies and got politicized in the process. Politics is another thing that baffles me like religion. It works for people who know how to manipulate it. I think Robert knew very well how to manipulate people the way he manipulated his camera and his models. Did he try to manipulate you?

Jack Fritscher: I could make a sex joke here. But, no, he didn't. We collaborated [on *Drummer* work and a potential book] without manipulation. He was good at manipulating himself in his self portraits where he'd do things like sticking a whip up his bum or putting on women's makeup.

Crawford Barton: Not in the same picture, thank God.

Jack Fritscher: Do you think with his S&M pictures and his role-playing auto-shots that he was trying to reach people or outrage them? Outrage is a political term. With Larry Kramer and Act Up, it's a virtue. Does outrage win people over? Outrage is a maneuver *The Advocate* doesn't like.

Crawford Barton: The way I would explain *outrage* if I had to is that, for instance, drag queens pave the road for ordinary gays to come out. Drag is not as shocking now as in the early days, but still, drag queens and S&M are the outrageous extremes. They may help some people come out, but most homosexuals are not like either one. To tell the truth, I've been in the gay community of San Francisco for so long that I don't know what's outrageous anymore. Is Mapplethorpe outrageous in our outrageous culture? Can anyone be? We've seen and done things in the 1970s that would shock ordinary American Nazis. That's where Mapplethorpe crossed the line. Maybe he was trying to educate people. But you have to do it gradually. You can't suddenly stick a bloody penis in front of their faces and expect them to accept it.

Jack Fritscher: And yet people applaud circumcision.

Crawford Barton: They think of that as a necessary religious and health experience. I'm a very sensitive person. I see a finger get cut and I have to turn away.

Jack Fritscher: What do you think of his presentation of women?

Crawford Barton: I think it's basically positive—although I think he portrays women as a gay man would do it. He chose muscular women, lesbians, or outrageous women. The women got off easy compared to how he sexualized men.

> Barton's undated photo, "Donna and Friend," San Francisco, and "Toby and Family (two lesbian mothers with their child)," pages 9 and 67, *DOH*, are very like Richard Avedon in his photo book *In the American West, 1979-1984*. In 1975, Barton documented Jo Daly, the first lesbian Police Commissioner in San Francisco.

Crawford Barton: His men and leathermen are more sensational. He'll be remembered for his S&M statements, then his blacks, but they will always be associated together as somehow forbidden. He probably wouldn't have made such a big splash without the S&M, but he may have helped education around race with his more wholesome pictures of blacks. I think the black pictures are fine.

Jack Fritscher: You don't find them stereotypical with the penises and muscles and bulging tights…and guns? ["Jack Walls (holding pistol parallel to his erect penis)," 1982.

Crawford Barton: I'm a documentarian. So, no, that's just how the models looked. They're not really exaggerated. He's not taking them to some extreme. They are what they are: black men. They just seem extreme because of racial fear of black men. I agree with him on his black interpretation. I think he is saying blackness isn't threatening. You just think it is because of racial problems in America.

> Robert had the good fortune of riding on what Tom Wolfe satirized in 1970 as "Radical Chic" after Leonard Bernstein invited high society to a Manhattan party he hosted for the Black Panthers so his rich friends could assuage their white guilt and feel liberal and grand, with no irony, lighting cigarettes and serving cocktails to black revolutionaries. A decade later, they were buying Mapplethorpe's blacks as trophies of their liberalism.

Jack Fritscher: Did your black friends who went with you to his show comment upon a white photographer presenting black males in this way? Is it documentary or stereotype when he poses a headless black model in a cheap suit with his prodigious penis hanging out, or a young nude black New Yorker draped with a cheetah skin and holding a spear? ["Isaiah," 1981]

Crawford Barton: No, they mostly said, "The model has great skin."

Jack Fritscher: Have you photographed many blacks? Castro Street where you find models is mostly white.

Crawford Barton: Not a lot. I had the same idea as Mapplethorpe about shooting black men because it was an area that had not been explored very much. There weren't any black gay photographers then that I can think of.

> Crawford Barton's photos representing black men include "After the Parade," 1974, page 22, *DOH*; "Jim McKell and

Friend," page 54; "Nude Study," page 56; "Romney (black man on bus bench)," page 60; and "Black Man Standing Shirtless in Front of Adult Movie Theater Posters," Tenderloin, San Francisco, 1970s.

Jack Fritscher: Perhaps you're aware of Craig Anderson [1941-2014] who is white and for years has shot rapturous pictures of black men for his Sierra Domino Studio here in San Francisco. [Unlike Robert, Anderson rented his models to his photography clients at his studio parties.] Do you know of any other whites photographing nude black men?

Crawford Barton: I don't know of any. You might ask Dan Nicoletta. He's a gay photographer who's been around a long time, He started working in Harvey Milk's camera shop at the age of seventeen. He ended up using my studio on Church Street. He may know of some. Do you want his number? It's 665-59....

Jack Fritscher: Thanks. He's in my Rolodex. I know him and his work. Prolific with a genius eye for catching both the moment and the character of his subject. What's your bottom line about Mapplethorpe? Was he anything besides sensational?

Crawford Barton: Yes. He was technically very good. But many of his images are very ordinary. I don't understand a lot of his work and why he did it. He created a whole series of picture frames for his photos and hung them like geometric arrangements and sculptures that I don't understand at all. In some of his series, it's the same subject shot from different angles forming a cross with a black center. What is that? I don't get it.

Jack Fritscher: Robert began studying sculpture at Pratt, built installations, and designed jewelry. Before he ever picked up a camera, he made lots of mixed-media collages using other photographers' erotic male images he found in 42nd Street adult bookstores. His repetitions are very Warhol. His crosses are Catholic. He works with religion. Like Fellini.

Robert Mapplethorpe, "Christ (photo of a crucifix)," (1988), Folded Card for the Exhibition *Three Catholics: Robert Mapplethorpe, Andy Warhol, Ed Ruscha*," Cheim & Read Gallery, 1998.

Crawford Barton: Well, I don't get that. I mean arranging pictures of an erect penis in three different positions? His geometric arrangements are not new. So you think that's a religious statement?

Jack Fritscher: As a main icon of western art, the Crucifixion plays a major part in his design and arrangement. In his *Creatis* catalog, which was the first gift he gave me, his cover shot is a self-portrait of just the upper quarter of his torso, and his grinning face, and his right arm stretched to the vast reaches of the frame, and his palm is open waiting for the nail to be driven in. Like a young artist exposing himself to critics for his own delicious crucifixion.

Creatis, La Photographie au Present, No. 7, 1978, was "un magazine bimestrial, vendu dans les galeries, les librairies specialisées," printed in Paris by Albert Champeau, publisher, and Mona Rouzies, art director. *Creatis* was published two years after Barton's primary reference book *Beautiful Men* and at the same moment Barton shut down his Arts Unlimited business.

In a tale of two cities, as the gentle Barton, a born Southerner, lived life without a *catalogue raisonné* in laid-back San Francisco, the prolific Northerner Mapplethorpe rose in the fast lane in New York. Crawford's layabout muse Larry Lara was no motivational Patti Smith. *Beautiful Men* surveyed Barton's past. *Creatis* projected Mapplethorpe's future.

By the 1976 American Bicentennial—coinciding with Barton's career high-point in *Beautiful Men*—Mapplethorpe was surrounding himself with observant writers and eye-witness photographers and the idle rich to build his brand.

Robert, the urban leatherman, was sitting front row at Paris Fashion Week rising to the full height of his powers, while Crawford, the hippie farm boy, cruised on shooting a confederacy of idle beauties in the Castro Street He-festival that was the "Golden Age of Sex" in San Francisco—that orgiastic decade of gay fraternity before the onslaught of AIDS in 1981 when Barton settled in as the local photographer of the San Francisco Gay Men's Chorus. Cities breathe. Sometimes they inhale you. Sometimes they exhale you.

Crawford Barton: I'm not tuned into religion or S&M. I see sex in the flowers, but I don't see religion in penises and bondage.

Jack Fritscher: Meaning like beauty is in the eye of the beholder. Some of his frames alternating three pictures in one line alongside one mirrored frame reflecting the viewer's face are meant to suck the viewer into the picture. The seer becomes the seen. Art is what you bring to it. You needn't see theology in his work, but it was part of Robert's creation.

> Robert who began his career creating picture frames carefully designed a layered presentation of the gay fetish for rubber gear in "Joe," 1978. He framed and mounted his photo flat on the center of a mirror placed behind a transparent pane of smoked glass whose reflective finish repeats, along with the mirror, the face—includes the face, makes an immersive montage of the face—of the viewer standing in front of the picture.

Crawford Barton: So…what do you do with his picture of a fish laid out on some newspapers?

Jack Fritscher: Maybe it's a comment on newspapers and publicity. On one level, it's a sports picture of a fish. On another level, it's a comment on the media. *Fishwrap* is a slang term for yellow journalism in newspapers like *The National Enquirer*. On another level, a deeper dive, it may be a comment on religion. The fish is an ancient symbol for Christianity.

Crawford Barton: Do you understand his fascination with socialites? Women with very pale light skin against a dark background?

Jack Fritscher: Women with wallets. Their socialite money fascinated him. He loved being the artist at their supper tables. He loved high society. Princess Margaret and all that. He took a lot of pictures of Greek and Roman female statuary which he applied to Lisa Lyon, and he gave some of his society women a classic-cool marbled look.

> Robert was genius at turning women and men to stone. He made glorious statuary of sitters like "Melody Danielson," 1987; "Ken Moody," 1983; "Desmond," 1983; and "Ken Moody and Robert Sherman," 1984. In 2014, the French paired Mapplethorpe with Rodin in the exhibit *Mapplethorpe - Rodin*, Museum Rodin, Paris.

Crawford Barton: Speaking of statues, why did the Whitney chose one of his statue pictures for the cover of his exhibit [*Robert Mapplethorpe,* Whitney Museum of American Art, curated by Richard Marshall, 1988].

Jack Fritscher: It was a metaphorical photo he shot of the profile of a white marble statue of Apollo. [*Apollo,* 1988] He was Apollo. He was dying. People were in a rush to create hooks to position him in art history.

Crawford Barton: Did he care about being a figure in history?

Jack Fritscher: Sam made him aware of history. He and Sam worked hard to convince collectors and critics and gallerists that there was a canon of historical fine-art photography that deserved respect in museums and galleries—and that Robert was a continuation of that canon. A passionate few can make a reputation.

Crawford Barton: I think I can tell what's good art and great art. I just have a feeling about it.

Jack Fritscher: Like the Supreme Court Justice [Potter Stewart] who said he couldn't define pornography, but he knew it when he saw it.

Crawford Barton: Yes. I have feelings about intuition, uniqueness, skill involved, beauty. There's so much junk being produced now. There always has been.

Jack Fritscher: What do you think of Herb Ritts?

Crawford Barton: He's another skilled technician. He's great with faces and bodies, but I think his pictures made into all the giant posters you see everywhere are just there to titillate gay people into buying them. Basically, it's just physical exploitation again. Just pretty bodies with carefully covered genitalia.

Jack Fritscher: Why do you think everyone gets so riled up over the penis?

Crawford Barton: Oh, lordy, lordy.

Jack Fritscher: I mean in art.

Crawford Barton: That's a very good question.

Jack Fritscher: People accept frontal nudity in women. Europeans don't care about frontal nudity of either sex. In America, there's this enormous fear of the penis.

In March, 1994, the year after Barton died, outré culture warrior Camille Paglia hosted the controversial program *Priapus Unsheathed*, for Rapido TV, Channel 4, London, in which she asked me to join with other talking heads to speak, as I had with Crawford, about cultural fear of the penis. Paglia included transcripts of that show in her book *Vamps and Tramps: New Essays*, 1994.

Crawford Barton: I don't know if I know the answer right off the bat. Nude females became acceptable and nude men did not. Are you talking about an erect penis or just a penis?

Jack Fritscher: Any penis.

Crawford Barton: Isn't penis what that one man [U.S. Senator Jesse Helms, Republican, North Carolina] got so bent out of shape about because Robert showed a black penis?

Jack Fritscher: It was "Man in Polyester Suit." Jesse Helms called it "filthy art." What do you expect of a single-minded fundamentalist who lacks visual literacy and whose religion is always bitching about sex? The only endowment they like is female breasts. Helms, by the way, is a Baptist.

Crawford Barton: All that religion and sex and race stuff. I had no religion growing up as a child of Baptist parents and brothers and sisters. I chose not to subscribe to all that although Jesus was my only role model. I grew up on a farm in Georgia. ["My Father in His Corn Patch," Northern Georgia, 1975, page 6, *DOH*] I didn't even know who the President was. Not until I was old enough to read did I realize there were gay men out there that I could pattern myself after. Maybe my early Jesus thing is why I deplore meanness and rudeness and aggression. I'm kind of Jesusy.

Jack Fritscher: Jesus took a whip and drove the money changers from the temple.

Crawford Barton: But I doubt if he drew blood. I think Robert produced several memorable images, certainly the whip picture ["Self-Portrait with Whip," 1978].

Jack Fritscher: What do you think that's about?

Crawford Barton: I think he was saying: This is my body. This is my asshole.

Jack Fritscher: That's very close to the declarative words of Consecration in the Catholic Mass. "This is my body. This is my blood." Robert lived that mantra.

Crawford Barton: Really? I think he's saying I'll do whatever I please with my body, and I'm going to make you aware of that. The fact that he is doing it with a leather whip and not a banana keeps it serious.

Jack Fritscher: Cool you mention that. Do you remember Warhol's silkscreen "Banana" on an album cover for the Velvet Underground? [*The Velvet Underground & Nico*, 1967] Referencing Andy, Robert did in fact shoot a campy banana with a leather strap wrapped around it with keys dangling from the strap ["Banana with Keys," 1973]. But regarding the whip does that seem at all scatological to you?

Crawford Barton: Not particularly.

Jack Fritscher: Maybe this campy picture is about pulling art out of your ass. Maybe it's about penetration, the way in, or is it about evacuation, the way out? The bullwhip's long tail evacuates out scat-like down its full braided length, and trails out the bottom of frame.

Crawford Barton: Considering what I've heard about him I suppose that's possible.

> It was the talk of the town when Robert shot his portrait of Katherine Cebrian, the elderly San Francisco *grande dame*, because the bright silver studs on the back of the big leather belt he wore at that time spelled out *shit*. "Katherine Cebrian," 1980]

Jack Fritscher: That's art interpretation for you.

Crawford Barton: Were you there for that shooting session?

Jack Fritscher: Oh, God, no. Not that one. But I enjoyed his psycho-drama take on things.

Crawford Barton: At a lecture?

Jack Fritscher: No. Role-playing during the three years of his high S&M period while we were dating before he switched to black men. The whip photo is like a still frame from a motion picture going on in his head. He's shot a couple of short films. His pictures are like still frames from a movie montage he's slowly assembling.

In the Chelsea Hotel in 1970, Robert appeared in the lap of his lover David Croland with Patti Smith nearby keening on the soundtrack in Sandy Daley's film *Robert Having His Nipple Pierced*. In 1977, he shot Patti solo for his thirteen-minute black-and-white film *Still Moving*.

Crawford Barton: That whip is very Satanic. Very sodomy. It's many, many things.

Jack Fritscher: He wanted it to look evil, but playful, the way Pan looks evil but fun. He shot himself as Pan with two little horns sticking out of his hair ["Self Portrait," 1985]. He loved playing at being Satan's bad boy like you tried to be Jesus's good boy. He tried holiness as an altar boy, and it didn't suit him. He tried being a hippie in the 1960s, but all he took from the Flower Child scene were the flowers. He tried being part of the gay scene, but he disliked gay ghettos except for recruiting the men and scenes he wanted to shoot in places like the Mineshaft.

Crawford Barton: I knew he didn't hang around the gay ghettos.

Jack Fritscher: He felt if you didn't move out of the ghetto, you're still closeted. Other photographers who envied him did not like that attitude.

Crawford Barton: Lucky for him, he could afford it because of Wagstaff. You know what else I think is an important image? The naked black man dancing with the white woman in a white gown. ["Thomas and Dovanna," 1986] If you hung that picture, or those two guys dancing [with crowns on their heads, "Two Men Dancing," 1984] on your wall in South Georgia, you'd be crucified, or the Ku Klux Klan would come burn you out.

Jack Fritscher: Fashion photography. That's a reason to be lynched? Here you are, Crawford, a nice man who doesn't like violence. You are an artist, and you are the child of a violent region. How do you account for your escape?

Crawford Barton: I *did* go around with men who are kind of like the wild mountain men in *Deliverance* [the 1972 box office hit in which primordial mountainmen attack a group of four civilized Atlanta businessmen—and rape one—on a weekend hunting trip in the Georgia wilderness]. Well, maybe not to that extreme, but those kind of men were there in the mountains around our farm. I was lucky I had such gentle loving parents. They went to church. They liked spiritual religious music, not classical. They had a garden. They cooked.

Jack Fritscher: So did Robert's parents. When did you first start shooting pictures? When did you first consider yourself a photographer? Were you born with a camera in your hand?

Crawford Barton: I guess the late 1960s. I took pictures when I was a child. I didn't just point and shoot. I composed them. Visually I was doing art, but I didn't know it. I still have some of those negatives. I got my first 35mm camera in the late 60s. I was also a painter and I was trying to be a writer. I wanted to be a filmmaker. So learning photography was something important for me to do that I could do readily.

Jack Fritscher: You're like Robert in that regard. He said something like "If I had been born a hundred years ago, I might have been a sculptor, but photography is a very quick way to see, to make sculpture."

Crawford Barton: Exactly.

Jack Fritscher: I mentioned Robert was a filmmaker. What did you think of his films?

Crawford Barton: I don't think I've seen any of them.

Jack Fritscher: I think he thought the same as you and Warhol that filmmaking is an extension of the still frame. Warhol moved from Polaroids to filmmaking and video portraits he called *Screen Tests*. Godard says "Photography is truth. The cinema is truth twenty-four times per second."

Crawford Barton: Yes, yes. Godard! In the 60s, filmmaking was the only art form for me when I studied film at UCLA because it combined all the art forms that I could do well. I have never had the opportunity to make a feature film. I have shot Super-8 movies and some of them are almost an hour long. [*Gay Parade 1978*, Super-8] I've been meaning to transfer them to videotape, but I hate TV.

Jack Fritscher: TV isn't video. Video is something other than TV.

Crawford Barton: You have to show videotapes on TV.

Jack Fritscher: No, you view them on a monitor.

Crawford Barton: Well, that's about as bad. I think TV distorts. I'm such a film buff. I get real angry if someone says I should put my films on a cassette. I wouldn't watch a videotape if you paid me.

Jack Fritscher: Actually, what we're doing right now on the phone without seeing each other is going to be prehistoric in a few years when we'll have videophone. Last summer when I was shooting erotic videos in West Berlin [1989], the producer showed me a tiny still camera that doesn't use film.

Crawford Barton: I think the making of a 35mm feature-length film is very archaic, but until they perfect the cameras and film stock, we'll never see the whole picture the way it was intended, clear and sharp and all that.

Jack Fritscher: They have. It's called high-definition television. In Europe, broadcast television looks glorious. It has 560 lines of resolution and we have about 250-350.

Crawford Barton: I also have a thing about watching a big picture on a big screen. I don't like sitting on my couch staring across the room at a small 8x10 TV image on a wall. That's what TV looks like: an 8x10. I realize all of this technology is going to work itself out.

Jack Fritscher: Maybe your next period will be as a great videographer, applying all your skills because video does make filmmaking accessible to people. That's why Robert was able to shoot videos of

Patti in the 1970s. Like Warhol, he was one of the first people to have a video camera.

Crawford Barton: Maybe videotape is the only way to reach everyone. Did you see the newspaper article a couple of weeks back on still photography done on computers?

Jack Fritscher: Yes. With computer manipulation, is still photography any longer only a document of truth? [Antonioni's] *Blow-Up* [1966] was an interesting study about finding truth in a photograph.

Crawford Barton: That's why technology bothers me being a candid photographer, a documentary photographer trying to capture what's actually there. Like *Blow-Up*. My work doesn't carry the weight it used to.

Jack Fritscher: There's an awful lot going on with all this change, isn't there? None of us knows what will be happening in fifty or a hundred years with your photographs.

> Twenty years later in 2013, Crawford Barton's photographs and Super-8 movies of his gay migration from Georgia to San Francisco were edited into existing Civil War historical photos to create *The Campaign for Atlanta: An Essay on Queer Migration* at the Atlanta Cyclorama and Civil War Museum. Curators "John Q" aka Wesley Chenault, Andy Ditzler, and Joey Orr saluted the value of Barton's queer eyewitness in his historical films and stills like his picture of his father on his farm in 1975 and his "Goat Man (with his Jesus sign)," Calhoun, Georgia, 1960s, to illustrate aspects of the great gay migrations of the 1970s.

Crawford Barton: I'm too tame to be remembered, but I do think I have captured some truly beautiful moments with truly beautiful men in a truly beautiful city. It seems the world is going in a violent direction rather than a peaceful direction.

Jack Fritscher: Endism is a philosophy that has become part of popular culture. Even among gays because of AIDS. I don't believe in it myself. Endism? Is the end really near? Not if you study history. Endism comes out of fundamentalist religion waiting for the Apocalypse which like Godot never comes.

Crawford Barton: All you have to do is go out your front door.

Jack Fritscher: Why, because it looks like the end of the world?

Crawford Barton: You can see anything by looking out your front door in San Francisco.

Jack Fritscher: What about those people back in Georgia looking out their windows? What happens when the Mapplethorpe exhibit comes to… What town were you born in?

Crawford Barton: Outside Calhoun where I went to high school. It was the nearest town. but I was born out in the sticks. But Mapplethorpe will never get there.

Jack Fritscher: AIDS got there.

Crawford Barton: Sooner or later, Mapplethorpe will be exhibited in Atlanta even though it's probably ten years behind California.

Jack Fritscher: The Mapplethorpe controversy has already gotten there on the news. Will Jesse Helms be as remembered as Robert Mapplethorpe in ten years? There will always be another reincarnation of Jesse Helms. That fascist mentality comes along on repeat in history, and each time that it does, it seems that art and homosexuality manage to beat it and survive.

Crawford Barton: I thought censorship was disappearing.

Jack Fritscher: Really? Today? [October 2] With the Mapplethorpe obscenity trial going on right now in Cincinnati even as we speak? [September 24 - October 5, 1990]

Crawford Barton: I don't watch TV.

Jack Fritscher: Government censorship is a bad mix of church and state. Do you think the government has the responsibility to fund art? That artists have a right to government grants?

Crawford Barton: No.

Jack Fritscher: Actually, censorship of Robert is not as much about art as it is about homophobia. When society won't let you kill the artist, kill the art.

Crawford Barton: I don't think Mapplethorpe should be censored anymore than I should be. If someone is into S&M, I'm sure some of his images are very pleasing. What pleases me is love, tenderness, and all that. Mapplethorpe made a leap, and he did it fast and just in time. If he did it my way, which is gradually, he wouldn't have become a star. I have AIDS. I don't care if you quote me. I won't last long enough to accomplish what he did.

Jack Fritscher: He died at 42. You're how old?

Crawford Barton: 47. And you?

Jack Fritscher: I'm 51.

Crawford Barton: AIDS?

Jack Fritscher: No.

Crawford Barton: You're lucky.

Jack Fritscher: Yes, but driven because AIDS exists. My first lover of ten years [photographer David Sparrow (1945-1992)] has AIDS. The horror of it all. I write to keep dead friends alive. Looking inside your own internal sensibility around AIDS, do you think the fact that Robert had AIDS caused him to speed up shooting everything in sight? In his last years, he shot more than he ever shot before.

Crawford Barton: That's probably a definite *yes*. Sometimes I think I've slowed my pace, but I'm working harder and I'm more productive than ever before, even with AIDS, maybe because of AIDS.

Jack Fritscher: Do you think speeding up your shooting has influenced your quality?

Crawford Barton: I think its gotten better. A kind of urgency has enhanced it.

Jack Fritscher: Has AIDS focused your art and life so you can capture the moment you want, your perfect moment, better in both the camera and the dark room?

Crawford Barton: AIDS has made me feel more urgent. I'm better because I've been shooting more, but that also comes out of my long years of experience. Without AIDS, I think I would have been doing the same quality, but not as fast. My art will last longer than I will.

Jack Fritscher: Your answer as a working artist is such an important insight because we can no longer ask Robert about his feelings around production, censorship, and AIDS.

Crawford Barton: AIDS forces you to get serious, to pick up your pace, to get rid of the nitpicking pre-occupying your time when you think you have all the time in the world. You have to boil it down to say: "That there's not important. I have something important to do over here." Work is the only thing that makes me happy anymore. I can't just go to the beach and waste time. I have to read a book or write something. Wasting time makes me feel very unhappy. So I just get down into the work.

Jack Fritscher: Robert had this sense, this urgency, about him even before AIDS. He was propelled by drugs, ambition, and the joy of working.

Crawford Barton: In the 70s, I medicated myself to enhance my work so I could be less hung up. The result was non-productive.

Jack Fritscher: Have you thought about the effect of AIDS on the artistic personality? Can AIDS be a source of gay art?

Crawford Barton: My physical reaction is to view AIDS as a reality, but not a reality I want to capture in my camera. Robert didn't take

AIDS pictures and neither do I. I refuse to take ugly, creepy pictures of people with spots and withering away. That's not my bag.

Jack Fritscher: He took self-portraits, almost time-lapse photos, of himself withering away.

Crawford Barton: Oh, yeah. I forgot about that. I may have blocked that out. The one of him looking about twenty years older all of a sudden. ["Self-portrait with Skull Cane," 1988]. I am trying to continue on and get down to the essence of my work. I'm trying to distill my work to its core essence to expand it into something new rather than keep making infinite variations of what I did before. I'd rather do that, simplify and expand my visions, rather than switching my whole thing to AIDS pictures.

Jack Fritscher: Are you now trying to capture in a single frame what you captured before in a series of images? Your own "perfect moment'?

Crawford Barton: Yes. Not that I don't still like sequential work. You could say I'm in search of the perfect moment, of doing it better, but I'm not searching any longer. I'm making each shot count more than I used to. The clock is ticking. I know how to make each shot count for more. My life is not like taking lecture notes in class any longer; it's about taking the final test.

Jack Fritscher: I think Robert did that same sort of creative distillation in his head all his life. His social life and his sex life were rehearsals for his pictures. What would you think if a model felt Robert misrepresented him, processed his face inside his camera into something beyond the personal? Like people who feel the camera steals souls. Is photography exploitation? The camera is a gun and the sitter sits like a target in the gunsite. He shot me, but are those single frames me? He Mapplethorped me. His perfect moment might not have been mine.

Crawford Barton: In relationship to models, all photographers including myself must deal with models who have egos and personalities that rise up the minute I set up the camera between us. That's why I like shooting Larry [Lara] and friends who understand how to make art.

Jack Fritscher: Inexperienced models like Robert shot maybe think you're shooting them personally when you are aiming for the platonic ideal of them, or, at least, the mystique you see in them.

Crawford Barton: Robert had to get releases from his models. There was a formal transaction. Whether he got the releases before he began to shoot, I don't know. They trusted him so he didn't exploit them unless they thought so.

Jack Fritscher: Like someone who regrets the sex they consented to the night before.

Crawford Barton: Anyone who is willing to be the subject for an artist has to be open ended about it.

Jack Fritscher: The person has to trust the photographer?

Crawford Barton: Yes. Otherwise they'll be uptight and the photographer won't get anything.

Jack Fritscher: That says something about the celebrities who trooped in front of his cameras as certainly as they did. ["Arnold Schwarzenegger," 1976; "Richard Gere," 1982; "Andy Warhol," 1986; "Yoko Ono," 1988]

Crawford Barton: They obviously trusted how he would present them. They wanted to be, as you say, Mapplethorped.

Jack Fritscher: The famous liked sitting for someone famous.

Crawford Barton: Yes. That's an age-old relationship. He didn't choose the celebrities as much as they chose him.

> Barton shot a portrait of Lawrence Ferlinghetti, founder of San Francisco's City Lights Bookstore, "Lawrence Ferlinghetti," in 1974, and several portraits of gay actor Sal Mineo a year before Mineo was stabbed to death in Los Angeles: "Sal Mineo," 1975, pages 68 and 69, *DOH*.

Jack Fritscher: While the celebrity and fashion photos are exquisite, there seems to be more of Robert personally in his sex and flower pictures that were not commissioned.

Crawford Barton: The portraits of women and socialites don't look as inspired as maybe the portraits he did of people he liked. I always revolted from shooting commercial stuff because I felt so "bought." I would become so bored and bummed out and angry with myself for accepting assignments. I turned down many more jobs than I accepted. I knew I would hate it. So, I'm not very well off. In fact, I'm rather bohemian dirt-poor.

Jack Fritscher: Well, you sound happy. Robert thought money was a way of keeping score in America. He thanked his lucky stars he found a rich and smart patron. Sam and he were born on the same day of the year, twenty-five years apart. His luck had something to do with their astrology.

Crawford Barton: That's one of the few things I do believe in: astrology.

Jack Fritscher: Have you looked at his Patti Smith photographs? What do you think of those as compared to his photos of Lisa Lyon?

Crawford Barton: Some of them with Patti were inspired. Some seem to be just trying to be weird, strange, vogue, just shadows of images. I don't know her, but I feel she is a brilliant person with lots of insight, a visionary, and he realized that—if you can project "visionary" in a photograph.

Jack Fritscher: I think if it can be done, he and she collaborated and did it. I can see it in his lighting and framing of her face and posture. I don't follow punk rock, but I read her book *Babble* and some other things she's written and she's clever.

Crawford Barton: I would compare her to Gertrude Stein.

Jack Fritscher: Someone told me Patti Smith is Gertrude Stein on drugs.

Crawford Barton: [Laughs] Which is a modern application.

Jack Fritscher: Gertrude ran a charmed circle and Robert liked the charmed circle he entered with Warhol and the Factory gang and *Interview* magazine. He was part of that 1960s-1970s world of art and commercial art.

Crawford Barton: At least, with Patti and Lisa, he didn't perpetuate the traditional female image which I have always hated and refused to do: the romantic woman on a pedestal, the sex symbol, the beauty. He didn't really perpetuate that. I always get angry when I go to movies. All of these romantic straight love stories and never any gay ones, or any sexy photography of men, although that's changing and has changed a lot in the last decade.

Jack Fritscher: Is sitting for the camera acting or being? When looking at his pictures of Patti and Lisa, Patti seems more personally "Patti" whereas Lisa's photos act out a more practiced pose about the faces and postures and power of women. He shoots Lisa, *posing*, from the outside in to capture her power as a platonic ideal. He shoots Patti, *being*, from the inside out to present her as herself.

Crawford Barton: Lisa is a bodybuilder and doesn't depend on her intellect, at least not in his images. My most photographed model is like that. He perpetuates the myth that he is a dummy. He's made himself into a living sculpture. He's very clever and very resourceful. Making a living with minimal effort.

Jack Fritscher: You mean Larry Lara. You shoot him both ways — as your personal lover, the way Robert shot Patti, and, because of his muscular body like Lisa's, as a platonic ideal of homommasculine perfection. He's still a throb on Castro Street.

> Born in the South on a farm in Resaca, Georgia, seventy miles from Atlanta where he studied art at the University of Georgia, Crawford Barton, for whom male beauty was a fetish, groomed himself as a ruggedly handsome romantic archetype of the blond Confederate Captain very like Ashley Wilkes played by Leslie Howard in *Gone with the Wind*.

He captured his own glory without vanity in "Self Portrait, Dorland Street," San Francisco, 1974, page 8, *DOH*. Long-haired and bearded and hot and beautiful himself, he set out to shoot beautiful men motivated by Diana Vreeland writing at *Vogue* about "Beautiful People" and the Beatles singing, "How does it feel to be one of the Beautiful People."

While he shot hippies, dykes on bikes, leathermen ["Julian Turk," 1976], Castro clones ["All-American Boy," 1977], trans-persons, San Francisco cops, Sisters of Perpetual Indulgence (a nun speeding past a MUNI bus on a motorbike in full habit with veil flying, page 35, *DOH*), Pride marches, and Harvey Milk, he specialized in lensing the hottest of the hot A-List hunks in the City as in his candid classic series of a dozen men perched on window ledges, provisionally titled here as *The A-List Lords on the Second-Floor Ledge* (overlooking the Castro Street Fair), 1978, and in his staged series *Castro Street, Men in a Truck*, 1978, which is one of the most accurate documentations of how entitled super-hot guys looked and acted in the 1970s.

It was apt high concept to title his 1976 book of men on Castro *Beautiful Men*. Crawford described Lara, his main subject, as the "perfect specimen, as crazy and wonderful and spontaneous and free as Kerouac. So I'm never bored and never tired of looking at him." Larry Lara (May 16, 1949 - January 9, 1992), whose pictures fill *DOH*, died age 42 from AIDS eighteen months before Barton died age 50, June 12, 1993.

Jack Fritscher: Larry is marvelous. Who hasn't lusted after that face and body?

On October 3, the day after this interview, Larry Lara arrived at my home and studio driven by his bodybuilder boyfriend Larry Perry, the hottest bartender at the Spike in LA, whom I'd hired to star in my newest Palm Drive video feature, *Naked Came the Stranger*. Lara, in an open relationship with Barton who got off shooting many photos of Lara with many other men, helped Perry get into character on set, and he signed his name as witness to Perry's signature on the model release.

I'd long been acquainted with the genial Lara who let me run a couple minutes of video on him outside on my deck. He didn't know I was screen testing him as a potential model, but he seemed more suited to pose for still photography than act in a solo video where he had to move and talk and hold down the screen himself. A still frame may freeze truth, but video exposes truth, faster than Godard, at 30 times per second.

Crawford Barton: Larry has a strong sense of what it takes to survive.

Jack Fritscher: Why is he your most photographed model?

Crawford Barton: Well, I've always been in love with him. We've been friends for years and years. I never get tired of looking at him. He was physically beautiful when I met him and has a great physique.

Jack Fritscher: So you have a personal lover's connection with your muse, the same as Robert and Patti, would you say?

Crawford Barton: I think so. I don't know if they were lovers, physical lovers.

Jack Fritscher: No one but Patti knows.

Crawford Barton: I don't know if Robert slept with women or not. I've never really read a biography of him.

Jack Fritscher: Only the women would know. As to books, there aren't any. That's why I'm writing this book.

Crawford Barton: So you're doing research into his background?

Jack Fritscher: As a pop-culture journalist, I have absolutely no intention of writing a biography of Robert *per se.* We live in an age of deconstruction. My memoir will be that, an offbeat pop-culture memoir, but not just my memoir. That's why I'm collecting the "memoirs" of artists who knew him. He's been dead for nineteen months. If these eyewitness testimonials aren't collected right now before their stories turn his myth into legend, people will forget the honest truth they felt about him and his work the moment he died.

Crawford Barton: I met him briefly.

Jack Fritscher: I remember. Robert and I went with Thom Gunn [British poet, 1929-2004] to the opening of your exhibit at the Ambush bar. Do you remember that Robert Pruzan [1946-1992] shot a photo of Mapplethorpe, Gunn, and you standing in the late afternoon sun outside the Ambush?

> In 1994, I published that Pruzan photo in my book *Mapplethorpe Assault with a Deadly Camera.* In the picture, the trio's clothing reveals the kind of diversity drag Walt Whitman liked in each one's fetish identity in their costumes: Thom in an original Levi's jean jacket, Robert in a bespoke leather jacket, and Crawford in an Army Surplus denim military shirt.

Crawford Barton: Oh, yes. The late 1970s.

Jack Fritscher: He came to see your work. What was that like?

Crawford Barton: It was cool. He affected me and my work a lot. He was aloof, withdrawn, quiet, didn't appear to be a happy outgoing person, dark and mysterious.

Jack Fritscher: He struck you as being unhappy then?

Crawford Barton: He didn't strike me as being desperately unhappy, just withdrawn, in his own world. I was surprised when I went to one of his exhibits and he was there, and he was doing a lecture, and he looked like he was uncomfortable doing it but he was forcing himself to. The show was the S&M stuff. It was at the Lawson-DeCelle Gallery on Langton. He was going to do it if it killed him, because he "had" to.

Jack Fritscher: I was there with him that night. Rink took several great pictures of us there. Robert and I had just had supper at Without Reservation on Castro with Lisa Lyon, Jim Enger [my bodybuilder lover of three years who posed for Robert] and Greg Day [New York and San Francisco photographer and college roommate of Enger], and we all arrived together tangled up in the back seat of a taxi. Robert was snorting MDA. He was a bit stoned. I remember him bitching about all the boring people he'd have to meet. His little talk answering questions was part of his show on the road, part of the "sell."

Crawford Barton: He was very interesting, but I got the feeling he might scream and run out of the room at any minute.

Jack Fritscher: I don't want to wear you out and wear you down. I think you, as a photographer, have given me a good picture of your feelings about him.

Crawford Barton: I hope I wasn't too negative.

Jack Fritscher: Not at all. Your memories belong to you.

Crawford Barton: I was trying to be honest. Robert and I were two very different personalities aiming in the same basic direction which is fine art.

Jack Fritscher: Despite some small commercial envy of his success, you felt close to what he was doing and could identify with it?

Crawford Barton: Oh, totally. I myself would never go in the direction he did, although I might have shot black men. I wasn't interested in naked women. I was interested in naked black men, sexual practices, and erotic images.

Jack Fritscher: Your point of view means so much. This has been great.

Crawford Barton: If you think of anything else when you go back over this, let me know. And please rearrange anything I've said to clarify it.

Jack Fritscher: That kind of gentle editing I do, if at all, very carefully and minimally. I try to be holistic.

Crawford Barton: I know how much trouble and how time-consuming it is to put something on paper from a tape.

Jack Fritscher: Exactly. Thank you for your time and your excellent insights into your own work. And into Robert. You said you'll be gone until October 28. When you return, let's get together again. I'd love to see some of your newest pictures and also some of your Super-8 films. If you want to get out of town, perhaps you can come visit and see my garden which is still blooming with a hundred of my six-foot-tall calla lilies that Robert thought were amazing.

Crawford Barton: That sounds perfect to me.

Other Works by Jack Fritscher

Novels

Some Dance to Remember:
A Memoir-Novel of San Francisco 1970-1982

Castro Street Blues
The Geography of Women
What They Did to the Kid
Leather Blues

Short Fiction

Rainbow County
Corporal in Charge of Taking Care of Captain O'Malley
Stand by Your Man
TITANIC: Forbidden Stories Hollywood Forgot
Stonewall: Stories of Gay Liberation
Sweet Embraceable You: Coffee House Stories

Non-Fiction

Profiles in Gay Courage Series
Vol 1 Leatherfolk, Arts, and Ideas
Vol 2 Dueling Photographers: George Dureau and Robert Mapplethorpe
Vol 3: Inventing The Gay Gaze

The Life and Times of the Legendary Larry Townsend
Gay Pioneers: How "Drummer" Shaped Gay Pop Culture 1965-1999
Gay San Francisco: Eyewitness Drummer
Mapplethorpe: Assault with a Deadly Camera
Popular Witchcraft: Straight from the Witch's Mouth
Anton LaVey Speaks: The Canonical Interview
Love and Death in Tennessee Williams
When Malory Met Arthur: Camelot
Television Today

www.JackFritscher.com